God's Politician

For Marie-Claire, with love

God's Politician

Pope John Paul II, the Catholic Church,
and the New World Order

DAVID WILLEY

St. Martin's Press

NEW YORK

Library of Congress Cataloging-in-Publication Data

Willey, David.
God's politician : Pope John Paul II, the Catholic Church,
and the new world order / David Willey.
p.   cm.
"A Thomas Dunne book."
Includes bibliographical references and index.
ISBN 0-312-08798-5
1. John Paul II, Pope, 1920–   . I. Title.
BX1378.5.W535   1993
282'.092—dc20
[B]   92-36031
                                                  CIP

First published in Great Britain by Faber and
Faber Limited.

First U.S. Edition: February 1993
10 9 8 7 6 5 4 3 2 1

Contents

Acknowledgements

I would like to thank Gianfranco Svidercoschi, religious affairs correspondent of the Rome newspaper *Il Tempo*, for use of an extract from his 1989 interview with Pope John Paul. I would also like to thank my news editors at the BBC for the sabbatical time they generously granted me. Without their forbearance this book could not have been written. Peter Hebblethwaite made valuable suggestions during the final stages of writing and I am indebted to him.

Prologue

The reign of the first Slav Pope, Karol Wojtyla, John Paul II, has occurred at one of the turning points of history. Communism has collapsed as a political creed, 'quiet' revolutions have transformed Eastern Europe, and the Gulf War has created a radically new situation in the Middle East. These and other developments – the soon to be celebrated birth of the six-billionth member of the human race, the rise of high-consumption societies in the rich world amid a developing world condemned to apparently endless hunger and poverty, the arrival of the global communications village and scientific advances in areas such as genetics – are reshaping the Catholic Church, the world's longest surviving international organization.

The Vatican is the smallest sovereign State, and has only the budget of a small to medium-sized company in the United States, yet it now wields huge political influence in the international field. John Paul II is not only a spiritual leader of the 900 million members of his Roman Catholic flock, but also a world statesman ranked in importance alongside presidents of the United States and Russia. The Pope's prestige has grown through his unprecedented series of world travels. Fifty major foreign pilgrimages have taken him to over ninety countries in every continent of the world.

The idea for this book first matured while I was accompanying him, reporting for the BBC on many of his strenuous journeys to Latin America, Africa, Asia and Europe. The apparently random selection of destinations to which we flew at first had little logic. What was the head of the Catholic Church doing, I asked myself, as we toured in Turkey, or Peru, or Japan, or Cameroon? The answer seemed to be: becoming visible to the maximum number of members of his Church, particularly in the poor countries of the Third World, which were rapidly overtaking the old Catholic strongholds in Europe as potential areas of major Church expansion in the next century. Then there were the return trips to the Pope's native Poland – key events, it later turned out, in the postwar political history of Europe. Finally there were visits which allowed him to drive home the message of Roman discipline among wayward Catholics whose religious practice did not conform with his interpretation of traditional teaching.

In many of the Pope's public speeches, politics and religion are inseparably linked, despite his attempts to draw the biblical distinction between the spheres of Caesar and of God, and his criticism of priests who engage in political activities. There was a moment in 1980 in Rio de Janeiro when the Pope had to tone down his text championing Brazilian workers' rights at a rally at the crammed soccer stadium. There was the amazing scene in Managua when the Pope reacted angrily to heckling from Sandinista supporters attending his mass. There was his triumphal mass in Warsaw during martial law in Poland when he preached an historical homily suited more to the uncrowned monarch of his beleaguered people than to the Vicar of Christ.

I later discovered that the Pope himself had no very clear idea of what he was trying to achieve when he first started jetting around the world. In a rare interview in 1989, on the plane back to Rome, during the eleventh year of his pontifice, he admitted that at first he had no systematic travel plan at all.

In contrast, Pope Paul VI, the first Pope since the wars of Napoleon to travel outside Italy, had carried out a well-planned series of foreign journeys beginning, logically, with the Holy Land where Jesus Christ was born, lived and died. In the last eight years of his life Paul made no more visits abroad. He had been invited by the bishops of Latin America to attend their meeting in Mexico in 1978. But Paul VI and then John Paul I died in rapid succession, and the conference was postponed. After some hasty preparations, the new Pope left Rome for Mexico only three months after his election, determined to crack down upon the liberation theologians who he believed were leading his Church astray. 'Then other invitations began to arrive. The idea of having the Pope present in person spread. And not only within the church. Waldheim invited me to take part in the General Assembly of the United Nations in September 1979. But this would have been a purely political visit and it had to be pastoral in nature. So that is how a visit to the north-east United States came to be added to attending the United Nations. Then, at the suggestion of my secretary, Father John McGee from Ireland, we added Ireland to the itinerary.'

Even at this stage, the Pope still had no long-term programme, just the increasing conviction that he had to travel, fuelled by the flow of pilgrims coming to the Vatican who asked: 'When are you coming to see us?' Invitations began to flood in from Catholic Bishops' Conferences around the world.

'The Second Vatican Council opened up a new way of performing my pastoral mission. This was not a tactical or strategic opening, but a form of dialogue. Paul VI had been to Constantinople to start a dialogue with the Orthodox Church. I felt I had to make the same pilgrimage to confirm this opening, even though in Turkey Catholics are a tiny minority.

'With the passing of time I found these travels more and more useful in developing policies. My presence in a particular country added a direct witness, something that was immediately understandable. To speak about peace at Hiroshima, for example, was to give a thousand times more meaning to the message. It gained eloquence and depth by being pronounced there.

'The problem about the Universal Church is how to make it more visible. There are tendencies in theology and above all in the Orthodox Church to reduce everything to the level of the local church. But the Church was born universal from the moment it began in Jerusalem. Saint Paul's travels, Saint Peter's coming to Rome, the Apostolic tradition, everything confirms the Petrine tradition of giving the church its universal dimension, and making all the local churches feel this universal dimension. And it seems to me that my travels help to make it more visible.

'I cannot avoid taking risks. I have to meet Heads of State, politicians as well as ordinary people. Sometimes perhaps politics is sinful, and sometimes there are sinful governments. But you cannot ignore this political dimension to life, especially in the life of a nation. When I went to Africa for the first time, it gave me great joy to see peoples who a few years before had been subject to colonial power finally enjoying their own sovereignty. Perhaps it was an imperfect sovereignty, not yet translated into democratic principles. But at least these people are their own masters.

'My Polish origins, the history of my people, the experience of my country has helped me a lot, above all to understand situations of injustice in the Third World. I tried to express this in my encyclical *Sollicitudo Rei Socialis*, which emphasized this phenomenon in countries which recently achieved independence, and their desire to be respected in their own sovereignty, national identity and culture.'

The Pope's travels, which quickly became part of his long-term political strategy, have been widely criticized. Non-Catholics were disparaging about the commercialization of papal journeys, which spawned such souvenir objects as lawn sprinklers in the shape of a mitred Pope, one-third life size; the three-dollar papal ring on sale in the United States complete with human lips – 'You kiss it, it kisses you back' – or the sponsored papal canned beer produced by an Australian brewery for an after-mass picnic in Adelaide. This all tended to trivialize the Papacy. And the international tours, an average of four each year, cost millions of dollars – money which some Catholics thought might have better been spent on the relief of poverty.

'Some people in the West say that the Pope ought not to carry out such celebrations, and cause such huge crowds to gather, because this is crass triumphalism which hinders progress towards Christian unity. It would be much better for him to come and engage in dialogue, they say. But that is exactly what I do every day with the people whom I see. I did it for example in the United States with the bishops, who then sent a return delegation to the Vatican. Is this not a dialogue? Was it not a dialogue that I had in the Scandinavian countries with the Lutherans?

'It is not possible to draw up a balance sheet. You cannot report upon a process which is still evolving. I shall go on as long as Providence gives me strength. What happened after the attempt on my life, my physical recovery and the ability to travel once again, has convinced me that the overseas visits are useful and that I should continue them. The Church asks for it. The Council demands it. And then, I repeat, it is Providence which decides everything and which writes everything down . . .'

Actor, priest, poet and professor of ethics, as well as the successor of both Saint Peter and Saint Paul, as he is fond of reminding us, John Paul II has spent a whole year of his reign away from Rome. The message he takes is that the coming millennium matters. He describes our predicament in apocalyptic terms. In one of his poems he compared himself to 'the herald who foretells disaster'. In one of his encyclicals he talks about the false idols worshipped by late-twentieth-century man – 'money, ideology, class and technology'. His Horsemen of the Apocalypse are hunger, nuclear war, abortion and genetic manipulation.

Papal speeches are not like ordinary politicians' speeches. The semantic problems are considerable: they may need an historian, a moral theologian, or a good translator from the Polish to make their meaning clear to those unskilled in Church jargon. The important speeches are normally drafted in Polish, then translated by the Pope's speechwriters into Italian, English, Spanish or German. 'Popespeak' has always been a form of human communication ill-adapted to ready comprehension. Papal style tends towards the generic and the abstract, and often towards the obvious and the repetitive. It is accepted usage for popes to quote themselves *ad nauseam*, repeating previous statements they have made on the same subject (with chapter and verse). The political point is often buried deep inside the text of a religious homily. During the heady period when Solidarity first blossomed, and the bitter months when it was suppressed by the Communist regime in Poland, the Pope's comments, his hopes and fears, became a matter of widespread international interest and comment. But they were often intermingled with prayers and pleas to Our Lady of Jasna Gora, the protectress of Poland, to whom Pope John Paul is particularly devoted.

As the frequency, scale and distance of papal journeys increased, a law of diminishing returns began to operate. Once the novelty of a travelling Pope had begun to wear off, the mystique behind the high office, formerly exercised only from Rome, weakened. A certain repetitiousness set in. The same set speeches to men of culture, to the faithful, to young people whether in Sydney, Australia or Bamako, Mali, somehow became less quotable.

But then the dramatic events in Eastern Europe of the winter of 1989 revealed a new direction and dimension to the pontificate. All the Pope's travels were merely stopping places on his road to Moscow, the Third Rome. The sudden demise of the Soviet Communist Party, the political fragmentation and death of the Soviet Union, and the creation of the new Commonwealth of Independent States opened up 'exceptional new opportunities' for the Vatican, in John Paul's own words. The Pope happened to be visiting Hungary when the abortive August 1991 coup against President Gorbachev took place in Moscow. The Soviet leader's temporary return to power brought a relieved 'Thank God!' comment from the Pontiff, who from the Vatican sent an immediate telegram of goodwill to Gorbachev expressing the hope that he would be able to continue his 'huge task of material and spiritual renewal of the Soviet people'.

The Pope received Mr Gorbachev's successor, Boris Yeltsin, at the Vatican during the leader's brief visit to Italy in December 1991. It was agreed to transfer diplomatic relations between the Vatican and the former Soviet Union to Russia, acting on behalf of the new Commonwealth. After also meeting Italian government leaders and industrialists, Mr Yeltsin left Rome directly for Alma Ata in Central Asia to establish the new Commonwealth.

Mr Gorbachev, in his new role as private citizen, head of a Moscow 'think tank' and international newspaper columnist, paid handsome public tribute to Karol Wojtyla, politician, in an article published in the Turin daily *La Stampa* in March 1992.

'Everything that happened in Eastern Europe in these last few years would have been impossible without the presence of this Pope and without the important role—including the political role—that he played on the world stage', Gorbachev wrote. 'Now that there has been a profound change in the history of Europe Pope John Paul will continue to have an important political influence'.

At a private audience with Paolo Meli, editor of *La Stampa,* who formally handed over to the Pope the full text of Gorbachev's article for his comments, John Paul played down his own role in changing the face of Europe during the 1980s, and expressed surprise at the speed of the political transformation.

'I do not believe that one can talk about a political role in the strict sense of the term', the Pope said, 'because the Pope's mission is to preach the Gospel. But in the Gospel, there is man, respect for man, and therefore respect for human rights and freedom of conscience. If this has a political meaning, then, yes, it also applies to the Pope. But always referring to man and defending man'.

'In 1978, when I became Pope, I did not think that I would be able to witness a transformation as radical as that which changed the face of Eastern Europe. I did not think about it because it was unthinkable, and not only at that moment. Even in the unforgettable year of 1989—the year of the "velvet revolution" as the Czechoslovak President Vaclav Havel defined it—there was only a sign, a glimmer of what was to come'.

But I suggest that Karol Wojtyla knew perfectly well, as did the Cardinals of the Roman Catholic Church who elected him Pope, that the first Slav ever to enter Saint Peter's throne would inevitably become the most politically influential Pope of modern times.

In order to keep the story flowing, sources are not given in detail. I sometimes refer to the Pope by his family name Wojtyla for the sake of clarity and variation of style, although I am aware this is not current usage in English.

Religion is a very personal matter and I should perhaps clarify my own beliefs and my credentials for writing this book right at the start. I was a cradle Catholic. My father was an Anglican; my mother, of Italian parentage, is a Catholic. I was baptized and brought up in the faith according to that strict marriage contract which used to be enforced by the Catholic hierarchy in England and Wales, aimed at capturing the progeny of mixed marriages. Long-time residence in Rome, under three popes, and growing familiarity with the Vatican and with Karol Wojtyla and his retinue during the worldwide peregrinations, have left me simultaneously fascinated and appalled by his Universal Church. My faith in God is intact, but my allegiance to the Roman Catholic Church has been suspended while I examine this brief Polish interlude in its long history.

Rome, September 1992

CHAPTER I

The Solidarity Pope

The inspirer of anti-socialist activities of the reactionary clergy in Poland.
Tass, quoting the Soviet political periodical *Politiceskoye*
Samoobrazovanie, December 1982

Thanks to Pope John Paul, the voice of the Vatican sounds an authoritative and important note all over the globe, for he is an objective judge of the reality of the contemporary world.
Pravda, January 1989

In the last week of August 1990 two Poles from very different backgrounds – a priest and a former shipyard worker – met south of Rome in the stately setting of an Italian Renaissance villa overlooking Lake Albano. They were celebrating the tenth anniversary of a revolutionary world event, the signing of the Gdansk accords which had established the Solidarity free trade union in Poland, the first democratic trade union in Communist Eastern Europe. Although this was only the fifth time that the two men had met, Solidarity had been in a real sense their joint creation. Together they had set off a train of events which led directly to the end of the Cold War and the breakdown of the postwar Soviet hegemony over Eastern Europe in 1989.

The shipyard worker was Lech Walesa from Gdansk, founder member of Solidarity, shortly to be elected President of Poland. The priest was Karol Wojtyla, Pope John Paul II. He had been second-in-command in the Roman Catholic Church in Poland before he was unexpectedly elected Pope in 1978. Their meeting place in the Alban Hills was the papal summer residence of Castelgandolfo.

The rise of the Solidarity movement, and indeed Poland's subsequent transition from Communist dictatorship under Soviet tutelage to the first non-Communist government in Eastern Europe, can be traced directly back to the sense of patriotism, purpose and optimism generated by the Pope's bold visit to Poland a decade before. That first crusading return visit, although it lasted a mere nine days, was a political as well as a religious triumph. Wojtyla gave his countrymen the impetus to invent a new challenge to the seemingly immovable Marxist dictatorship in Warsaw.

Lech Walesa was unknown among the thirty-five million Polish Catholics in 1979. Yet by January 1981 the walrus-moustached shipyard electrician, whose face had already become famous on television and in newspapers all over the world, was considered important enough to be invited to Rome for a special Vatican audience. On each of the Pope's subsequent visits to Poland, even during the martial law, there was a top-secret meeting between the two men.

In 1989, after Lech Walesa had attended early morning mass at the Pope's private chapel in the papal summer villa, he joined Karol Wojtyla for breakfast, the Pope's preferred meal of the day. The two men remained closeted together for more than three hours. Walesa sought the Pope's blessing on his candidature for the Polish presidency. The Pope wanted to hear why the Solidarity movement had split into two hostile factions, and he wanted to discuss the political future of his country. Although we do not know the details of what was said that humid summer morning, we do know the Pope's mind. He had told a visiting group of fellow countrymen the day before, 'It is not an exaggeration when we say that it was Poland that resolved the gigantic dilemma of the division of Europe into two opposing blocs.'

It was logical that the first Slav Pope should view the Cold War from a viewpoint profoundly different to that of his Italian predecessors. Karol Wojtyla had witnessed the events which cut Europe in two. He saw the Nazis occupy his country. He had lived as priest, bishop and cardinal under the political shadow of the Soviet Union for three decades, and possessed a visceral knowledge of the political and religious divisions of central Europe. His long-held ambition to visit the Soviet Union, whose border lies only a short distance from his native city of Kraków, now stands a strong chance of being fulfilled.

Shortly before Mikhail Gorbachev's rise to power in the Soviet Union, I asked Pope John Paul, while we were flying across the South Atlantic at the start of one of his Latin American pilgrimages, if and when he planned to travel to Moscow. This was four years before the crumbling of the Berlin Wall.

'Ah, Moscow,' he replied immediately, his face lighting up. 'Yes, the third Rome.'

For anyone unversed in Church history, the reference might seem puzzling. What connection has Moscow, capital of the world's first atheist state, with the centre of Christendom? In order to understand the thrust of John Paul's extraordinary pontificate, it is necessary to look back to the end of the first millennium of European history and to travel beyond the boundaries of the Roman Empire.

The second Rome was Constantinople, the capital of Byzantium, whither much of the spiritual and temporal power and Christian heritage of Rome migrated after the disintegration of the Roman Empire.

A Russian legend relates that the tenth-century ruler of Kiev, Prince Vladimir, after uniting by military conquest a vast area extending from the Baltic Sea to the Ukraine (thus founding the kingdom which was to be the precursor of modern Russia) sent out envoys to the leaders of the world's major religions. Their task was to choose a religion for his people and so strengthen his rule. Rome, Cairo and Jerusalem failed to impress. Prince Vladimir was attracted by the Muslim attitude towards polygamy (he had already accumulated seven wives), but was less keen on Islamic restrictions over the consumption of strong liquor and pork. So one after another he rejected Latin Christianity, Judaism and Islam. Finally his choice settled upon the eastern branch of Christianity, whose centre was Constantinople.

This story is related in the mediaeval chronicle *Tales of Bygone Years*, written by the Kievan monk Nestor a century after Saint Vladimir's death. Nestor wrote that Vladimir's envoys reported from Byzantium, quite overcome by the beauty of the architecture and the liturgy chanted at the great basilica of Saint Sophia in Constantinople:

They led us to edifices where they worship their God and we knew not whether we were in heaven or on earth. For on earth there is no such splendour or beauty and we are at a loss how to describe it. We only know that God dwells there among men and their service is fairer than the ceremonies of other nations. For we cannot forget the beauty.

Vladimir's decision may also have been influenced by the fact that he wanted to marry Anne, sister of the Byzantine emperors Basil and Constantine. He obtained her hand in exchange for military aid to the Emperor, and was accepted on condition that he renounce his former wives and be baptized into the Christian faith.

On a warm summer's day in the year AD 988 on the banks of the broad river Dnieper, 1,500 miles east of Rome, Prince Vladimir directed his subjects to wade into the river, cast away their pagan idols, and be baptized by immersion into the Christian faith according to the

Byzantine rite. This remote event was celebrated in 1988 in Moscow and Kiev – the 1,000th anniversary of the baptism of the Land of Rus.

Vladimir's main adversaries to the west of his kingdom, the Poles, had opted for the Latin branch of Christianity and their ruler had sworn allegiance to the Pope in Rome. A great cultural and religious divide thus opened in this part of Eastern Europe, one whose political consequences are still important today. The Russian Orthodox Church, as it later developed, was the child of Constantinople, not of Rome.

The baptism of the Land of Rus took place a few decades before the final split or schism of AD 1054 between the Eastern Church and the Western Church. From that moment Christendom was formally divided.

With the decline of Byzantium and its eventual extinction by the Turks in 1453, the concept of a 'third Rome' began circulating in Muscovy. About this time the princes of Muscovy assumed the title of 'Tsar', the Slavic equivalent of 'Caesar' or Emperor. A monk from Pskov named Philofei wrote to Prince Vassily, ruler of Muscovy at the beginning of the sixteenth century: 'Attend to it, pious Tsar, that all the Christian Empires unite with your own: for two Romes have fallen, but the third stands, and a fourth there will not be.'

The Tsars did not follow Philofei's advice. They did, however, set up a Moscow Patriarchate in 1582 when Patriarch Jeremiah travelled from Constantinople to Moscow to grant self-governing status to the Russian Orthodox Church. More than four hundred years were to pass before there was another visit to Moscow by the spiritual leader of world Orthodoxy. Moscow never made a former claim to universal primacy, and ecclesiastically has always recognized the seniority of the patriarchs of Constantinople, Alexandria, Antioch and Jerusalem.

However, the concept of Moscow inheriting the legacy of Constantinople and becoming the defender of Eastern Christianity attracted Russian and Slav intellectuals for centuries. It was only natural that Karol Wojtyla, the first Slav pope, should also be fascinated by the idea of the 'third Rome'. The idea of a papal visit to Moscow would have been inconceivable until his reign. In 1978 when the College of Cardinals chose him as head of the Roman Catholic Church, the world was still locked into the East-West Cold War confrontation.

As late as 1987 the Pope distinguished between dictatorships he still regarded as permanent, such as that in his own country, Poland, and those which were transitory, such as that of General Pinochet in Chile, where, as he correctly forecast, democratic rule might one day return.

The sudden and total collapse of Communism as a political system and creed in Eastern Europe, the crumbling of the Soviet Empire and the quiet revolutions of 1989, however providential they may have seemed in Rome, apparently took even Pope John Paul by surprise.

For many centuries the Papacy had been a Western-centred institution, intimately involved with the history and politics of the nations of Western Europe. The Catholic Church travelled to the New World with the armies of the Spanish *conquistadores*, and to Africa and Asia led by a small band of Western European missionaries.

The Reformation was regarded by Rome as a purely European affair. Until the reforms of the Roman Curia carried out under Pope Paul VI in the 1970s, the Vatican was a Roman organization run and dominated by Italians, and the election of a non-Italian pope would have seemed unlikely. The last non-Italian pope – Hadrian VI, a Dutchman – was elected four hundred and fifty years ago.

In just over a decade, John Paul has transformed the minor international presence of the Papacy into one with an altogether higher profile. But apart from his unprecedented travels, many of the key events of this pontificate are related to the Slav world – to Eastern Europe, the Pope's home for the first fifty-eight years of his life.

When the Pope was born, Poland had just been restored to the map of Europe after more than a century. His father had been an army quartermaster in the employ not of the Polish republic, but of the last Austro-Hungarian Emperor, Franz Josef I. During his own lifetime Karol Wojtyla has seen the invasions, persecutions, genocides which brought about the frequent shifting of the borders of central and Eastern European states. Witness to the sufferings and wanderings of millions of European refugees, victims first of Nazi, then of Soviet tyranny, it is not surprising that Wojtyla's constant theme is that the quintessential Europe is formed by its peoples, not by its states. And looking back at the early history of these peoples, he cannot help noticing the frequent coincidence between the first affirmations of national identity of the Slav nations and their conversion to Christianity, often by missionaries from Byzantium.

There are four events which mark the political ascent of Karol Wojtyla to world statesman.

The first was his first return visit to Poland only eight months after his election, in June 1979. During this trip, at Gniezno, the Pope made a crucial decision. He decided to ignore the artificial political divisions of the Iron Curtain and to remind the world that Christian Europe's historical and geographical limits included the Soviet-controlled parts of Eastern and central Europe.

'After so many centuries,' he announced to the bishops of Poland and the crowd assembled in the ancient capital of Polish kings, 'the Slav peoples have heard the Apostle of Jesus Christ speaking in their own tongue. And the first Slav Pope in the history of the Church cannot fail to hear these closely related Slav languages, although they may still sound strange to ears accustomed to the Romance, Germanic, English and Celtic tongues. Is it not Christ's will that this Pope should manifest at this precise moment the spiritual unity of Europe?'

The Pope's words were applauded by his enthusiastic audience. But their full import was not immediately recognized. The Gniezno ceremony was networked neither on Polish State television, nor on Eurovision for the benefit of viewers in Western Europe: the Pope's words were only transmitted locally in accordance with the strict conditions imposed on media coverage by Warsaw's Communist authorities.

Pope John Paul recalled the intermarriage which had taken place between the first Christian rulers of the Polish and Czech peoples. 'On the occasion of the millennium of the baptism of Poland, we must also call to mind the baptism of the Slavs, the Croats, the Slovenes, the Bulgarians, the Moravians, the Slovaks, the Czechs, the Russians, and the Serbs,' he said.

Finally he recalled that it had been the baptism of Lithuania in 1386 that had marked the completion of Europe's conversion to Christianity. Catholic Lithuania's independence struggle with Moscow lay ten years ahead, but John Paul was reminding Europe that the history of the continent as it was being taught in the schools of the West was incomplete. In his list of Slav peoples, he had prophetically identified the cauldron of latent nationalisms which was soon to start bubbling away all over Eastern Europe.

As soon as he returned to Rome, John Paul organized a meeting at the Vatican of scholars from both sides of the Iron Curtain who specialized in relations between Eastern and Western Europe, in the fields not only of theology but also the visual arts, history, music, literature, philosophy and, of course, politics.

Meanwhile the red-brick church of Saint Brigid near the Lenin shipyard in Gdansk quickly became one of the focal points of the rapidly growing Solidarity movement. As the Pope pointed out in his annual address to diplomats accredited to the Vatican just over ten years later in 1990, the sparkpoints of several of the successful challenges to Communist regimes in Eastern Europe in 1989 were also churches.

But he did not mention that Protestant churches were also involved.

In East Germany, the Leipzig Sunday-night demonstrations which in the end swept away the Honecker regime stemmed from the Nikolaikirche in Leipzig and the Gethsemanekirche in Berlin, while the trigger for the dramatic overthrow of the Ceausescu regime in Romania was the imprisonment of the popular Reformed Church Pastor, Laszlo Toekes.

Six years before Mikhail Gorbachev came to power, Karol Wojtyla sowed the first seeds of political change inside Poland. From Rome the Pope encouraged, advised and provided a constant reference point for Lech Walesa and the strongly Roman Catholic Solidarity movement. He is also believed to have channeled funds to Solidarity through the Vatican's offshore bank, the Institute for the Works of Religion, with the aid of his controversial former private banker, Archbishop Paul Marcinkus.

When General Jaruzelski banned Solidarity, arrested its leaders and declared martial law, the Pope made a series of impassioned pleas on behalf of human rights in his country. His words were beamed back to Poland by Vatican Radio's powerful shortwave transmitters, unjammed by the Russians or the Poles. Speaking to the College of Cardinals in Rome a few days after martial law was imposed, the Pope announced, 'The Church is on the side of the workers!' A few weeks later, speaking to pilgrims gathered in Saint Peter's Square after Sunday mass, he said that respect for the civil rights and the sovereignty of Poland was a condition for true social justice and peace in the rest of the world. 'My land is bathed with the blood and sweat of its sons and daughters. I put this problem before the conscience of the whole world,' he said, uncharacteristically raising his voice almost to a shout.

Although the Pope was usually careful to speak in the name of his Polish bishops, it was in the Vatican that the policy guidelines for statements put out from Archbishop Glemp's residence in Warsaw were actually given shape.

It was not the first time that the Vatican had overseen bloodless political transitions from totalitarianism to democracy. Although the Vatican's record in relation to the rise of Fascism in Italy and the Nazi regime in Germany in the 1930s was sometimes ambiguous, after the Second World War the Church firmly supported the ascent to power in Italy of the Christian Democrat party. In the late 1940s the Italian Catholic hierarchy joined in the political fight led by the Christian Democrats against the establishment of a Popular Front of Communists and Socialists. Had the proposed Front not been roundly defeated in the critical elections of 1948, the Italian Communist Party would have been tempted to set up a regime in Rome very similar to the puppet governments of Eastern Europe.

The peaceful transition from the dictatorships of Salazar in Portugal and Franco in Spain to liberal democracies was also aided by the local churches' decision, strongly supported by Rome, to opt for democratic institutions and avoid inciting vendettas against the former ruling classes. Here were other models for the 'soft' revolutions which took place in 1989 in Eastern Europe.

The second key event marking the rise of Karol Wojtyla as a world figure was the attempt on his life in Saint Peter's Square in May 1981. A Turkish gunman, Ali Agca, tried to kill the Pope as he was being driven in his Popemobile through the crowds of pilgrims and tourists. Although the hypothesis of a KGB plot has never been proven, and although the trial of Bulgarians accused of doing the KGB's dirty work ended in their acquittal, there are plausible reasons for believing that Ali Agca did not act alone in his attempt to kill a man who was becoming a serious threat to the Communist empire. In an interview on Italian television in 1991 President Zhelyu Zhelev of Bulgaria said he was sure that the previous Communist regime was capable of such a plot, although it would have been carried out on the orders of a 'larger headquarters'. He did not specify whether this meant the KGB.

Victor Ivanovich Sheymov, a former major in the cipher section of the KGB who defected to the United States in 1980, alleged at a news conference in the United States ten years later that when he was working in Warsaw the year after John Paul's election, he read a classified telegram signed by KGB chief Yuri Andropov (later to succeed Leonid Brezhnev as Soviet leader) ordering the collection of information about how close it was possible to get to the Pope when he appeared in public. The implication was that the Pope was already a candidate for the KGB's hit list.

The Pope had been informed by Vatican security of a possible attempt on his life. His answer, characteristically, was to refuse any curtailment of his public appearances, or his international travel programme.

The third key development in the international rise of Karol Wojtyla was his decision to send to Moscow ten cardinals – the highest level Vatican delegation to visit Russia since the October Revolution – to attend the 1988 millennium celebrations of Russia's conversion to Christianity. The delegation was led by the Pope's deputy, Cardinal Agostino Casaroli, Vatican Secretary of State, and included two other Curia cardinals from Rome. Cardinal Casaroli carried with him a letter to President Gorbachev in Russian in the Pope's own hand. The text of this letter has never been published, but according to reliable Vatican sources it contained proposals not only to ensure religious freedom for Catholics in the Soviet Union, but also about how the Roman Catholic Church might assist President Gorbachev in carrying out his *perestroika* policies and in tackling his country's grave social ills by allowing churches to resume medical, educational and charitable activities.

Problems relating to family breakdown, AIDS, drug and alcohol abuse, prostitution of minors and juvenile crime are rife in Russian society: President Gorbachev, conscious that the disintegrating Soviet State could not combat such problems by ordinary legislation, found the Pope's views on the importance of an ethical approach to social problems coincided unexpectedly with his own.

Such information as is available about the state of Russian youth suggests an appalling situation for a country that, until recently, congratulated itself that the only privileged class in the Soviet Union was its children: 200,000 under-sixteens with police records for crime or drug addiction; 300,000 orphans or abandoned children imprisoned in state institutions; 400,000 children suffering from congenital brain damage – the result of one or both parents' addiction to alcohol or drugs. Glue and solvent sniffing, which produce quicker and more serious brain damage than more common narcotics such as heroin or hashish, are prevalent.

Abortion remains the main method of contraception. The Soviet Union may have one of the highest number of obstetricians and gynaecologists among industrialized countries, yet it also has the highest infant mortality rates. Dirty needles and vaccines produced without sufficient controls are another menace to child health.

The resumption of charitable and nursing activities by the Russian Orthodox church after the passing of the 1990 law on religious freedom had little immediate practical impact, given the magnitude of the Soviet Union's social problems. The Pope's first priority was to supply the Russian Orthodox with bibles; but then he ordered the Catholic Church's international charitable network Caritas Internationalis to give maximum priority to setting up branches inside the Soviet Union, and by 1991 Caritas was already operating in Moscow, Kiev and Lithuania.

The fourth and last key event in John Paul's pontificate, grew directly out of the 1988 meeting at the Kremlin between Cardinal Casaroli and Mikhail Gorbachev. This was President Gorbachev's official visit to the Vatican in December 1989. On this historic occasion the decision was taken to restore diplomatic relations between the Holy See and the Soviet Union, which had been suspended for over seventy years.

In order to appreciate the unprecedented nature of this meeting, which was followed by a second visit to the Vatican by President Gorbachev a year later, and was the culmination of decades of behind-the-scenes Vatican diplomatic attempts to regain contact with the suppressed and persecuted churches of Eastern Europe, we need to recall briefly the later history of the Land of Rus, today known as the Ukraine.

The name Ukraine comes from the Slavic 'Okraina', meaning 'borders'. It was upon the Soviet Union's south western borders with Poland, Czechoslovakia, Hungary and Romania, that the attention of the Pope and President Gorbachev was focused at their historic Vatican meetings.

Under the Russian empire of the tsars, the Ukraine had no separate political existence. War divided the territory between the Poles, who took that part of the Ukraine west of the Dnieper river, and Moscow, which seized the part to the east.

In 1596, under the treaty with the Vatican called the Union of Brest, the Ukrainian Church split away from Constantinople and went over to Rome. In return, the Pope allowed the Ukrainians to continue their Byzantine traditions and forms of worship, which meant keeping their own liturgy in their own language and permitting married men to become priests.

The Orthodox have always regarded this as an act of treason, and they still call the Ukrainian Catholics 'Uniates', which in Russian has a strong pejorative ring.

The majority of Ukrainian Catholics lived for a century and a half under Austro-Hungarian rule, then more briefly under Polish government. During the Russian Revolution in 1918 a short-lived Ukrainian National Republic was proclaimed in Kiev. With the collapse of the Austro-Hungarian monarchy later that year, a West Ukrainian Republic was also declared in Lvov. A merger was announced in 1919, but the union never took place because war with the Bolsheviks and the Poles led to the formation of a Soviet Ukrainian republic, which in 1922 became part of the USSR.

From the outset of the 1918 Revolution, the Soviet authorities attacked all religious institutions, falsely accusing them of political opposition and of collusion with internal and external enemies of the Bolshevik regime. The aim was to discredit religion in the eyes of the masses. During the 1920s the tactics shifted to allow limited tolerance for those individual churches and sects willing both to accept far-reaching controls over their activities and to declare their loyalty to the Soviet State. The Moscow Patriarchate of the Russian Orthodox Church decided to accept these conditions – at the price of the alienation of many bishops, clergy and believers, who found such a compromise with the atheist State unacceptable. In the 1930s Stalin embarked on a harsh anti-religious campaign, and by the end of the decade institutional religion in most of the Soviet Union had been almost totally suppressed.

The Western Ukraine formed part of the Polish republic established after the First World War and then dismembered by Hitler and Stalin in 1939. It was not until the Soviet occupation of western Ukraine and western Byelorussia in 1939 that Stalin was presented with the problem of aborting a new religious community. His answer was predictable – liquidate the Ukrainian Catholics.

Stalin had to wait to recover the Ukraine from the Nazis at the end of the Second World War before he seriously set about the systematic destruction of the Uniate Catholics. The Soviet secret police, the NKGB, arrested or eliminated the entire hierarchy of the church. In 1945 and 1946 800 priests were arrested. Most were deported to Siberia. A fake Synod was summoned to end formally the 350–year-old Union of Brest and announce the 'reunification' of the Ukrainian Catholics with the Russian Orthodox. All Church property and assets were taken over by the Orthodox. The Ukrainian Catholics went underground for two generations.

The celebration of the millennium of Christianity among the East Slavs prompted the Vatican to take a fresh look at events in mediaeval and contemporary history which had been distorted or manipulated by the Soviet authorities for political reasons. Whose baptism exactly was being celebrated? That of the Ukrainians or the Russians or the Byelorussians, the inhabitants of the region west of Moscow known as 'White Russia'? The Ukrainian Catholics claimed it was the commemoration of the founding of their Church, as Prince Vladimir of Kiev was undisputably a Ukrainian. Russians, however, saw the Prince as the first of a long line of Christian rulers of the whole Russian Empire, descending through the princes of Muscovy to the tsars.

There was also an awkward historical slight against the White Russians to be explained away. The pious Prince Vladimir, before leading his subjects down to the river Dnieper to be baptised, had previously espoused a Byelorussian Princess from Polotsk called Rahnieda. He had carried her off and married her against her will, only to repudiate her, along with his six other wives, on the eve of his conversion in order to marry the Emperor of Byzantium's sister. So the Byelorussians had nothing much to celebrate in 1988, and were forced to concentrate on other less distressing events in their religious history.

The Gorbachev-Wojtyla meeting in Rome must also be viewed in the context of the Vatican's painstaking efforts to re-establish contact with the Soviet Union which began during the remarkable pontificate of Angelo Roncalli, Pope John XXIII. What later became known as the Vatican's 'Ostpolitik' could be said to have begun in 1962 in the Turkish capital, Ankara. Karol Wojtyla at that time was still auxiliary Bishop in Kraków, southern Poland. Pope John XXIII was preparing the Second Vatican Council and desperately wanted representatives of the Catholic bishops of the Soviet Baltic Republics of Lithuania and Latvia to come to Rome to take part. Pope John, who had once been the Vatican's diplomatic representative in Istanbul, chose the method of indirect negotiation. The Pope instructed a Vatican diplomat called Francesco Lardone, the Holy See's representative in Ankara, to put out feelers to the Russians by calling upon the Soviet Ambassador to Turkey, Nikita Semionovich Rijov. (Three years later Rijov was to be appointed the Kremlin's Ambassador to Rome, a post he held right up to the election of Karol Wojtyla.)

On his eightieth birthday in November the previous year, Pope John had received an unexpected message of congratulation from the Soviet leader Nikita Khruschev, praising the Pope for his encyclical *Pacem in Terris* – 'sincere good wishes of health and success in your noble aspiration of contributing to the reinforcement and consolidation of peace on earth'. John XXIII glimpsed the tiniest of chinks in the Iron Curtain. Despite advice from the Curia against trying secret diplomacy with the Kremlin, John went ahead with his negotiations. 'It may be a thread of Divine Providence and I haven't got the right to break it,' he said.

Lardone was received cordially by the Soviet Ambassador, who spoke feelingly about his own mother's attachment to the Russian Orthodox Church, and promised to ask Khrushchev for permission for a representative of the Lithuanian Catholic bishops to travel to Rome for the Council. Within a week he had the Kremlin's approval, and even offered Lardone the use of his diplomatic bag to send the invitation.

Encouraged by this encounter, Lardone called upon the diplomatic representatives of other Communist states of Eastern Europe in Ankara. Most, taking note of the Lithuanian example, were only too willing to make a similar good-will gesture to the Pope. The Council opened on

11 October 1962 in the presence not only of bishops from many parts of Eastern Europe, but also observers from the Russian Orthodox Church.

Other gestures followed. That Christmas Khrushchev sent a telegram of seasonal greetings, and shortly afterwards announced from Moscow that the Ukrainian Catholic Church leader, Metropolitan Josef Slipyi, had been released from a labour camp in Siberia, where he had been confined for almost eighteen years after Stalin's attempt to liquidate his flock. Slipyi was allowed to leave the Soviet Union to travel to Rome, where he was to die in exile in 1984.

The following March, Pope John XXIII received in private audience Alexei Adzhubei, Khrushchev's son-in-law, and his wife Rada. In April the Pope decided to send Agostino Casaroli, then a bishop and a senior member of the Curia, on a confidential mission to Budapest and Prague. At that time Casaroli had no particular experience inside Eastern Europe.

In Budapest Casaroli was able to meet Cardinal Mindszenty, the Hungarian primate who for seven years had been a virtual prisoner inside the American legation. He had sought asylum there after being freed from a Communist prison during the 1956 uprising. He had been arrested in 1948 for refusing to allow the secularization of Catholic schools in Hungary, and was sentenced the following year to life imprisonment for 'treason'.

Casaroli then went on to Prague, where he was able to meet another key figure of the Catholic Church in postwar Europe, Cardinal Beran, Archbishop of Prague, who was under house arrest. The two prelates communicated by writing notes to each other on scraps of paper to avoid being overheard in the Archbishop's bugged house. Although almost on his deathbed, Pope John received Casaroli for two hours when the Vatican diplomat returned to Rome. His last words to Casaroli were, 'We must not be in a hurry. These things must mature. In the meanwhile, let us continue with good will and confidence.'

Despite the continuation of the Cold War for almost three more decades, that thread of Divine Providence offered to Pope John by Nikita Khrushchev was never completely severed. Casaroli travelled tirelessly through Eastern Europe, creating a small team of travelling ambassadors in the Holy See who succeeded in maintaining relations with even the harshest of Communist regimes.

Andrei Gromyko, the longest-serving Soviet Foreign Minister, later a figurehead President of the Soviet Union in the early days of the Gorbachev regime, became a regular visitor to the Vatican. He had a total of eight meetings with three popes between 1963 and 1985.

Gromyko's first meeting with Pope John Paul was in 1979, shortly after the Pope's election, and his second came in 1985. According to Cardinal Casaroli, Gromyko was quite blunt at their 1979 meeting in his reaction to what he regarded as an over-modest assessment by the Pope of the Vatican's influence. 'Perhaps the Holy See itself does not fully realize just what strength it possesses,' he said.

In his memoirs Gromyko recounts the subtlety of Vatican diplomacy:

The first initiative always came from the Vatican and usually in an ingenious form: not hard enough to be regarded as a formal invitation but quite definite enough to suggest that the head of the Roman Catholic Church was ready for an exchange of views with the Soviet Foreign Minister about certain problems. In general this coincided with out point of view; it is well known that the Vatican never remains isolated from world politics.

Gromyko never hid his disapproval of the Pope meddling in Polish politics. 'The events of the summer of 1980 in Poland went beyond the limits separating religion from politics,' he wrote.

While Gorbachev was consolidating his position as the new Tsar of a post-Communist Soviet Union, the Pope kept up a steady stream of signals showing his interest in Soviet developments. These included the despatching of Mother Teresa of Calcutta to Moscow, where she obtained permission to open a religious house and hospice. Charitable works by religious orders inside the USSR had been banned after the Bolshevik Revolution, but they were authorized again in 1990.

There was no immediate response to the Pope's signals. The first sign that Gorbachev was interested in a direct dialogue did not occur until Cardinal Casaroli, in Moscow to attend the millennary celebrations as guest of the Russian Orthodox Church, was invited by the Soviet leader for an unscheduled meeting at the Kremlin.

After sundry visits by Soviet astronauts, circus artists, actors, soccer teams and journalists to the regular Wednesday papal audiences, in February 1988 the Red Army Choir entered the Vatican for the first time at the invitation of the Pope. In full military dress, the 100–strong choir gave a performance of Schubert's 'Ave Maria' in the Clementine Audience Hall and presented the pontiff with a Russian bear carved in wood. The Pope blessed the choir members and their families and gave them all rosaries or souvenir key rings.

The crowning event, the official visit by President Gorbachev to the Vatican in December 1989, was sandwiched between a State visit to Italy and a summit with President Bush in Malta. But there was no doubt in the Soviet leader's mind about the overriding importance of his Vatican appointment. He told his aides that he was fascinated by the similarities between his own headquarters inside the Kremlin, a walled-fortress complex of churches and palaces, and the Vatican, another walled city within a city crammed with a mixture of religious and secular buildings. During his stay in Rome, the Soviet leader eschewed most of the tourist opportunities offered by his Italian hosts apart from a walk around the Colosseum, and concentrated upon his historic encounter with the head of Christendom, writing and reviewing the speech he was to deliver inside the Vatican. Soviet public opinion had been softened up ten days previously by an article in *Komsomolskaya Pravda* announcing that the Soviet Union no longer subscribed to Karl Marx's opinion that religion is 'the opium of the people'.

The Soviet leader entered the tiny Vatican State through Gate of the Bells at the side of Saint Peter's basilica, his bullet-proof Zil limousine, specially flown in from Moscow, sandwiched in the middle of a twenty-vehicle motorcade. His Italian police motorcycle escort, which had preceded him everywhere during his Rome visit, had to be left behind at the frontier, Saint Peter's Square.

President Gorbachev's limousine drew up at the entrance to the papal apartments in the courtyard of Saint Damasus to the sound of heels clicking and a halberd salute from a detachment of the Pope's private army, the Swiss Guard, which has protected the lives of Roman pontiffs for four centuries. The Guards still wear the dashing burgundy and mustard-coloured Renaissance uniforms which the guide books insist were designed by Michelangelo, although there is doubt about this. The Internationale was played by a Vatican band, followed by the papal hymn. After the welcome by Vatican officials, Raisa Gorbachev, dressed in a startlingly bright cherry-red suit – defying Vatican protocol that women at formal papal audiences always wear black – was taken to see some of the Vatican's art treasures while her husband was closeted with the Pope in his private library.

Both men seemed tense as they strode towards one another, but they relaxed quickly and shook hands warmly. The Pope ushered his guest into the library where the two leaders, sitting facing each other across the Pope's massive mahogany desk, remained alone with their interpreters for seventy-five minutes. John Paul's interpreter was a Polish priest, born in White Russia. The Pope understands Russian well, but is not a fluent speaker and preferred to address Gorbachev in his native Polish or in what has now become his working language, Italian.

The last occasion upon which a Russian leader had visited the Vatican was in the middle of the nineteenth century. Tsar Nicholas I had travelled to Rome to be received in audience by Pope Gregory XVI on two occasions in December 1845. The subjects on the agenda were broadly the same as in 1989: the Pope complained about the difficulty of nominating bishops in the Tsar's Empire, and Nicholas promised to do what he could to bring his laws into line with Roman Canon Law.

Top of the agenda for Pope John Paul was to hear at first hand how Gorbachev's promised new Soviet law on freedom of conscience and religion was progressing. The treatment accorded to the persecuted Ukrainian Catholic Church would be proof of Soviet commitment to reversing policies that had been in force since the 1917 Revolution.

President Gorbachev, who once described himself to a high-ranking Vatican official as a 'non-practising aetheist' and has admitted he was baptised into the Russian Orthodox Church, explained to the Pope his concept of renewing Soviet society through his *perestroika* policies.

Later in the day he was to tell a news conference in Milan, 'I feel that my thoughts and preoccupations have been well understood, as has my explanation of the problems existing in my country, including Church-State relations. The Pope and I speak the same language. We moved from politics to morals. And as far as *perestroika* is concerned we heard words of support from the Pope for our people.'

The evening before his meeting with the Pope, Gorbachev spoke in public about religion during his address to the Italian people at the Campidoglio in Rome. 'We have changed our attitude to religion – which admittedly we used to treat in an over-simplified way,' the Soviet leader said. 'Now we proceed from the assumption that Church and State are separate and no one should interfere in matters of the individual's conscience. The moral values which religion generated and embodied for centuries in our country can help in the work of *perestroika*.'

Gorbachev was referring to the role which he hoped the Russian Orthodox Church might play in his new Utopian Soviet society. The Orthodox Church has been associated by ordinary Russians since the days of Peter the Great more with the world of politics and government than with the exercise of moral authority. But the Soviet leader was also aware that crime rates and the incidence of violence in parts of the Soviet Union where Catholics are present have generally been lower than, for example, in republics of the USSR with a large Muslim population. Despite allegations by the Russian Orthodox of violence displayed by Ukrainian Catholics towards their fellow Christians, by and large

Catholic political dissidents never indulged in the sort of ethnic protest and violence which occurred in Azerbaijan and Armenia.

Gorbachev asked the Pope for a moral contribution to his efforts to reform Soviet society.

The Pope replied that the Second World War had taught us that 'if fundamental ethical values are forgotten, fearful consequences can result and even the greatest of enterprises can end in failure'. He said that the Holy See had been following with great interest the process of renewal which Mr Gorbachev had set in motion in the Soviet Union and wished him success. 'The Holy See declares itself ready to support every initiative that will better protect and integrate the rights and duties of individuals and peoples, so that peace may be ensured in Europe and the world.'

After their private session, Mr Gorbachev introduced his wife Raisa and members of his suite including the Foreign Minister Eduard Shevard-nadze to the pontiff. And, as expected, he announced that he had invited the Pope to visit the Soviet Union. John Paul was guarded in his reply. He thanked the Soviet leader for the invitation, but said his visit would have to depend upon developments inside the Soviet Union – code for the extent to which Ukrainian and Lithuanian Catholics would be allowed to benefit from *perestroika*'s promised greater religious freedom.

In a short address the Pope announced a major step forward. He and President Gorbachev had agreed to re-establish diplomatic relations. 'Mr President, our meeting today will hardly fail to have a powerful impact upon world opinion. Not only is it something new and unusual. It will also be interpreted as singularly meaningful, a sign of the times that have slowly matured, a sign that is rich in promises.'

There was no doubt about the mutual fascination these two Slavs felt for each other. 'Holy Father,' said Gorbachev, just before they parted, 'you are the highest religious authority in the world – and you are also a Slav.' The Pope accompanied his guests down the long corridor leading to the Apostolic Palace's Throne Room, where he bade them farewell. At dinner that night with one of his aides, the Pope was to ponder aloud about the origins of Mikhail Sergeyevich, whose concept of Holy Russia and whose attitude towards religion was so profoundly different from all previous general secretaries of the Soviet Communist Party.

Long before Gorbachev's visit, Soviet media comment about Pope John Paul had begun to switch from vicious condemnation and slander to praise. The first signs of change came as early as 1982, when Moscow's *New Times*, commenting upon a meeting between President Brezhnev and a delegation of scientists from the Pontifical Academy of

Sciences in Rome, congratulated the Roman Catholic Church on its 'new look'. 'The Church which once upon a time called for anti-Communist crusades is now favourable to arms limitation,' the Soviet monthly said. The official Novosti news agency said the Moscow leadership had welcomed the Pope's support for arms control.

However, later that year the Kremlin launched a series of broadsides against John Paul for his encouragement of the Solidarity free trade union movement in Poland. Not since the death of Pope Pius XII in 1958 had the Russians directly attacked a pope. Three separate articles were published by the official press in Moscow, accusing him of 'anti-Communist propaganda on a vast scale and of actively helping Solidarity'. Some observers thought this was simply a ploy to get the Pope's next return visit to Poland postponed for as long as possible.

Just after Christmas 1982 came the strongest attack. The Pope was accused of meddling in the internal affairs of the Eastern bloc. He was behind the 'anti-socialist activities of the reactionary clergy of Poland'. He was also described as being responsible for 'subversive activities' by innumerable agents, including propaganda specialists throughout Eastern Europe. The Vatican formally rejected the Kremlin's charges in an official statement, pointing out previous Russian praise for the Pope's 'tireless work' for peace.

Détente slowed for several years, but then the new Soviet leader, Mikhail Gorbachev, used a significant phrase when he received Jean Cardonnel, a French Dominican priest, at the Kremlin on what the Frenchman reminded him was his name day, the feast of Saint Michael Archangel, 29 September 1987. Questioned about future relations between Marxists and Christians, the Soviet leader replied in prophetic tone with a quotation from Ecclesiastes 3:5. 'To everything there is a season . . . a time to cast down stones, and a time to gather them together.' He declined to elaborate on his hint that Soviet policy on religion was not immutable.

The following month representatives of the Vatican and the Russian Orthodox Church met in Venice for the first time in seven years. There had been five previous sessions of these theological conversations in the USSR and in Italy since the Second Vatican Council. Metropolitan Filaret of Kiev briefed the Vatican delegation led by Cardinal Willebrands on the significance of *perestroika* for the ecumenical movement and later travelled to Rome for a private meeting with the Pope. The Russians made clear there would be no invitation to the Pope himself to visit the Soviet Union for the millennium celebrations because of his support for the Ukrainian Catholics, a perpetual thorn in relations with the Russian Orthodox Church.

In the Ukraine on Easter Sunday, 1990, I had the opportunity to see for myself some of the benefits – and the limitations – of *perestroika* as applied to Catholics in the Soviet Union.

Throughout Easter week, crowds of worshippers thronged the nine-teenth-century Church of the Transfiguration in Lvov under the gaze of newly burnished icons of the Virgin and saints. The icons gleamed in the golden light of banks of electric candelabra and thousands of yellow wax candles. While a near-by former Dominican church was still func-tioning as a 'Museum of Religion and Aetheism', and the former Latin-rite Roman Catholic cathedral stood abandoned with broken windows and shored-up doors, the Eastern-rite Catholic Church of the Trans-figuration was a showpiece of fervent devotion.

To anyone accustomed to the casual cafeteria-style churchgoing preva-lent in Western Europe, the atmosphere of reverence and the attention given by Ukrainian worshippers to the posture and gestures of prayer was striking. The choir could be forgiven for fumbling for words and harmonies in the complicated Byzantine liturgy, for there were no printed prayerbooks or hymnals. Everything had to be copied by hand and learned afresh as most of the transmitters of ancient Church traditions had been wiped out by Stalin.

This was the first Easter celebrated as a public holiday in the Ukraine for over forty years. The traditional Easter greeting 'Christos Vaskres' – Christ is risen – exchanged in the Ukraine since the times of the legendary Saint Vladimir took on more than liturgical significance.

It was difficult to believe that only one year before many members of the congregation had been in prison for declaring their faith, and that no nun dared wear her habit in public. Blushingly, a nun told me it was only the second time she had worn her distinctive black and white habit in the street. One of the priests celebrating the Easter liturgy had been doing forced labour stoking furnaces near the damaged nuclear reactor at Chernobyl, where he had told soldiers and decontamination workers that the best protection against radioactivity was the Gospel and had joked that priests are immune to nuclear fallout.

On Easter Monday I set off into the countryside, defying official restriction on the movement of foreigners in an area where at that time Soviet nuclear missiles were still aimed at Western Europe. The legalization of the Ukrainian Church had not yet touched a small mon-astic community living at a hilltop shrine in rolling wooded country at

Hoshiv, 100 kilometres from Lvov. Father Mikhail Havryliv was in charge of a group of seven monks including one of the only two original members of the religious community to have survived deportation to Siberia in 1950. Brother Makalis Gren, who used to teach Latin and Greek, had just celebrated his eighty-third birthday, returning from a Siberian prison cell after exactly forty years. He passed no judgement upon the politics of persecution, but told me he was content to celebrate the 'miracle' that had taken place for him.

Father Havryliv, now forty-nine, had originally been ordained priest in the Russian Orthodox Church in Leningrad, where he studied at one of the few seminaries permitted to operate inside the Soviet Union. There, he told me, he had developed a close friendship with Metropolitan Nikodym, former leader of the Russian Orthodox Church in the Soviet Union's second largest city. From Nikodym Father Havryliv learned at first hand of the manipulative relationship between the Russian Orthodox hierarchy and the KGB. Father Havryliv was secretly ordained into the Catholic Church in 1979. 'You cannot be an honest Orthodox priest; the Orthodox church is too close to the Soviet state. Priests and bishops are regularly asked to work as informers for the KGB. I refused,' he told me.

The walls of the sixteenth-century Church and Monastery of the Transfiguration were cracked and the cupola appeared to be in imminent danger of collapse. But Father Havryliv could do little to restore the monastery. 'The change is that they have stopped persecuting us. Yet we cannot sign a contract to repair the building. We cannot have a bank account. Officially we still do not exist.'

Negotiations for the legalization of the Ukrainian Catholic Church began in Kiev in March 1990 between representatives of the Vatican, the Russian Orthodox Patriarchate in Moscow and Ukrainian Catholics. The talks started badly when the local Catholic leader in Lvov, Archbishop Sterniuk, walked out in protest at the lack of support he felt he was getting from the Vatican and at what he regarded as the manipulation of the negotiations by the Orthodox clergy.

The Russian Orthodox delegations steered discussions away from the Catholics' demands for legal status to be restored to their church, and the talks centred merely on the division of disputed church property between the two sides. What rankled with the Catholics, Archbishop Sterniuk told me, was the refusal of the Orthodox to admit any responsibility for past persecutions. The Ukrainian Catholics said they wanted to go back to the status they enjoyed before 1939, when Western Ukraine was part of Poland. The Orthodox replied that this was unrealistic and impossible. The Vatican, anxious not to upset the friendly relations with Moscow established by the Vatican Gorbachev-Wojtyla meeting, seemed to be more intent on compromise than on standing up for the 5 million Ukrainian Catholics unjustly deprived of their right to worship. When the talks resumed in Moscow in the autumn of 1990, it was the turn of the Orthodox to walk out.

Pope John Paul was praised in Lvov for his efforts in bringing the rights of Ukrainian Catholics to the world's attention. But he was criticized for what they considered the weak attitude shown by his Vatican representatives in dealing with the Orthodox Patriarchate in Moscow. 'If those Vatican bishops dare show their faces in Lvov again they will be pelted with rotten eggs,' was a typical comment. People like Ivan Hel, the Ukrainian Church's lay leader, who spent eighteen years in Soviet labour camps, found the Vatican attitude inexplicable. The Easter before I met him, Hel had still been in prison, he reminded me in an interview.

'The meeting between President Gorbachev and Pope John Paul did not give us the result we hoped for,' Hel said. 'Our Church was given no legal status. The Russian Orthodox Church continues to refuse to give back property taken in 1946. Moscow fears that giving back the churches will strengthen the Ukrainian independence movement.' Hel believes the Vatican was deluding itself by attaching importance to the idea of encouraging ecumenical relations with the Orthodox Church.

'They don't understand that the Moscow patriarchate is not interested in Christian love. The Pope ought to know better: he knows the Communist world well. We hope our Church will play the same role as in Poland in the dismantling of the system. That is why the Russian imperial system is so afraid of us.

'Thanks to the reforms of Gorbachev, repression is taking place surreptitiously and secretly. Acting according to the principles of Machiavelli, the authorities say one thing and do another.'

The relationship between the Ukrainian Catholics and the budding Ukrainian independence movement is symbiotic. Rukh, the new political movement for the independence of the Ukraine, works closely with the Catholics. But how much real power had Rukh, I wondered? When Lvov city council issued an order to the Russian Orthodox occupiers of Saint George's cathedral to hand the building back to the Catholics, at first they simply ignored the order, but within a few months they complied.

Saint George's has special significance for the Ukrainian Catholics – it is their cathedral church and the official residence of their Metropolitan Cardinal Lubachivsky. He lived abroad for fifty-four years until at Easter 1991 he was finally permitted to return to the Ukraine from exile in Rome and take up permanent official residence at Saint George's, which he had last seen on the day he was ordained priest more than half a century before.

I received a useful indication of President Gorbachev's awareness of the continued sparring between Ukrainian Catholics and Russian Orthodox over the custody of churches, at a time when he was trying to calm nationalist passions, during a chance meeting at the Danilov Monastery in Moscow on Good Friday, 1990. Raisa Gorbachev was accompanying the daughter of the former Polish President, Barbara Jaruzelski, on a tour of the restored church complex handed back to the Moscow Patriarchate in 1988. Raisa said that she was optimistic about the future of the Ukrainian Catholics. Why could not the Russian Orthodox communicants and the Catholics celebrate Easter together in the name of the unity and concord of all people on earth, she suggested, tongue in cheek. It seemed clear to me that the Gorbachevs had discussed together how the Ukrainian Catholic Church might fit into the putative brave new Soviet Union.

Gorbachev fulfilled his promises to the Pope about allowing greater freedom in the former USSR. The Supreme Soviet, before its dissolution, passed the new law of freedom of worship in October 1990.

But events moved even more swiftly than we imagined was possible at the time. The sudden political collapse of the Soviet Empire in 1991 caused the postponement of the Pope's long-awaited visit to Moscow to an uncertain date in the future. The splitting of the former Soviet Union into its component parts did, however, open up possibilities of separate Papal pastoral visits to the Catholics of the Ukraine and of Lithuania, now that there was no political necessity for the Pope to pay his respects first to the leadership in Moscow.

Yet John Paul's desire to visit the 'Third Rome' remains undiminished. He sees the end of seventy years of Communism as an unprecedented opportunity for spreading the Christian religion in Russia.

The first Russian Ambassador to the Vatican since the days of the tsars is Yuri Karlov, a 53-year-old lawyer who submitted a thesis on legal aspects of the Vatican's international relations for his doctorate from the Soviet Academy of Sciences.

The first diplomatic representative of the Holy See in Moscow is

Archbishop Francesco Colasuonno, an Italian career diplomat who served in the United States, India, Taiwan and Yugoslavia before becoming the Holy See's roving envoy in Eastern Europe in 1986.

One of the Vatican Ambassador's first priorities was to select a candidate to be nominated by the Pope as the first Roman Catholic Archbishop to be appointed to the new Latin rite diocese he set up in Moscow. The post went to a 45-year-old Byelorussian of Polish origin, Monsignor Tadeusz Kondrusiewicz. Since before the Second World War a single chaplain had served the mainly foreign Roman Catholic community in the Soviet capital.

Monsignor Kazimier Swiatek, a 76-year-old Estonian who had spent ten years in Soviet labour camps, was named Metropolitan Archbishop of the new diocese of Minsk, capital of the Byelorussian Republic. A German-born Jesuit, Joseph Werth, thirty-eight, was appointed Apostolic Adminis trator in Siberia. Six new Soviet bishops were appointed in all, apparently without Moscow raising any objections.

But the Russian Orthodox Church was angry at what it regarded as unwarranted interference by the Pope in attempting to set up new Catholic Church structures in lands which had traditionally belonged to Eastern Christendom. The Moscow Patriachate refused to send representatives to the special Synod of Bishops from Eastern and Western Europe summoned to the Vatican in December 1991. The other Orthodox Churches of Eastern Europe also boycotted the Pope's meeting.

Relations between the newly reestablished Ukranian Catholics and their Orthodox brethren in the Ukraine also remained tense. The Pope had to realise that the political rapprochement he had established with Moscow during the rule of President Gorbachev might not endure, given the strength of the Russian Orthodox Church.

One person who has no hesitation in attributing radical political change in the Soviet Union and Eastern Europe to divine intervention during the pontificate of John Paul is a Carmelite nun now well into her eighties, Sister Lucia dos Santos. Sister Lucia is the only survivor of three Portuguese shepherd children who claimed to have witnessed a series of apparitions of the Virgin Mary and strange phenomena – such as the sun spinning like a top – at Fatima, north of Lisbon, beginning on 13 May 1917 and ending six months later.

In her last apparition, the Virgin entrusted three 'secrets' to the shepherd children. The first secret was that the two younger children would die soon and that Lucia would be responsible for spreading the messages of Fatima. Lucia's cousins Jacinta and Francisco died shortly afterwards, from complications following influenza, aged ten and eleven. In June 1989 Pope John

Paul confirmed the decision of the Vatican's Congregation for the Causes of Saints to recognize the 'heroic virtues' of the two children, thus putting them forward as official candidates for sainthood.

The Vatican, always reluctant to pronounce upon modern manifestations of the supernatural, had recognized the Fatima apparitions as genuine as early as 1930.

The second 'secret', revealed by Cardinal Idelonso Schuster of Milan in April 1942, was that if Russia were to be reconverted to Christianity 'wars and persecution' would be avoided. Later that year Pope Pius XII, in a clear reference to Russia, prayed to the Virgin Mary for 'peoples separated by error and discord, and particularly those who profess a singular devotion to you and in whose houses your venerated icon was held in honour. Give them peace and bring them back to the true fold of Christ under the one true shepherd.'

The third 'secret' of Fatima was written down by Sister Lucia in her convent in Portugal in 1957, forty years after the apparitions, and sent by diplomatic pouch through the Apostolic Nuncio in Lisbon for safe keeping in Rome.

During a visit to West Germany in 1980, Pope John Paul talked in confidence to a group of German prelates and lay people about the 'third secret'. They later claimed to have recorded his words. They said the Pope spoke in frighteningly apocalyptic terms about 'oceans invading entire continents and millions of men losing their lives from one second to the next'.

According to Sister Lucia (in a 1990 interview with the right-wing Italian Catholic periodical *Trentagiorni*), it was the Pope's consecration of Russia to the Virgin Mary on 24 March 1984 that helped set off change in Eastern Europe. Mikhail Gorbachev emerged as Soviet leader one year later. Sister Lucia says she firmly believes that the rise to power of Mikhail Gorbachev was 'an action by God in the world to free it from the danger of a nuclear war'. As far as I know she has not yet pronounced on the role played by Karol Wojtyla in pushing the world back from the brink.

For those who find significance in dates, there is another strange coincidence to note. Ali Agca's attempted assassination of the Pope took place on the anniversary of the first appearance of the Virgin at Fatima, on 13 May 1981; the Pope has publicly attributed his survival to the intervention of his patron and protectress. As soon as he was fit enough to resume his travel programme the following year, he went on a pilgrimage to Fatima in Portugal to pay homage at her shrine. In 1984 he presented to the shrine the bullet which had almost killed him and which surgeons had extracted from his body. Church officials in Portugal set the bullet among 313 pearls and 2,679 precious stones decorating a crown placed on the Virgin's statue in Fatima on special church festivals. And on 13 May 1991 the Pope returned yet again to Fatima to pray to the Virgin Mary, now wearing in her solid gold crown the bullet from Ali Agca's gun.

In a special supplement that was published on the occasion of John Paul's latest Fatima visit, the Vatican newspaper *L'Osservatore Romano* printed interviews with two leading churchmen, Cardinal Ugo Poletti, former Vicar of Rome, and Bishop Alberto Cosme do Amaral, within whose Portuguese diocese the shrine of Fatima lies. In these interviews the collapse of Communism is attributed to Our Lady of Fatima. Neither of the prelates mentioned the roles played by Pope John Paul or by Mikhail Gorbachev.

CHAPTER 2

The Actor from Kraków

It is necessary to have the courage to walk in a direction in which no one has walked so far.
Karol Wojtyla on leaving Kraków after his first return visit to Poland, 1979

Two days after his election as Pope, Karol Wojtyla summoned the ambassadors of almost a hundred countries accredited to the Holy See to make the first 'political' speech of his reign. He emphasized his new supranational as well as his supernatural responsibilities as head of the Universal Church. He also made a plea for what was to be one of the main themes of his pontificate, the struggle for human rights and religious freedom.

Pope John Paul tried to play down his Polish nationality. 'From now on', he said, 'the particular nature of our country of origin is of little importance.'

But the origins and nationality of the Polish Pope have always deeply coloured his policies and decisions. He thinks in Polish, he writes his most important speeches in Polish, and inevitably he views the world from a Polish perspective. Poland, the country of shifting frontiers, four times partitioned or wiped off the map of Europe by its more powerful neighbours, remains his touchstone. A witness to the Holocaust, Wojtyla can never forget his country's human tragedy; one-third of his nation has been slaughtered in war during his lifetime.

The Roman Curia, with roots in Western Christendom, never found it easy to absorb the new Slav slant of John Paul's pontificate. Conversation at the Pope's dinner table is normally in Polish, and the Italian who was his Deputy or Secretary of State for over twelve years until his retirement in 1990, Agostino Casaroli, realized very early on that he would have to become fluent in the Pope's native language. I remember meeting him strolling one day in the Vatican Gardens with a Polish grammar in his hand.

On the plane to Mexico during the Pope's first foreign trip in 1979, one of my colleagues asked him what favour he would ask of the Madonna of Guadalupe, patroness of Mexico. 'I shall ask her to pray for the Mexican people who have suffered a lot, just like the Polish people,' he replied.

In 1988 on a visit to Uruguay he preached to impoverished cowboys in cattle country at Melo, championing their right to form a trade union and to go on strike. In a country where strikes are perfectly legal and even commonplace, his thoughts were clearly a hemisphere away with the striking steelworkers of Silesia locked at that moment in confrontation with the Communist government.

Poland is ever present in his mind and heart. Apart from living for two years at the Belgian College while studying in Rome from 1946 to 1948, Pope John Paul spent his childhood, his adolescence, most of his early manhood and all his middle age in Poland. He was fifty-eight when he was elected Pope, not an age when a man changes in character or outlook. So his family, education, student days and career as priest, bishop and then cardinal in Kraków are more than mere passing biographical interest.

Karol Wojtyla was born on 18 May 1920, in the small town of Wadowice, not far from today's border with Czechoslovakia, in the newly independent Poland, which had emerged from the dismembered Austro-Hungarian Empire at the end of the first World War. The rebirth of Wojtyla's country preceded his own birth by only eighteen months.

Wadowice lies in green, rolling countryside, in the foothills of the Carpathian mountains. The Wojtyla family house, the onion-domed church across the road and the village school remain a central European rural Arcadia, where the young Karol passed his childhood amid the gathering storms of another, even more tragic and horrifying war.

There were three Jews out of forty-one students in Karol's year – the class of 1938 – at the Marcin Wadowita Grammar School in Wadowice. This was less than the normal ratio of Jews to Catholics in this part of southern Poland. Before the Nazi holocaust Wadowice had about 2,000 Jews among its 9,000 population.

One of them was Jerzy Kluger, whose father, a prosperous lawyer, was leader of the local Jewish community. Today, by some quirk of chance, Karol and Jerzy, the two former fellow students, both live in Rome, Karol in the Apostolic Palace in the Vatican, Jerzy in a modest flat in the Parioli suburb. While Karol runs the Universal Church, Jerzy runs a two-man business, Kluger & Rosenberg, specializing in the sale of second-hand earth-moving equipment, from somewhat dingy offices two miles away from the Vatican.

The two boys used to play soccer during their free time. Anti-semitism had little hold in Wadowice and Jews and Catholics often teamed up to play friendly matches against each other. Sport was important both at school and after hours, Jerzy remembered when I interviewed him at his office.

'Karol kept goal in the school soccer team, and was a deft hand at pingpong. There were two afternoons of compulsory sports at school, volleyball or basketball in summer and skiing in winter. Skiing could be a dangerous sport in pre-war Poland. There were no safety bindings and no ski lifts. If you wanted to enjoy the pleasures of ten minutes downhill skiing, first you had to slog on foot up the slopes for half a day.'

He and some of his friends set up a ski-jump near Wadowice with the aid of a trampoline. Jerzy fell and broke his hip, but this did not kill his love for the mountains. Today his office wall is covered with pictures of his family on climbing expeditions. When he meets the Pope (he is regularly invited to the Vatican to share a meal and talk about old times), he still relishes with Karol the pleasure of recounting long-past hikes and skiing expeditions in the Tatra mountains.

Jerzy's family used to own half the property around Marshal Pilsudski square (later renamed Red Army Square and now restored to its original name) in Wadowice. Another Jewish friend, Goldberger, was a skilled musician who later became a composer. He was among those invited to one of the regular re-unions of schoolfriends which the Pope has organized each year in Italy, usually at the papal summer residence at Castelgandolfo south of Rome. Often there is a sing-song, for old times' sake. Photographs of the group (with wives) clustered around the Pope record fifty years and more of friendship. Jerzy picked out one of the photographs for me to list the subsequent careers of the rest of the Wadowice class of 1938: 'This boy became a mathematician, this one a mining engineer, this one a taxi driver, that one an accountant; the balding one is now a farmer who augments his income with a bit of beekeeping on the side, another is now a doctor, and, inevitably, one member of the group became a senior Communist Party official.'

Jerzy explained that there had been many misunderstandings about Karol's reported adolescent love affairs.

'You have to remember that in Poland in 1938 you had to plot and concentrate pretty hard to get and keep a regular girlfriend. There was nothing between Halina – she was the headmaster's daughter – and Karol. I know, because I taught Halina to play tennis.

'Karol simply did not spend any time on getting a steady girlfriend. His studies took up all his energies. He knew more and studied more than anyone else did. For example, he used to read pure philosophy, which was not even taught at school. He came out top in every subject.

'My father, who ran a big lawyers' office, had an assistant called Kuczkowski. This young man fell in love with a local girl who later worked for the Resistance when the war started. The girl was arrested and taken to the gas chambers at Auschwitz and the young man was so upset that he decided to become a priest. Today Monsignor Kuczkowski still lives in Kraków. This story of frustrated love has been mistakenly attributed by some journalists to Karol, but it is simply not true.'

When it became dangerous to associate with Jews as the Nazi threat increased, Karol's attitude to his Jewish friends never wavered. 'You cannot imagine what it was like to have such a warm, human and brotherly friendship,' Jerzy told me.

And they are still able to discuss the painful relations between Jews and Catholics today. The Pope's controversial decision to invite Austrian President Kurt Waldheim, suspected of having taken part in anti-Jewish activities when he was serving with the Wehrmacht in the Balkans, to the Vatican for a State visit is among the subjects the two friends have discussed in private. 'Above all, we Poles know about tragedy and injustice,' Jerzy said.

Jerzy's grandmother, mother and sister all perished at Auschwitz. He escaped from Poland in 1939 with his father, but fell into the hands of the Russians. Unlike his friend Karol, he has never been able to return to Wadowice, although he still has a large collection of photographs and postcards and talks familiarly about the square and the church and the building where his father's office was, and the grammar school just around the corner.

On the Pope's first visit home after his election in 1979, we spent a day in Wadowice. Karol's former grammar-school headmaster reported favourably and proudly upon his now eminent pupil. Bouquets of flowers were presented and the town band played at a mass in the square where Jerzy and Karol used to play football after school. I visited the modest two-storey corner house near the Church where Karol lived until 1936.

His mother Emilia, a schoolteacher of Lithuanian origin, died when he was only six. Psychologists have suggested that the origin of Pope John Paul's fervent devotion to the Virgin Mary – her initial M is emblazoned on his papal coat of arms – and attraction towards Marian shrines may be traced to maternal deprivation during his early childhood. Four years later there was another bereavement in the family. Karol's much older brother Edmund, who had qualified as a doctor, contracted scarlet fever and died. As soon as the young Karol had passed his matriculation examination, his father, a retired army quartermaster who had begun his military service when southern Poland was still part of the Austro-Hungarian Empire, took his son to complete his studies in the near-by university city of Kraków. They lived in this handsome city in a very modest basement flat in the suburb of Debniki.

Karol's father died when the future Pope was barely twenty. 'At twenty,' Karol later recounted, 'I had already lost all the people I loved and even the ones I might have loved, such as my big sister who had died, I was told, six years before my birth.' A student friend, Juliusz Kydrynski, remembers Karol at the age of eighteen as a strongly built youth with a round face, thick, dark blond hair and an aversion to wearing a tie. They shared an interest in the theatre and poetry. Karol, had a deep, resonant voice and was a born actor, liked to take part in public readings. They had many friends, Tadek, Marek and Wojtek, and Krysia, Danka and Halina. Karol was not averse to female company although he never had a steady girlfriend, according to Juliusz.

Karol first got to know Halina Krolikiewicz – the headmaster's daughter – in amateur dramatics at school in Wadowice. They played leading roles in a parish hall production of *Sigismond Augustus*, an historical and patriotic epic about the first kings of Poland. Later they took part in more serious theatre together in the Rhapsody student theatre company in Kraków. When he was elected Pope, all sorts of wild rumours flew around Rome about his youthful love affairs; he had had a secret affair with Halina, he had been engaged to another girl who died in a concentration camp, he had even contracted a secret marriage and had a daughter who was now a journalist in Warsaw.

In a play about marriage called *The Jeweller's Shop*, published under a pseudonym after the war in a local magazine, Karol had written:

Sometimes human existence seems too short for love. At other times however it is the other way round, human love seems too short in relation to existence, or rather too shallow. In any case every person has at his or her disposal an existence and a love. The problem is: how to build a sensible structure out of it?

Halina in fact fell in love with Tadek, another member of Karol's group of friends, and married him during the Nazi occupation. Shortly after their wedding, Karol began his studies for the priesthood. One of the first children he baptised after his ordination was their infant daughter Monika, who when she grew up wrote for a Communist Party publication in Warsaw.

While Karol rose to become Bishop and Cardinal, Halina became leading lady of the Stary theatre company in Kraków. Every Christmas she still receives a greetings card from her best friend at the Vatican.

Often after lectures or in the evening Karol's student group used to repair to a café: Michalik's or the Little Cross, just off the Market Square, were their favourite haunts. But Karol did not seem to be interested in carousing and drinking. He tended to disappear after a while to read or study at home.

Karol became a frequent visitor at the Kydrynskis' flat, where he found an affectionate welcome from Juliusz's mother. It became his second home. Nearly always he wore the same black jacket and worn grey trousers, and he never complained about the lack of money at home.

Karol was also cool in the face of danger. When the Germans started bombing Kraków on 1 September 1939, he and Juliusz loaded some food, bedlinen, clothes and household equipment on to a handcart to push them to safety at a friend's flat in the suburbs. But the Germans dive-bombed the radio station just as they were trundling through the empty streets, and they were forced to seek refuge in the porch of an empty house. As the silver-painted German fighters screamed down on their target, the two students must have thought their last moment had come.

'Karol remained totally calm. We did not talk,' Juliusz remembers. 'Even during the worst explosions we did not exchange a word. If Karol was praying, he did it inwardly without crossing himself. He was very grave and calm and eventually his calmness spread to me.'

When his father died in February 1941, Karol moved in with the Kydrynskis. In order to avoid deportation by the German occupation forces the two friends found jobs as labourers in a quarry belonging to a local chemical factory. The work was backbreaking. During the most severe of the wartime winters, with temperatures falling to minus thirty degrees Centigrade, they smashed lime rocks with sledgehammers and loaded the rubble on to the skips of a narrow-gauge train, which carried it to the factory. Later they were transferred to a slightly less strenuous indoor job as stokers at the water-purification plant. Thus Karol had his first direct contact with the labouring classes, an experience which stood him in good stead when he came to formulate his own ideas on the dignity of human labour in his encyclical *Laborem Exercens* and *Centesimus Annus*.

Then there was his life in the intellectual underground, the secret world of Polish culture. In his free time, Karol studied, wrote and organized the clandestine theatre. All such gatherings for cultural purposes were forbidden on pain of immediate deportation. If the police had found out about the readings and performances at the Kydrynskis' flat on Felicjanek Street, performers and audience alike would have ended up in a labour camp. Karol was an industrious writer. On the eve of his twentieth birthday, he borrowed a typewriter and tapped out his first play, a biblical drama entitled *Job*. It was an allegory of the tragedy of Poland. Job, the man who dared to argue with God about the injustice of his sufferings, was, at the end of the play, raised to life again.

Juliusz, an easy-going person, spoke of Karol's powers of concentration and discipline, of how he used to pace around the room for hours with a French textbook in his hand going over words and phrases.

From underground theatre, Karol moved on to underground theology. He enrolled in 1942 at a part-time seminary whose students were scattered all over the city. As the war drew to an end and the Germans started exacting reprisals, rounding up all males between the ages of fifteen and fifty, Kraków's Archbishop, Prince Adam Sapieha, gave Karol asylum by inviting him to take up residence inside the Archbishop's palace. The future Pope's priestly vocation was by now confirmed. He devoted himself entirely to his studies. Finally Kraków was liberated by the Russians and Karol was able to complete his theological studies at the re-opened Jagellonian University. He was ordained priest on 1 November 1946 by Archbishop Sapieha, who immediately sent him on his first trip abroad, to begin two years' study for a doctorate at the Angelicum College run by the Dominicans in Rome. There he boarded at the Belgian College, which enabled him to become fluent in French as well as Italian. He travelled with friends to France and Belgium to study the problems facing working-class young people in shattered post-war Europe.

Karol returned to Kraków in 1948 during the height of the Stalinist terror, after being awarded top marks for his thesis on the Spanish mystic Saint John of the Cross. He was given his first job as vicar in a country town 200 kilometres east of Kraków, not far from the Soviet border. He moved back to Kraków to take charge of a city parish and continue his studies. Ten years later he was promoted at the age of thirty-eight to become the youngest bishop in Poland and one of the youngest local leaders in the Roman Catholic Church. He was already a full Professor, holding the chair of ethics at Lublin University, the only Catholic university allowed to operate in Eastern Europe. He used to commute the 220 miles from Kraków to Lublin by night train in order to save time on those days that he had to lecture.

The rigorous organization of his working day, begrudging time off for rest or recreation, was a characteristic that marked Karol Wojtyla's whole life. When he became Bishop, he had a reading light and folding desk fitted in the rear of his car so as to be able to continue reading and writing while he was driven around on official business. As Pope he was a glutton for work even during the most strenuous of his intercontinental travels. He did pause for a short stroll in some woods during a visit to Canada, and he spent half an hour watching the animals at a game reserve while in Kenya. But foreigners unused to his gruelling non-stop touring schedule sometimes wondered why he never even bothered to look out of the window of the plane during his travels. Usually he had his face buried in a book.

Monsignor Stanislaw Dziwisz, the Pope's private secretary, told bemused Australian reporters who wondered why they always saw John Paul immersed in some philosophical tome instead of relaxing on take-off and during the long flights across the Australian continent: 'He is not a tourist. He does not look at the countryside or the buildings. He is a pastor and this is a pastoral mission.'

The seriousness with which he accomplished his religious mission did now, however, mean that he was standoffish. The difference in style between Wojtyla and Prince Sapieha, his protector and sponsor, an ecclesiastic of noble birth, could not have been more striking. Whereas one could only approach Prince Sapieha on bended knee, Wojtyla never stood on ceremony. He was prepared to sit on the floor to talk with students. A sportsman at heart, he liked the open air and spent his free time camping, hiking, canoeing, mountain climbing, bicycling and swimming.

He remained a keen skier. One of his friends in Kraków told me, 'When he became Bishop he used to stay at a convent in Zakopane, the winter sports resort near the Czechoslovak border and take the cable car to the highest peak in the Tatra mountains, Kasprowy Wierch, skiing down nonstop at high speed. He relished the thrills and the danger.

33

Wojtyla's first visit home in the summer after his election in Rome
was a unique chance to observe him in his familiar native context. He
could use his own language, see his old friends, sleep in his former bed
in the Archbishop's palace in Kraków, worship at the tomb of former
kings of Poland, visit his country's holiest shrine, that of the Black Virgin
of Czestochowa. The atmosphere was very different to that of his new
habitat, Rome.

The emotion he felt during those eight days was evident from the
moment he boarded the Alitalia jet in Rome for the flight to Warsaw. I
asked him what it meant to him to be going back home. The reply came
in ponderous English (he spoke the language poorly in those days)' 'I . . .
could . . . not . . . not . . . go.' He was unable to hide the joy behind the
confusing double negative.

The reaction of the Polish people, 95 per cent of whom are Catholics
according to the Vatican, was equally enthusiastic. Although the official
airport reception by the Communist authorities when we taxied to a
halt at the military side of Warsaw airport was stiff and formal, there
was no mistaking the explosion of popular feeling as soon as the official
motorcade swung into the broad avenue leading to the city centre.
Although Poland and the Vatican at that time had no diplomatic
relations, the Pope was received with full military honours as a visiting
Head of State. His first public engagement was to celebrate an open-air
mass in Victory Square, in the centre of Warsaw, just opposite the small
memorial to the unknown soldier with its goose-stepping guards.

A million people crammed the square. Yet there was total silence as
the Pope raised the Eucharist. 'Christ cannot be kept out of the history
of man in any part of the globe,' Wojtyla triumphantly proclaimed in his
homily. Applause kept on drowning out his words. There was repeated
chanting of 'We want God'. The Pope made no attempt to quieten the
crowds.

The moment he stepped down from the white-draped platform on
which an altar had been raised, workmen moved in to dismantle the
huge wooden cross which had formed the backdrop to the proceedings.
Two hours later there remained no visible trace of the symbols of religion
in Victory Square.

The following day, speaking to the bishops of Poland in the ancient
city of Gniezno, the Pope boldly sketched out what was to become the
theme of his reign, his belief in the unity of the European continent
through its common Christian origins, all the way from Russia in the

east to France in the west, from Britain in the north, to Italy, Spain and Greece in the south.

At the same time he distinguished between what he considered 'good' frontiers and 'bad' frontiers. In 1982 ambassadors accredited to the Vatican were taken by surprise when he offered his view of the 1942 Yalta Conference at which European borders were delimited by the Soviet Union, Britain and the United States.

The continuing existence of 'spheres of hegemony' was not justified, he told the ambassadors, 'especially if they tend to limit the sovereignty of other nations. Each people must be entitled to the free determination of its own fate. The Church cannot fail to give support to such convictions.'

It was a message that he was to return to many times; at Santiago de Compostela near Spain's Atlantic coast later that same year, at Speyer near the frontier between the East and West Germany in 1987, and on the eve of the tenth anniversary of his pontificate, at Strasbourg, the seat of the European Parliament located on the banks of river Rhine, which marks the frontier between France and West Germany.

But to return to Poland in 1979, was it not perhaps God's will, he now asked the splendidly mitred bishops at Gniezno, that he, the Pope from Poland, the first Slav Pope in history, should show the way forward to the world by proclaiming the essential spiritual unity of the whole of Western culture and civilization? Could not Eastern Europe and Western Europe transcend the divisions of the Cold War by going back to their common spiritual roots?

Of the two great Christian traditions of Europe, Eastern Orthodoxy and Western Catholicism, Poland had chosen that of the West, together with fellow Christians from Lithuania and Ukraine, both now within the borders of the Soviet Union.

Poland had been celebrating the thousandth anniversary of the conversion of its people to Western Christianity, but had always respected the traditions of Eastern Christianity, the Pope said. Significantly, nowhere did he mention that other later, great divide of Christendom, the Protestant Reformation of the sixteenth century.

The Pope's nostalgic and patriotic pilgrimage to the familiar places of his life as schoolboy, university student, priest, bishop and cardinal, now turned southwards. He travelled to the monastery of Jasna Gora ('Bright Mountain' in Polish) to pay homage at the shrine of the Black Virgin, a holy icon that Poles believe turned the tide of war in their favour when they were under attack from a Swedish army in the seventeenth century.

In Poland, as in Ireland, the Church has always been the guardian not only of the national religion, but also of national identity in times of repression.

The crowds were so dense that it was impossible to move on the hillside leading up to the monastery. I walked around to the back of the buildings and found a group of people listening to the Pope's words on a transistor radio. I was puzzled and asked what station they were tuned in to, as the service taking place only half a mile away was not being relayed by the State-controlled Polish radio. 'Vatican radio on short-wave' a priest replied triumphantly. It was a first lesson in the Pope's grasp of the importance of the electronic media. Twelve years later he was to install big-screen television inside Saint Peter's basilica.

Next day the tour continued with a pilgrimage to Auschwitz. the concentration camp a few miles from Kraków where millions of victims of Hitler's extermination programme of Jews, Gypsies and other non-Aryan races were gassed and cremated. The death factory has not been razed; the camp buildings in red brick, the wickedly misleading slogan 'Arbeit macht frei' (Work brings freedom) over the main entrance, the railway sidings where truckloads of deportees from all over Europe arrived on their final journey, have all been preserved. German tourists were among those who came to view the monstrous piles of spectacles, and the mounds of human hair shorn from those about to be slaughtered. It was a perfect summer day and there were wild flowers growing near the ruins of the cremation ovens. The Pope prayed for some time alone in the prison cell where a Polish priest, Father Maximilian Kolbe, died after offering himself for execution in place of a man who had a wife and family. Later the Pope was to declare Kolbe the first saint of the Second World War. Among those attending the Pope's mass were former Auschwitz inmates who knew Kolbe, wearing their striped prison-camp uniform, the badge of their survival.

The Pope spent his two final days in Kraków. His popularity in his home town was such that revellers would simply not allow him to go to bed. Outside the Archbishop's palace singing, clapping and impromptu speeches continued until the early hours. The Pope kept on coming out on to the balcony and exchanged banter and songs with the crowd until he was exhausted and asked to be allowed to sleep.

On the Blonie meadows, along the river Vistula, what must have been the biggest crowd ever to assemble in Poland gathering during the Pope's final night at home. As dawn broke I climbed to the roof of the eight-storey Cracovia Hotel near by and saw a sea of people which seemed to stretch for more than a mile. The gathering was estimated by the authorities at about two million, more than twice the entire population of Kraków. Polish State television, unsure how to portray such an act of unofficial homage in a land unused to genuine manifestations of public enthusiasm, fixed its cameras on a small section of the crowd, and avoided any wide-angle shots. The event was a foretaste of the multitudes that were to become a feature of the Pope's presence when he first visited a country during the early days of his travels. Everywhere second and third visits drew smaller crowds – except in Poland.

The departure for Rome direct from the small civil airport near Kraków was another emotional occasion. The Pope kissed his native soil before leaving and bade his public farewell to his country, 'from which my heart can never be parted'. He had sown seeds of confidence which one year later were to take root with the creation of the first free trade-union movement in Communist Eastern Europe, Solidarity. The Polish Church had shown its strength and self-discipline. He had demonstrated that he was not pushing for change in the political *status quo*, but could not be prevented from carrying out his duty of reminding the Polish people of their inalienable human rights.

The Pope had to watch from a distance the rise – and the subsequent temporary fall – of Solidarity, whose name was incessantly on his lips during the coming years. The Vatican's most influential political act of the century, the commanding influence that Pope John Paul had established in his country, was about to bear fruit. If anyone had asked him whether his motives were political or religious in trying to influence the course of modern European history, I am sure he would have found the question as absurd as if it had been asked during the Middle Ages of one of the crusading kings of France or England. For Karol Wojtyla the divisions between Polish patriotism, faith and politics are happily blurred.

Portraits of the Pope hung alongside the holy icon of the Madonna of Czestochowa on the gateway of the Lenin Shipyards in Gdansk where Solidarity was born. Flags of the new trade union were blessed in the churches. The Pope was able to welcome Lech Walesa, the architect of Solidarity on a visit to the Vatican in January 1981, just over four months after the signing of the Gdansk agreements authorizing the free trade union put an end to the longest strike recorded up to that moment in a Communist-controlled country in Eastern Europe.

However, 1981 turned out to be a bitter year for the Pope.

On the afternoon of 13 May, as he was being driven around Saint

Peter's Square in his Popemobile during a general audience, the Turkish gunman Ali Agca fired three shots at close range and almost killed him. The Pope was rushed to hospital and an emergency operation performed. From his hospital bed the Pope publicly forgave his would-be assassin. There also, on 28 May, he learned of the death of Cardinal Stefan Wyszynski, Primate of Poland, his close friend from his earliest days as Bishop.

Recovery was slow, and he had a relapse because of infection, which forced him to return to hospital for a spell. Ali Agca, who had previously threatened to kill the Pope during his visit to Turkey at the end of 1979, was tried for attempted murder by an Italian court and sentenced to life imprisonment. There was speculation in the Western media that the Russians, worried about the politically destabilizing effect of the Pope's visit to Poland, might have been behind the assassination attempt, acting through their surrogate Bulgaria. These allegations led to another trial at which Agca and several other Turks and Bulgarians were acquitted for lack of evidence on charges of conspiring to kill the Pope. The court rejected circumstantial evidence of an international plot uncovered by American and Italian intelligence. The Italian judges ruled that the Turkish Mafia, who operated drugs and arms smuggling rackets throughout Bulgaria, hired Agca, a professional killer, to assassinate the Pope and then abandoned him to his fate when he bungled the attempt. What the judges were unable to explain was who actually commissioned the crime and why just two hours after the attempt on the Pope's life, a pantechnicon owned by the Bulgarian government left the Bulgarian Embassy in Rome carrying diplomatic baggage for Sofia. Agca always maintained that this was meant to be his escape vehicle, but he was captured by police before he could rendezvous with it. During the whole of 1981 the Bulgarian Embassy requested no import or export authorization from Italian customs – other than for this one heavy goods vehicle.

The most bitter blow to the Pope was the outlawing of Solidarity and the declaration of martial law in Poland on 13 December. This put paid to any prospect of his second Polish visit in 1982, as originally planned to coincide with the six-hundredth anniversary of the founding of the monastery of Jasna Gora.

The Polish bishops played a key role in persuading the government in Warsaw gradually to release Solidarity political prisoners, including the future President of Poland, Lech Walesa. Paradoxically, the Church strengthened its position under martial law as its ministered to working people and political prisoners and their families. Perhaps the most remarkable development was the adherence to the Church of many members of Poland's intellectual élite, scientists, journalists, academics and artists, who had hitherto been lukewarm Christians. Churchgoing, which had been on the decline, suddenly increased. Attendance at mass by university graduates doubled during these years.

John Paul had to be content with the canoniszation ceremony in Rome in October 1982 for Maximilian Kolbe, which attracted tens of thousands of Polish pilgrims. His chief informant in Warsaw, Cardinal Glemp, in Rome for the ceremony, brought an offer from the Polish government. In exchange for the Polish Church's condemnation of further strike calls by the underground Solidarity movement, a papal visit would be permitted the following year. Replying to the strike threats, Cardinal Glemp said, 'The church is firmly opposed to this initiative, whose only consequence would be heavy repression . . .'

I found the atmosphere in Warsaw when John Paul arrived on 16 June 1983, with martial law still in force, much more oppressive than on his first visit four years before. The Pope stood up boldly in front of an unsmiling General Jaruzelski and said he hoped that the social reforms 'so painstakingly worked out during the critical days of August 1980' would gradually be put into effect.

At a papal mass celebrated in the Warsaw football stadium, hundreds of thousands of people squeezed into the terraces and stands. Hundreds of thousands more stood patiently outside. The Pope appealed to the Polish people's innate sense of history. Behaving more like the King of Poland than the Vicar of Christ and Bishop of Rome, mitred and dressed in imposing new vestments, John Paul implied that the current masters of his country only had the right to govern if they respected the moral laws of the Church. In the course of Poland's long and tormented history, he said, the people had suffered worse troubles than the current state of martial law, and they must look forward confidently to the next millennium.

The speech was peppered with historical references ranging over a thousand years of Poland's past. It was received by the huge crowd with cheering, applause and chanting. The people of the drab city of Warsaw had identified their hero and were confident that the Pope's long view of history would eventually be vindicated.

Next day the weather was rainy and the fields surrounding Saint Maximilian Kolbe's former religious house at Niepokalanow near Warsaw quickly turned into a quagmire as John Paul celebrated another open-air mass, this time in honour of Poland's new saint. Although he pronounced the word 'solidarity' in his homily, the Pope did so only in a general sense, and could not be accused of political provocation by the government. But he was treading on a tightrope. Solidarity banners were flashed at him suddenly in the crowds attending his masses, and were hidden again just as quickly to avoid incidents which might cause the omnipresent police to intervene at a religious gathering. The Pope spoke in a coded language that was understood perfectly by the millions who flocked to see him in Warsaw and central and southern Poland. The authorities had made it clear in advance that he would not be welcome anywhere near Gdansk.

An emissary from General Jaruzelski was despatched to the monastery of Jasna Gora on the fourth day of the visit to protest to the Vatican Secretary of State that the Pope's speeches were becoming dangerously political. In reply, the official Vatican spokesman put out a glib statement confirming the purely religious and pastoral nature of the Pope's second return visit to his native country.

In Czestochowa, however, John Paul made one gesture which did please the authorities. Quoting Saint Paul's words to the Christians of Corinth telling them not to change their social condition because of their religious conversion, he appealed to the young people of Poland not to abandon their country and seek political refuge and a new life abroad because of the current troubles. Polish pilgrims visiting Rome had frequently failed to rejoin their tourist buses. Thousands of young Poles emigrated, many of them via Rome, during the years following the imposition of martial law.

Continuing his tour in Poznan, the scene of serious rioting in 1956 when there had been an explosion of popular protest against food shortages and rising prices, the Pope paid tribute to the seventy-two dead and 1,500 injured of that year commemorated by two huge monumental crosses. After he left I saw police tear-gassing Solidarity demonstrators near by. Later that day the Pope went on to the industrial centre of Katowice to address Silesian miners and steelworkers. In driving rain he told them of their right to organize themselves in trade unions, and of the religious significance of the events of August 1980 which led to the legalization of the Solidarity movement and which had been followed, he said, with great emotion by people all over the world.

At Wroclaw, where the banned free trade union had gone underground, the police were again seen in action against demonstrators. But by now the Pope had the measure of just how far he could go with public references to 'solidarity'. Once again the tour ended in Kraków, where there was a moment of tension when he dedicated a new church in the industrial area of Nowa Huta, another hotbed of Solidarity. The symbolic importance of the new ultra-modern church in this desolate industrial landscape was clear. It was Wojtyla himself who had fought with the Communist authorities for permission to build the church in the days when he was Archbishop.

Before leaving for Rome, the Pope took a few hours off for a brief private visit and a reflective walk in his beloved Tatra mountains. There, a private meeting had been arranged with Lech Walesa, who was allowed to travel down from Gdansk with his family to meet the pontiff on the understanding that no publicity would be given to the event, which was censored in the local Polish press.

The official departure ceremony at the airport in Kraków again provided proof of the homage that Poles felt due to their spiritual leader. Although all roads leading to the airport had been closed by police, we could see hillsides two and three miles away covered with swarms of people who had to be content to say farewell from a distance. The Pope noticed them and paused for a long final wave before he boarded his special LOT charter plane.

The day after his return to Rome, there was an unexpected sequel to his meeting with Walesa. *L'Osservatore Romano*, a semi-official publication which is nevertheless regarded as the authoritative voice of the Vatican, came out with an astonishing front-page editorial headlined 'Honour to Sacrifice' signed by the priest acting as deputy editor, Don Virgilio Levi. The article suggested that the Pope had decided to distance himself from Walesa in exchange for a promise for concessions by the Polish authorities, including the lifting of martial law.

'Officially, Walesa is leaving the scene once again. We might say that he has lost his battle . . . Sometimes it is necessary to sacrifice awkward people in order that a greater good may be created for the community.'

The article almost sounded like an obituary.

What Walesa has meant for Polish workers can never be cancelled. By receiving him, the Pope gave satisfaction to his people. But by receiving him so privately he avoided harming the delicate phase of national reconciliation. Not all will agree. In Poland, practically no one. But there were reasons of *'force majeure.*

Let us honour Walesa's sacrifice!

The Pope was furious. He sent for Don Virgilio and told him he had to resign. There was an internal enquiry into the editorial policies of *Osservatore*. The incident revealed that the Pope would not tolerate anyone in the Vatican playing politics in his native country. In fact Don Virgilio was quite right. The Pope had agreed with the Communist authorities that for the time being Walesa should be regarded as a non-person inside Poland. But he could not have this made public in his own newspaper.

Four years later the Pope returned for the third time. The mood had changed. Martial law had been abolished, yet Solidarity remained an outlawed organization. But on this occasion the Pope used the word Solidarity without worrying too much whether it was understood by his listeners to be written with a small 's' or a capital 'S'.

Cities exlcuded by the authorities on former visits on the grounds that they might become centres for political provocation by dissidents became the setting for noisy celebrations, with heavy forces of police kept in reserve well out of sight. In Lublin, only a few miles from the Soviet border, where the Pope had been Professor of Ethics at the Catholic University, he now ordained twenty-three new priests in front of a crowd of hundreds of thousands gathered against a background of dismal high-rise workers' flats. Under the inspiration of John Paul, Poland led Europe in new vocations; in 1990, 28 per cent of all students for the priesthood in Europe were Poles.

In Szczecin, on the East German border, the Pope was only a short hop east of Berlin, for until 1945 this was a predominantly Protestant German city called Stettin. It was also the city that Winston Churchill fixed as marker for the northern end of the Iron Curtain in his famous 1946 Fulton, Missouri speech. ('From Stettin in the Baltic to Trieste in the Adriatic, an Iron Curtain has descended across the continent.')

Here the Pope mentioned in public in Poland for the first time the agreements signed between Solidarity and the Polish authorities in 1980 on which Warsaw later reneged. 'What was the meaning of those agreements? Was it not everything concerning the dignity of man's work?' he asked.

Later he flew by helicopter across the farmlands of Pomerania, the so-called Gdansk corridor, which Hitler had annexed to give him access to the German-speaking free port then called Danzig. Hitler's invasion of western Pomerania marked the start of the Second World War in September 1939. Everywhere the Pope went, there were memories of Poland's and Europe's tragic recent past.

In the early evening he arrived at the port of Gdynia, developed as Poland's main Baltic waterway after the Versailles peace treaty at the end of the First World War had limited Polish shipping activity from

Danzig. This was the occasion for the keynote speech of the Pope's 1987 visit, addressed formally to the fishermen of the Baltic sea, but in fact to every Pole. Speaking in Kosciuszko Square, in the centre of the port area, he used the word solidarity no less than seven times within the space of three minutes. He had repeatedly to break off from his text and ask for silence so that his words could be understood properly. The tone was fatherly and measured. Every window, every balcony overlooking the square was crammed to bursting point. Some people around me in the densely packed crowd were weeping openly.

'Not only does the sea separate men and nations, it also unites them,' the Pope said. 'It speaks to men of the need for meeting each other, for collaboration, in short for solidarity.

'In the name of the future of man and mankind, this word "solidarity" must be pronounced. Today it is still spreading like a wave throughout the world which recognizes that we cannot live according to the principle of "all against all" but only according to a different principle of "all with all", "all for all". This word has been pronounced here in a new way and in a new context. And the world cannot forget.'

The Pope was officially adopting the Solidarity agreements as part of his Church's social teaching. His papal predecessors and the Second Vatican Council had all taught these same principles of solidarity, he said.

Out of sight, just behind the square, were parked the dozens of blue buses which brought the grey-uniformed police who had been shadowing him in every city he visited, officially to protect him from acts of terrorism, in fact to intervene with tear gas and water cannon the moment a pro-Solidarity demonstration threatened.

Later that night, at the house of the Archbishop of Gdansk, his host, the Pope had a private meeting with Lech Walesa. The Archbishop had been told by the authorities to ensure that no Solidarity banners were unfurled by the crowds at the shipyard workers' mass to be held on the drab housing estate in Gdansk where Walesa used to live with his large family, in the days before he moved into the Belvedere Palace in Warsaw. When he heard about this condition Walesa reportedly said that if there were no red and white Solidarity banners on display, he would write the name across his own t-shirt using his wife's lipstick.

This was the first of two unscheduled private engagements. The other was in the early morning of the day of the Pope's departure from Warsaw, a Sunday. Before celebrating his final mass, the Pope went to the suburban church where the popular Father Jerzy Popieluszko was the parish priest before he was murdered by security police in 1984 for openly preaching in favour of Solidarity. The Pope knelt and prayed before Father Jerzy's simple grave in the churchyard, and placed on it a wreath of yellow and white flowers – the Vatican colours. By nightfall there rose over the tomb a mountain of fresh flowers, representing a small fortune in zlotys, the Polish currency.

The Pope's final public appearance was a set-piece mass in front of central Warsaw's principal eyesore, the Palace of Culture. The ugly skyscraper was Stalin's gift to the Polish people, a cynical gesture considering that the Soviet leader had allowed the Polish capital to be razed by the Germans at the end of the Second World War while the Red Army stood by and watched. Here the Pope gave a telling Slavic slant to the Universal Church: 'The Church which is in Rome and in Antioch and in Jerusalem and in Alexandria and in Constantinople. The Church which is in Lithuania and in Byelorussia and in the Ukraine, and in Kiev and in the territories of the great Russia and of our brother Slavs (and also the non-Slavs) to the south in the countries once visited by the saintly brothers Cyril and Methodius [of whom more later]. And in all of Europe and in the Americas now preparing to celebrate the five-hundredth anniversary of their evangelization. In Africa, in Australia and in Asia, and in all the islands and archipelagos of all the seas and oceans . . .'

Non-Slav Europe came some way down the list.

There followed a remarkable pageant. A long religious procession wound slowly through the centre of Warsaw. The Pope was sandwiched between serried ranks of hundreds of priests and nuns and members of religious orders, all marching more or less in step to the music of factory brass bands from the industrial areas of Silesia.

John Paul was encased in an enormous, gleaming, bullet-proof glass cage on wheels with a chauffeur up front and security men as outriders – a stretched Popemobile. The Pope knelt in front of the exposed sacrament. He remained completely immobile, his head bent in prayer, his brow furrowed, eyes closed, hands clasped in supplication before him, along the whole two-mile route. Here being played out before our eyes was an allegory of the Polish church militant on the eve of the third Christian millennium.

The Pope's prayers were to be answered with unexpected rapidity. Economic pressures, and a green light from Moscow, finally convinced the Communist authorities in Warsaw that they should enlist the help of Solidarity to solve the country's serious economic problems. The first free elections since the Second World War were held and Solidarity triumphed. The Roman Catholic Church was granted full legal recognition. The Catholic press was allowed to print as many newspapers and periodicals as it could sell in competititon with a newly free press. And so an era came to an abrupt end. The old opposition between an oppressive State and a Church which represented true national and social identity no longer held.

For forty years, with no independent expression of opinion allowed, the Church hierarchy had acted for and spoken out on behalf of the largest section of Polish society. It did not matter that it had no legal status. It had authority.

Now that a pluralistic society has emerged, the Church in Poland is faced with a series of fundamental questions. What is to be the future of folk Catholicism, that attachment to quaint ceremonies and customs which was the dominant model of religiosity during the years of oppression? And how is the Catholic Church to compete with other groups who present themselves in the religious market-place?

Bishops, and above all the Primate of the Church Cardinal Glemp, who have grown accustomed to being obeyed unquestioningly while defending their community against a hostile State, have to learn that they are now themselves open to political criticism.

It is clear that the Catholic Church in Poland will retain its dominant position only in so far as it derives its strength from the active faith of its members, not from its institutional power.

Zbigniew Nosowski, editor of the Polish Catholic monthly *Wiez* put it like this:

It is questionable whether the Church in Poland is prepared to face the challenge. In the years when educated people were being attracted, the response was very low in the countryside. In the rural areas there was even a decline of as much as 30 per cent. So what will happen when it appears that ceremonies are no longer sufficient? The sociologist in me is concerned when he notices an amazing passivity among laypeople, and on the other hand growing disrespect by the clergy for those lay men and women who do take a moral lead in society. It is difficult to be optimistic when one sees the narrow-mindedness of many priests who can only criticize Western Europe as an excellent negative example of the effects of materialism. They are not able to recognize the similarity between their own situation at present and that which previously existed in the West, and the necessity of Poland being open to the positive values that the Churches in the West grasped too late, thus losing many of their members.

New attitudes towards religion to suit the changed political circumstances of the 1990s are the concern not only of the Church in Poland but also of the other Catholic hierarchies of Eastern Europe.

The Ukrainian Catholic Church for example, at present engaged in what it sees as a righteous struggle with the Russian Orthodox Church for repossession of its former churches, has little understanding of or admiration for the new spirit of ecumenism which has swept the Churches in the West since the Second Vatican Council. The Ukrainian Catholic Church has been dormant for over forty years and does not hide its aversion to some of the attitudes it hears being expressed by Church leaders in Rome.

Andrew Sorokowski, Head of Research at the Ukrainian Catholic Church headquarters in Rome, explained that his Church has traditionally been one of a people 'living on the frontier of civilization, concerned primarily with physical and spiritual survival.

'It is the Church of a fundamentally insecure – and therefore deeply conservative – people, determined to preserve its cultural identity, but reluctant, in view of the overwhelming risks, to experiment or innovate. In this role as spiritual and cultural fortress, the Church has helped us to survive the onslaughts of the centuries from the Mongols to the Bolsheviks. In the emigration [there are two million Ukrainians living overseas, mainly in Canada and the United States] it has even helped us to stave off alien moral and cultural values. But is this a sufficient model for the future?'

A survey carried out in 1989 by the Soviet Academy of Sciences among Ukrainians found 56 per cent of those interviewed in Lvov were in favour of legalization of the Ukrainian Catholic Church, but this fell to only 34 per cent in rural areas, where almost as many people, 32 per cent, said they opposed it. So the widely held view that the strength of Catholicism lies in the countryside of Eastern Europe rather than the cities may be as false in western Ukraine as it is in Poland.

Meanwhile Poland seems more preoccupied with its economic rather than its moral future. The Solidarity trade union felt obliged to organize strikes and protests against the draconian economic austerity programme decreed by the first Solidarity-led government. Cardinal Glemp, perhaps sensing the winds of secular change blowing through his country, said he would have no objection to the future separation of Church and State in the newly democratized Poland.

President Lech Walesa was received with full honours on his first visit abroad as Head of State – a State visit to the Vatican in February 1991. Walesa and his family received a particularly warm personal welcome from the Pope, who had been ultimately responsible for the former shipyard electrician's dramatic ascent to the presidency of his country.

Speaking at a news conference after his meeting with the Pope at the Vatican, President Walesa ventured his opinion about possible future developments in the Soviet Union based on his political experiences in the 1980s.

'If the Soviet Union wishes to continue to be a world power,' Walesa said, 'it should dissolve itself as soon as possible and then form a new federation based on new principles of freedom, democracy and pluralism.

'Otherwise the future of the Soviet Union will be marked by a string of funerals, clashes and negative developments. The Soviet Union will become weaker and weaker until it crumbles into dust.

'I am convinced that in the future new solutions will be enacted, solutions which will offer new possibilities. Pluralism and freedom are the challenges of the new era we are entering.'

CHAPTER 3

Christians of the East

My wish, knowing the aspirations of the Slav people, is that one day, through the creation of free institutions with sovereign power, Europe may once again cover its true geographical and even more important, historical, dimensions.

Pope John Paul II, addressing the European Parliament,
Strasbourg, October 1988

The events of 1989 are a warning to those who in the name of political realism wish to banish law and morality from the political arena.

Pope John Paul, encyclical letter, *Centesimus Annus*, May 1991

During 1989 the French celebrated at length the bicentenary of their historic Revolution. But 1989 may well go down in history as a year of more fundamental importance, not least for the future of the Roman Catholic Church in Europe, than the anniversary of the storming of the Bastille. Eastern Europe was the theatre for an unparalleled sequence of political changes as Communist governments fell one after another. In the final months of the year, revolutions broke out almost every week in those buffer states which had been under Soviet control since the Second World War. Following Poland's peaceful transition to democratic rule in the spring, Hungary threw off the shackles of Communism, the Berlin Wall was dismantled and Bulgaria threw out its dictator. Then Czechoslovakia and Romania followed suit. Early in 1990 Catholic Lithuania and the other Soviet Baltic Republics began to implement plans to cut their ties with Moscow and revert to the independent status they had lost half a century before when a secret pact between Hitler and Stalin led to their annexation. And finally even Albania, that last bastion of pure Marxism in Europe, crumbled.

Although the Pope was undoubtedly surprised by the rapidity of political change, the new situation was one for which he had been preparing throughout his pontificate.

In his encyclical *Centesimus Annus* published in 1991 to celebrate the hundredth anniversary of *Rerum Novarum,* the Roman Catholic Church's first major document on social issues, the Pope claimed credit for the Vatican's contribution to these changes as a result of his strong stand on human rights.

The decisive factor which gave rise to the changes was the violation of the rights of workers. It cannot be forgotten that the fundamental crisis of systems claiming to express the rule and indeed the dictatorship of the working class began with the great upheavals which took place in Poland in the name of solidarity.

While Marxism held that only by exacerbating social conflicts was it possible to resolve them through violent confrontation, the protests which led to the collapse of Marxism tenaciously insisted on trying every avenue of negotiation, dialogue and witness to the truth.

It seemed that the European order resulting from the Second World War and sanctioned by the Yalta agreements could only be overturned by another war. Instead it has been overcome by the non-violent commitment of people who, while always refusing to yield to the force of power, succeeded time after time in finding effective ways of bearing witness to the truth. This disarmed the adversary, since violence always needs to justify itself through deceit, and to appear, however falsely, to be defending a right or responding to a threat posed by others.

The Pope quickly took advantage of the opportunity to appoint new bishops to vacant sees in formerly hard-line Communist countries. He also re-established diplomatic relations which the Holy See had suspended when Soviet armies took over Eastern Europe, if not before.

First on the list, of course, came Poland (July 1989), then Hungary (February 1990), the Soviet Union (March 1990), Czechoslovakia (April 1990), Romania (May 1990), Bulgaria (December 1990) and finally Albania (September 1991).

Five years previously, in 1985, Pope John Paul had devoted his fourth encyclical letter to his Slav heritage and its importance for the modern world. The fifty-page letter, entitled *Slavorum Apostoli* (Apostles of the Slavs), argued that the only way for Europe to end its political divisions was for it to return to its common Christian roots. The Apostles of the Slavs he was referring to were Cyril and Methodius, two Greek monks from Salonika who had brought Christianity – and an alphabet – to the Slav world a thousand years before. They symbolized for the Pope the undivided Church which had existed before the 1054 split between Constantinople and Rome. Not only did the monks translate the Bible into Slavonic languages, and thus begin the Christian conversion of the pagan tribes of central and Eastern Europe, but Cyril is credited with being the inventor of the Slavs' written language and grammar. Today the Cyrillic alphabet is still in use in Bulgaria and former Yugoslavia, as well as in the Soviet Union.

The Eastern or Byzantine rite of the Roman Catholic Church evolved from liturgies originally used in Palestine, Antioch and Cappadocia. Their use spread gradually from Constantinople through the eastern Mediterranean and the Balkans; today the Eastern rite is followed by more than 100 million Christians, both Catholic and Orthodox. The national Churches include the Albanian, Armenian, Bulgarian, Byelorussian, Georgian, Greek, Hungarian, Melkite, Romanian, Russian, Ruthenian, Serbian, Slovak and Ukrainian Catholic and Orthodox Churches.

Pope John Paul implicitly drew a telling comparison between the countries of the Warsaw Pact and the Holy Roman Empire of the Middle Ages. The two missionary brothers, he wrote, 'took as their own the difficulties and problems inevitable for peoples who were defending their own identity against military and cultural pressure'. Cyril and Methodius brought religion and culture together in a way that, as the Pope said, overcame political divisions between the Slavs.

CZECHOSLOVAKIA

John Paul had originally hoped to deliver his message of East-West unity in person at the ecclesiastical celebrations held in July 1985 at Velehrad in Moravia. Now part of Czechoslovakia, this is where Methodius is reputed to have died eleven centuries ago. (Cyril's body rests in the church of San Clemente in Rome.) However, the Communist government in Prague refused to allow the visit, so the Pope had to send Cardinal Casaroli instead as his envoy. The event turned into the biggest Church gathering ever held in Communist Czechoslovakia. Fifteen thousand people booed Communist officials, who vainly tried to turn the eucharist into a peace rally, and chanted, 'We want the Pope.'

In 1990 the Pope was finally able to visit Velehrad in person. A brief weekend trip to Czechoslovakia provided him with a new bridgehead in his campaign to gather the Christians of the east back to Rome. Prior to this the nearest he had come, apart from his travels in Poland, was in Austria in 1988 when he had sent messages to Catholics in neighbouring Yugoslavia, Hungary and Czechoslovakia. In Helsinki during his 1989 tour of Scandinavia, he received a small group of Catholics from Soviet Estonia.

The modern State of Czechoslovakia, like twentieth-century Poland, was the creation of the peace settlement which re-apportioned the old Hapsburg Empire at the end of the First World War. With two-thirds of its population, about 6 million Slovaks and 4 million Bohemians and Moravians, baptised as Catholics, Czechoslovakia contains one of the Pope's largest Catholic communities in Eastern Europe, second only to 35 million Catholics of his native Poland. In common with Poland, Czechoslovakia had to surrender its independence, first under military pressure from Hitler in the west and then from Stalin in the east.

Relations between the Vatican and successive Communist governments in Prague had been poor for decades. For fifteen years, between 1973 and 1988, there was a stalemate over the Czechoslovak government's rejection of new bishops nominated by Rome. The Prague authorities insisted that new bishops should belong to the government-sponsored Church organization Pacem in Terris, which the Vatican refused to recognize. When Bishop Julius Gabris died in 1987 at the age of seventy-four, he was by then the youngest of the Czechoslovak bishops. His fellow bishops were mostly sick or infirm, and nine out of the country's thirteen bishoprics were vacant. The Pope described the situation as 'without parallel in countries with a Christian tradition'.

Although the Cardinal Archbishop of Prague and Primate of Bohemia, Frantisek Tomasek, was then aged eighty-eight, he was a towering figure who had fought tenaciously for many years for religious freedom in his country. Each day during Communist rule he had had to endure the humiliation of asking for the key to unlock the doors of his own cathedral. Strongly encouraged by Pope John Paul in Rome, he drew up a petition demanding from the Communist authorities more liberty for Catholics and organized the collection of over half a million signatures. His voice became the symbol of a new will to resist, more particularly of a new militancy within the Czechoslovak Church.

The dramatic juxtaposition of the seats of ecclesiastical and temporal power on the Hradcany hill overlooking old Prague and the Vltava river neatly illustrates the importance of Christian tradition in this ancient European capital. The castle has for centuries, been the official residence of the ruler of Prague, be he Holy Roman Emperor, German, Pole, Hungarian, Austrian, Hapsburg, Nazi, Communist, or the playwright President of a new democratic Czechoslovak Federation, Vaclav Havel. From this natural vantage point ruled the first Catholic kings of the Czech nation, including Good King Wenceslas himself. And at its side were laid the foundations of the great, towering Gothic cathedral.

The Pope was finally able to accept an invitation to travel to Prague in the spring of 1990. He received an emotional greeting at Prague airport from the leading champions of human rights in Czechoslovakia during the long years of Communist rule: Alexander Dubcek, who had tried – and failed – to create Communism with a human face during the brief Prague Spring of 1968; Cardinal Tomasek, still actively in command of his Church at the age of ninety-two; and President Havel, founder member of the Charter 77 movement, who had spent over five years in prison for defending the right to free expression.

'Your Holiness,' said the President, in what was perhaps the most poetic and moving speech of welcome that the Pope had heard in all his years of globetrotting, 'Your Holiness, I do not know whether I know what a miracle is. None the less, I dare to say at this moment that I am party to a miracle. A man who only six months ago was taken prisoner as an enemy of his own State is welcoming today, as President, the first Pope in the history of the Catholic Church to set foot in Czechoslovakia. For long decades the spirit has been chased out of our homeland. I have the honour to be a witness to the moment when its soil is being kissed by the Apostle of spirituality.'

Keeping to his usual whirlwind timetable, the Pope managed to cram into that day's schedule a visit to the famous Gothic cathedral of Saint Vitus next to Prague Castle, an open-air mass for half a million people, an address to his bishops, another to priests and yet another to leading intellectuals, as well as a private meeting at the castle with President Havel, before leaving early the following morning for Velehrad.

The Pope warned both Czechs and Slovaks not to underestimate the moral dangers which their country faced as Czechoslovakia began to renew contracts with the West. The people, who he said had been living for years as though behind locked doors, now needed to be immunized by their pastors against contagion by the 'viruses' of rampant materialism, indifference to ethical values and the consumer society.

The Pope referred to the moral as well as the economic bankruptcy of the previous regime. The Communists he said, had paralysed the nations of central and Eastern Europe by the violent application of a materialistic ideology which had corresponded neither to their traditions nor to the needs of their peoples.

He said that he, a Pole, understood the languages of Bohemia, Moravia and Slovakia. During the long years of Communist oppression he had understood their silence and he had considered it part of his own mission to be their voice.

For most of the day the voice of the Pope boomed out in Czech from loudspeakers placed along the Royal Route, the processional way of the former kings of Bohemia, and in Wenceslas Square, the focal point of political opposition to the Communists during the dark days of oppression. Just five months before, in November 1989 at a ceremony at Saint Peter's in Rome, Pope John Paul had canonized Blessed Agnes of Bohemia, sister of the thirteenth-century Czech King Wenceslas I. Saint Agnes was the first Czech to be canonized in Rome for three centuries. Her cause had lain forgotten in the Vatican's archives, but was re-opened by John Paul. Ten thousand Czech and Slovak pilgrims travelled to Rome to celebrate her canonization. The following week a student demonstration was violently suppressed and the surprising 'velvet' revolution took place in Prague. Few political observers connected the two events at the time, although their significance was immediately understood by Czech believers. Just as in Poland, the Pope had helped to provide the courage for bold political change behind a religious happening.

The village of Velehrad does not figure large on tourist itineraries. It is situated in what is almost the geographical centre of Czechoslovakia, an area which at one period in European mediaeval history was called the Great Moravian Empire. A Cistercian monastery was built in Velehrad at the beginning of the thirteenth century – four centuries after the death of Saint Methodius – but it was not until the eighteenth century that it became a popular pilgrimage centre associated with Cyril and Methodius, those parton Saints of Moravia who would later to be promoted by John Paul to become patrons of the whole of Europe.

In Velehrad the Pope was even nearer to his beloved Kraków than in Prague. 'Here are our roots!' he proclaimed. Velehrad, he declared, this little known Moravian village, was one of the cornerstones of Europe. He compared the importance of this shrine for the Catholic Church in the East to that for the Latin Church of Monte Cassino, the famous monastery between Rome and Naples founded by Saint Benedict.

While the Pope was speaking at Velehrad, I went to visit a retired 77–year-old Moravian priest and theologian, Father Josef Zverina, who until only a few months before our meeting had led a dramatic cloak-and-dagger existence in the service of the Catholic Church. After being interned by the Gestapo for four years during the Nazi occupation of Czechoslovakia in the early 1940s, Father Zverina had then been sentenced to another twenty-two years' imprisonment on high treason and espionage charges by the Communists when they took over the country at the end of the war.

'The espionage consisted in having sent two or three letters to friends abroad,' Father Zverina told me. 'The treason was starting a Catholic Action group.'

After he had served fourteen years in various gaols, Amnesty International managed to secure Father Zverina's release. He was given the jobs traditionally reserved for priests by Communist regimes – as stoker at a central-heating plant or manual labourer in an uranium mine with no protection against contamination from radioactivity. After the Prague Spring, Father Zverina served quietly for five years as a country parish priest. Then began what he regarded as the culmination of his life's work: fifteen years of teaching at the Flying University. This was a clandestine theological school which changed premises every few days. Each week he travelled around Czechoslovakia by car, visiting some of his thirty different student groups. The students remained permanently on the move in order to minimize the risk of arrest.

'I have the satisfaction of knowing that 500 young men and women graduated under my tuition, and five hundred more have been prepared for their degree. I developed a theology for the Second World, the formerly Communist world stretching from the river Elbe to the China Sea.

'As we live in a world of hate and ignorance, my first principle is to apply the teaching of Saint Augustine and Saint Francis that we must show charity and love. My second principle is that we need a new system of practical theology, a new style of preaching and Christian witness to approach modern man and give him access to the truths of the Christian religion.'

Father Zverina, with President Havel a founder member of the human rights group Charter 77, was not overly optimistic about the task his Church faced in the newly democratic Czechoslovakia. He estimated that only about 15 per cent of urban Catholics now go to mass regularly, and believed the figure was even lower in the countryside, where Communist pressure against the practice of religion had been more overt.

'The Pope knows about my ideas, I met him in Prague and he told me to come and see him in Rome.' Father Zverina did meet the Pope but, tragically, never had the opportunity to develop his 'Second World theology'. He drowned accidentally while swimming in the Mediterranean near Rome soon after he had had a private audience with the

Pope at Castelgandolfo in August 1990. But the debate over the proper role of the Roman Catholic Church inside the new Eastern Europe continues.

How far is a strongly secularized post-Communist society interested in moral as opposed to economic renewal? My own impression is that the end of Communist rule finds the Czechs more involved in the parochial problems of how to keep their uneasy federation with the Slovaks working at a period of rampant nationalism in the Slav world than with working out a new ethic for the beginning of the third millennium or in delving back into the histories of Cyril and Methodius from Macedonia. Predominantly Catholic and agricultural, Slovakia is showing strong secessionist tendencies against the Czechs of Bohemia, where protestantism is stronger. But as Father Zverina had reminded me, 'We Czechs are an enigmatic nation. We have always renewed ourselves. Look at Baroque Prague, and look at the Prague Spring!'

LITHUANIA

When Lithuania was incorporated into the Soviet Unionin 1940 it had a small but flourishing Catholic Church. According to the Vatican, about 85 per cent of the population was baptised and there were 1,450 priests, 717 churches and 4 seminaries. Soviet persecution was both violent and systematic. Four bishops and over 300 priests were arrested and many were deported to Siberia. By 1947 only one bishop remained in his diocese. From 1955 onwards, the situation improved slightly: two bishops were released from prison and some priests were allowed to return from Siberia. The Holy See never recognized the Soviet takeover and for years described the Lithuanian bishops as being 'impeded' from carrying out their duties. However, by 1986 the situation had improved considerably, with many churches re-opened. The Pope decided to use celebrations planned that year for the 600th anniversary of the country's baptism to push for yet greater relaxation of restrictions by the authorities. Pope John Paul is a strong believer in the value of anniversaries as an occasion for hammering home political points. He sent a special message to the Catholics of Lithuania, which the Soviet authorities permitted to be read out over loudspeakers in the capital Vilnius, and church bells rang out for the first time since the Second World War.

At that same moment inside Saint Peter's basilica in Rome, the Pope was celebrating a mass for Lithuania, beatifying one of their early twentieth-century bishops. The ceremony was attended by thousands of

Lithuanians living in exile. To make his point even clearer, the Pope was joined at the altar by the head of the Yugoslav Church, Cardinal Kuharic, and by Church leaders from Hungary and Poland.

The Pope's mass and his message to Lithuania coincided with the first major nationalist upsurge in neighbouring Latvia. This is a country with a much smaller Catholic population, so small that the Catholic seminary in Riga was the only one in the Soviet Union which was allowed to function during the worst years of religious persecution.

The Vatican's refusal to recognize the inclusion of the Baltic Republics within the Soviet Union's postwar frontiers was the reason Moscow gave for not inviting Pope John Paul to lead the Vatican delegation for the official 1988 celebrations marking the millennium of Christianity. 'You must admit it is not comfortable to invite guests into your home if they do not recognize you as a master there,' joked Konstantin Kharchev, head of the Council for Religious Affairs in Moscow, a touch uneasily.

Yet by the end of 1988 the Soviet authorities felt sufficiently relaxed to allow the leader of the Lithuanian Catholic Church, Archbishop Julijonas Stepanovicius, to travel to Rome for the first time since he had been arrested and sent into internal exile in 1961. (Archbishop Stepanovicius was erroneously believed to be the 'secret' Cardinal appointed during the Pope's first year of his reign using a special procedure designed to avoid difficulties for local churches suffering persecution – in fact the 'secret' Cardinal turned out to be the imprisoned Archbishop of Shanghai, Gong Pin Mei. He received his red hat from the Pope in person in 1991.)

On his return to Vilnius, Stepanovicius was allowed to celebrate mass in public at Vilnius's fourteenth-century cathedral for the first time since the Second World War. The building had been converted first into a warehouse and later an art gallery. There were so many worshippers that the ceremony had to be held in the open-air outside the cathedral. Local television broadcast the mass. Many worshippers carried the yellow, green and red Lithuanian flag which had been banned in 1940, the year the persecutions began. Politics and religion were once more inextricably linked. The Church supported demands that Lithuania's students should be exempted from the military draft and that all her young people should be allowed to perform compulsory military service within the Republic.

In the spring of 1989 the reconsecration of Vilnius cathedral was carried out by Archbishop Stepanovicius. 'We are witnessing the rebirth of a nation,' he told the joyous congregation which packed the cathedral and spilled out into square.

The silver casket containing the remains of Saint Casimir, patron saint of Lithuania and ruler from 1475 until 1484, who had been canonized by Pope Clement VIII in 1604, was carried in solemn procession through the streets of Vilnius. The saint's bones were accompanied back to the cathedral, where they had lain undisturbed for centuries, followed by a large procession of believers singing hymns. The Polish pattern of public liturgical demonstration of the Church's strength was proving successful, even within the borders of the USSR.

Alfonsas Svarinkas, the last Lithuanian priest held by the Soviet authorities, was released from prison in November 1988. He had spent more than five years in gaol and eighteen months in exile having been found guilty of spreading anti-Soviet propaganda.

After his meeting with Gorbachev in December 1989 and the exchange of ambassadors with the Kremlin, the tone adopted by the Pope in his references to Lithuania became increasingly statesmanlike. Cardinal Casaroli had called for 'wisdom and moderation' when trouble had broken out in Azerbaijan just after Gorbachev's visit to the Vatican. Now the Pope asked both Catholic Lithuania and the Soviet President to show prudence and keep talking when there was a risk of a military showdown. The Pope prayed for 'illumination and strength' on both sides. He was sending the same signals to Moscow as President Bush and the European Community leaders, but his moral authority seemed to give his word more weight.

The Pope kept up this even-handed attitude towards Lithuania even when the new Cardinal he had appointed in 1988, Vincentas Sladkevicius, was giving interviews saying that the Catholic Church gave its full backing to the Sajudis independence movement.

On the plane taking him for his second visit to Mexico in 1990, Pope John Paul told Vatican correspondents that the desire of the Baltic states for political independence was a complex situation which had to take into account not only the aspirations of their peoples, but also the wider interests of the Soviet Union. The Lithuanians had to remember 'the whole dimension of an immense country made up of many peoples'. In other words, the Pope seemed prepared to help Mihkail Gorbachev restrain the resurgent nationalisms of the Soviet Republics in order to prevent the Soviet Empire from falling apart. Could there have been a secret exchange of messages between the Kremlin and the Vatican about papal mediation in Lithuania after Gorbachev's visit to Rome?

Nikolai Kovalski, one of President Gorbachev's leading foreign-policy advisers, said in an Italian newspaper interview that he found the Pope's pronouncements on Lithuania 'coincide with the fundamental directives of Soviet foreign policy and create a good basis for co-operation with the Vatican.'

The Pope was cautious about ratifying the accreditation to the Holy See of Stasys Lozoraitis, for many years described in the Vatican *Year Book* – the official listing of Curial appointments – as representative of the Lithuanian government in exile. During the Lithuanian parliament's struggle for independence from Moscow in 1990, special powers were delegated to Mr Lozoraitis 'in the event that through acts of violence Parliament cannot express the will of the Lithuanian nation.' But the Pope refused to get personally embroiled in the dispute between Moscow and Vilnius, and would not receive Mr Lozoraitis in private audience.

ROMANIA

About three-quarters of Romania's twenty-three million people are estimated to be members of the Orthodox Church. The Catholic Church in Romania, as in the former Soviet Union, is divided between Eastern and Latin rite believers. Statistics are unreliable, in the aftermath of the 1989 political upheaval, but each rite claims about a million and a half members, which would put the combined strength of the Pope's followers at just over 10 per cent of the population.

The reason for the division among Catholics in Romania is to be found in the decision by the members of the Transylvanian Orthodox Church to go over to Rome at the end of the seventeenth century, a hundred years after the Ukrainian Uniates. The Romanian Eastern rite Catholics played a prominent part in fostering Romanian nationalism during the period when the country formed part of the Austro-Hungarian Empire. When Nicolae Ceausescu took over the country in 1948, he followed Stalin's example, cancelled Romania's concordat with Rome and decreed that henceforth all Eastern rite Romanian Catholics should consider themselves members of the Orthodox Church. The Latin rite Church, whose membership was predominantly Hungarian, Moldavian and German, was not abolished, but it was severely persecuted. All the Latin rite Catholic bishops and many of their priests were thrown into gaol and the Pope's Ambassador was expelled from Bucharest in 1950.

In 1973, Pope Paul VI received President Ceausescu and his wife Elena in private audience at the Vatican and spent fifty minutes with the Romanian dictator talking mainly about measures to increase understanding between the two Cold War blocs and so preserve peace in the world. Paul VI, having involved the Vatican in significant international diplomacy with the Holy See's accession to the Nuclear Non-Proliferation Treaty (which had been the pretext for sending Cardinal Casaroli on his first mission to Moscow), now gave the Catholic Church's support to the holding of the thirty-four-nation European Security Conference in Helsinki. Pope Paul considered this an important platform for the Church's stand on human rights, and he wanted to obtain the diplomatic support of Romania despite the Romanian communists' own appalling human rights record. I remember Cardinal Casaroli telling me in 1971 that he believed Vatican policy should be to maintain a presence in Eastern Europe *at all costs*. If Communist regimes did not want to talk about religious freedom, he said, then he was perfectly prepared to talk only about world peace. 'We can wait for decades if necessary,' the Cardinal said.

It is not recorded whether Ceausescu asked Paul VI about his *Humanae Vitae* encyclical, which confirmed the Catholic Church's ban on all forms of artificial birth control including, of course, abortion.

Abortion and contraception were treated as serious crimes in Ceausescu's Romania for all women who had not produced at least five babies. His ban led to one of the world's highest rates of infant mortality, and to countless deaths from backstreet abortions and to the widespread abandonment of infants. There were thirteen thousand children under the age of three in 1990 living in State orphanages, in conditions which in any other country would have been the cause for prosecution on the grounds of criminal neglect.

Women from the ages of sixteen to forty-five were subject to medical checks to detect any secret abortions, and doctors supplying contraceptives were sent straight to gaol. Hospital gynaecological and obstetric departments had as many Securitate spies as paramedics on their staff.

When President Ceausescu came to power, Romania's population stood at about 19 million. His aim was that the nation should increase to 25 million by 1990, and 30 million by the year 2000. Latest estimates suggest that at the time of the revolution Romania's population had increased to about 23 million. Immediately after the call of Ceausescu, the black market price of an abortion dropped by 2,000 per cent. The French Medical Aid Group, Médécins sans Frontières, began helping immediately with advice on the creation and organization of a state family-planning policy.

Like its Russian counterpart the Romanian Orthodox Church had seriously compromised itself with the Communist regime. Religious books were only printed if they contained portraits of the dictator and his wife alongside icons of the saints. Up to a week before the dictator's execution by firing squad, the Orthodox Patriarch Teoctist was sending him formal telegrams of congratulation as protocol required. As part of his national reconstruction programme Ceausescu bulldozed twenty-three Orthodox churches in Bucharest alone. Only his death saved the Orthodox cathedral, next on the list for demolition. Lazlo Toekes, the Protestant pastor from Transylvania whose arrest and deportation triggered the 1989 Romanian revolution, said the leaders of the Romanian Orthodox Church had done more damage to their Church by collaborating with the regime than the Securitate police ever did.

Before taking up his appointment as the Holy See's diplomatic representative in Moscow, Archbishop Colasuonno was sent by Pope John Paul to make contact with the National Salvation Front in Bucharest. The Romanians agreed that Ceausescu's decree abolishing the Romanian Easter rite Catholic Church would be immediately rescinded. The Pope nominated seven new Latin rite bishops and five for the Eastern rite. Two aged bishops who had been consecrated in secret in 1949, and had spent over thirty years in prison, were promoted to the rank of Archbishop. Diplomatic relations were re-established after forty years.

Dan Lazarescu, a senior opposition politician and editor of the Liberal Party daily newspaper, became Romania's first Ambassador to the Vatican, while Pope John Paul appointed Monsignor John Bukovski as Apostolic Nuncio in Bucharest. The new Romanian leader Ion Iliescu visited the Pope on his first foreign trip in 1991 and invited the pontiff to visit Romania. The Pope replied that there would have first to be some progress recorded in the return of Church properties confiscated by Ceausescu.

BULGARIA

Bulgaria, where Orthodox Christianity is the dominant religion, is estimated to have only about 40,000 Catholics out of a total population of 8 million people. Pope John XXIII began his rise to the top at the

Vatican with a diplomatic post as Apostolic visitor in Sofia, where he served for ten years from 1925 to 1935. He would tell the story of how he received the following brief from the then Secretary of State, Cardinal Gasparri, upon his appointment: 'Listen Monsignore, the situation in Bulgaria is very confused. I can't tell you in detail what is going on. But everyone seems to be fighting with everyone else, the Moslems with the Orthodox, the Greek Catholics with the Latins and the Latins with each other. Could you go there and find out what is really happening?'

After the Communist takeover at the end of the Second World War, the Vatican's formal diplomatic ties with Sofia were suspended. Later the so-called 'Bulgarian connection' in the terrorist attempt upon Pope John Paul's life in 1981 led to an all-time low in relations between Rome and Sofia. At the trial of the Turkish and Bulgarian conspirators, the prosecution stated that Bulgaria had acted as surrogate for the Soviet KGB in trying to kill the Pope. The court acquitted the accused for lack of evidence. After Todor Zhivkov's fall from power in 1989, the new Bulgarian regime said it would make available documents proving that there never was a conspiracy. The Sofia government has now officially invited the Pope to visit their country. Full diplomatic relations were restored in December 1990, after the Vatican declared that the Holy See and Bulgaria now 'mutually desire friendly relations'. The Italian judiciary re-opened enquiries into the shooting of the Pope ten years after the assassination attempt. Rome magistrate Antonio Marini said he had been promised 'full co-operation' on his return to Italy from a visit to Sofia, but no significant new evidence emerged.

HUNGARY

Saint Stephen, the first Catholic ruler of Hungary, died in 1038, so his millennium cannot be celebrated under Karol Wojtyla's papacy. During Communist rule, Stephen temporarily lost his saintly status. For the 950th anniversary celebrations in 1988 Wojtyla had to send as his representatives Cardinal Glemp from Poland and Archbishop Colasuonno, at that time his roving Ambassador in Eastern Europe. Pope John Paul was subsequently invited to pay the first-ever papal visit to Hungary in August 1991, shortly after his fifth return visit to Poland.

Relations between the Holy See and Hungary were marred for years by the dramatic show trial and imprisonment of the Catholic Primate of Hungary, Cardinal Josef Mindszenty, in 1949. The Vatican's Ambassador in Budapest had been expelled the day after Soviet tanks rolled in to liberate the country from Nazi rule in 1945. Cardinal Mindszenty was a stubborn adversary of the Communists when they came to power in 1947–8. He excommunicated all those responsible when the State took over Catholic schools. He was sentenced to life imprisonment on trumped-up charges of treason and black marketeering, enjoyed a brief period of freedom during the 1956 uprising, but was then virtually incarcerated for another fifteen years after seeking political asylum inside the American Legation in Budapest.

The first breakthrough came in 1964, when Cardinal Casaroli was allowed to meet Mindszenty inside the American Legation. The Vatican's new roving envoy in Eastern Europe signed the first agreement between the Holy See and a Communist regime since the Bolshevik Revolution.

Another five years passed before Pope Paul VI was able to appoint four new Hungarian bishops. Just before he died in 1978, Pope Paul was able to make more new Church appointments in Hungary, and also to reshuffle existing bishops with an ease undreamt of before Cardinal Casaroli began his 'softly, softly' diplomacy in Eastern Europe.

The safe-conduct agreement with the Hungarian Communist authorities, which finally allowed Cardinal Mindszenty to leave Budapest for Rome and then for exile in Vienna in 1971, stipulated not only that he would never be allowed to return home, but also that he must never make any political statements. It took another three years of anguished correspondence before Pope Paul VI could convince Mindszenty, considered to be one of the great anti-Communist heroes of postwar Europe, to offer his resignation at the age of eighty-two, and to allow a younger prelate to take over as Primate of Hungary.

Finally Mindszenty was reluctantly forced to concede that his resignation was necessary for an improvement in Church-State relations. In 1974 Cardinal Laszlo Lekai took over as Primate. Cardinal Mindszenty died in Vienna in 1975. The Hungarian Communist Party Secretary Janos Kadar was received in audience at the Vatican in 1977 by Pope Paul, who publicly acknowledged that his policies of keeping diplomatic contacts with an atheistic regime had left some Catholics perplexed, but explained it was all in the long-term interests of the Church.

He was right. Cardinal Lekai's policy of patient accommodation with the regime enabled the Church to maintain a position of considerable influence in Hungarian society. This line was also adopted by his successor, Cardinal Laszlo Paskai. In 1988 the Hungarian Communist Party announced that it no longer required Party members to be atheists and that it would stop interfering in Church affairs. And Pope John Paul was promised a full review of the 1949 trial of Cardinal Mindszenty, together with that of other prelates tried for alleged crimes committed against the Hungarian State between 1945 and 1962.

FORMER YUGOSLAVIA

The former Federal state of Yugoslavia is a classic example of the way a history of past invasion and occupation can spill over into the twentieth century. The northern Yugoslav provinces of Slovenia and Croatia, once part of the Austro-Hungarian Empire, and now independent states, remain predominantly Catholic. Serbia is mainly Orthodox, and Bosnia retains the Muslim heritage of Turkish occupation.

The civil war which broke out in 1991 as Yugoslavia fell apart was caused by the eruption of ancient ethnic and religious feuds which had been smothered by decades of Communist rule. The Pope's calls to Catholics, Orthodox and Muslims for an end to fighting fell on deaf ears.

Sarajevo was the city where a Bosnian Serb assassinated Archduke Francis Ferdinand, heir to the Austro-Hungarian throne in 1914, precipitating the First World War. The savage fighting in Sarajevo, the Bosnian capital, in September 1992 reminded Pope John Paul of the outbreak of the Second World War, fifty-three years before. 'Old wounds are reopening', he commented, recalling 'past and present tragedies'.

Diplomatic relations between Belgrade and the Vatican had been broken off by the Yugoslav government in 1952 as a result of Pius XII's decision to give a cardinal's hat to Archbishop Aloisius Stepinac, Primate of the Catholic Church in Croatia during the Second World War. Stepinac had been sentenced to sixteen years in prison in 1945 for collaboration with the Nazi puppet regime in Croatia, and the Pope's gesture was interpreted by Tito as a political slap in the face.

Gradually relations with Rome thawed, to the extent that a new Church-State agreement was signed in Belgrade in 1966 by Cardinal Casaroli. The Vatican promised that its bishops and priests would never abuse their functions 'for political ends' and formally condemned 'all acts of terrorism and similar forms of political violence'. In 1970, relations were upgraded with a formal exchange of ambassadors, so this was the one part of Eastern Europe with which Karol Wojtyla enjoyed normal diplomatic contacts from the start of his pontificate.

During the 1980s, the increasing involvement of the Catholic Church in Slovenian and Croatian nationalist and separatist movements led to attitudes hardening in Belgrade against a papal visit. Although a formal invitation was issued to the Pope by the then President of Yugoslavia, Cvietin Mijatovic, when he was received in audience at the Vatican in 1980, it was made clear later that 'the conditions were considered inopportune'. This did not prevent the Pope from dropping a heavy hint when he accepted the credentials of Stefan Cigoj, a new Ambassador from Belgrade, in 1985: 'When the Pope visits the many countries that invite and welcome him, he has the comforting evidence of being part of a family', he said. 'My gratitude towards these populations and the leaders who allow me to meet so many Christian communities there is immeasurable'. But there was no response. Nor was there any response to the peace feelers the Vatican put out during the height of the fighting in Bosnia-Herzegovina. The Serbs organised anti-Vatican demonstration outside the office of the Papal Nuncio in Belgrade.

The strange goings-on in the village of Medjugorje, in western Herzegovina, where six local children reported almost daily apparitions of the Virgin Mary from 1981 onwards and in doing so attracted hundreds of thousands of pious Catholic pilgrims from all over Europe, were not encouraged by the Pope in Rome. On the contrary, he banned Church-organised pilgrimages to Medjugorje. Cardinal Ratzinger disciplined one German Bishop for ignoring Rome's instructions and accompanying an official pilgrimage from his diocese.

The six children have now grown up. They still receive alleged messages from the Virgin, but the pilgrimages have been disrupted by the fighting. One of the Virgin Mary's 'messages' deplored that her calls for peace had not been heeded. 'Satan is playing with your souls and I cannot help you because you are far from my heart', she said.

The Vatican ordered an official inquiry into the phenomenon by Yugoslav bishops, but the bishops decided to refrain from pronouncing on the authenticity of the apparitions. The local Catholic Bishop Monsignor Pavao Zanic of Mostar-Duvno was highly skeptical about the visions.

ALBANIA

The Albanian government closed all places of worship in 1967, and many Christians were killed in Enver Hoxha's efforts to create an atheist state. The situation improved after the death of the hard-line Albanian Marxist leader in 1985, but it was not until 1990 that the authorities in Tirana lifted their ban on religious propaganda. The Vatican believes that about 300,000 Catholics, one-tenth of the population, may still be practising their religion now that the country has held its first free elections and discarded Communism.

On 15 November 1990, mass was celebrated in public in Albania for the first time since 1967 at a cemetery chapel in Shkoder, the only religious building in the country not to have been converted to secular use. The service was conducted by Archbishop Simun Yubani, who had spent twenty-two years in prison for violating the atheism laws of the Tirana government. A congregation of about 5,000 people, both Catholics and Muslims, attended. At Christmas church bells rang out again in Tirana, and by September 1991 formal diplomatic relations had been re-established between Albania and the Vatican, completing the process of the normalization of relations between the Holy See and the whole of Eastern Europe.

THE FORMER SOVIET UNION

Just before Mikhail Gorbachev's first visit to Rome, the Vatican took the opportunity to publish its first-ever official report on the state of the Church and the number of Catholics living inside the Soviet Union.

Because the Vatican never recognized the postwar territorial expansion westwards of the Soviet Union, eleven formerly Polish and Lithuanian diocese were partly or wholly situated within Soviet political boundaries in Byelorussia and the Ukraine. These include archbishoprics created six centuries ago, such as those of Vilnius and Lvov, as well as some much later territorial divisions created by the Vatican after the 1917 Revolution. There were thus some complicated overlapping diocesan boundary questions to resolve with Moscow.

Latest estimates (dated 1986) show about 2.5 million Catholics in Lithuania, 2.3 million in Byelorussia, 500,000 in Latvia, 50,000 in Estonia, and a rapidly diminishing Catholic population of about 1.5 million ethnic Germans and Poles in the Soviet Asian republics of Kazakhstan, Kirgizstan and Tadzhikistan. These Catholics all belong to the Latin rite. Then there are the Eastern rite Catholics of the Ukraine, the largest single national group of Catholics in the Soviet Union, numbering about 4 million, plus a much smaller group of about 500,000 Latin rite believers also in the Ukraine. The total number of Catholics formerly living under Soviet rule was not limited to 11–12 million people.

The diversity of Christian belief inside the Soviet Union is not limited to the major divisions between the Orthodox, Catholics and Protestants. There are also about a million churchgoers in Armenia. Echmiadzin, a small town near the Armenian Republic's capital of Yerevan, seat of the Catholicos, Head of the Armenian Church, claims to be the centre of the world's first Christian state, as it was founded AD 301.

Religious activities inside the former Soviet Union are controlled by a governmment department called the Council for Religious Affairs. It was run between 1984 and 1989 by Konstantin Kharchev, who was apparently ousted from his post by Communist Party bureaucrats who opposed Gorbachev's efforts to increase religious tolerance. In a significant interview with the Moscow weekly *Ogonyok* after his forced resignation, Kharchev said that some senior Party officials were unhappy with the new *perestroika* policies as applied to religion. 'Many of our ideological officials remain convinced that the current democratization of relations between Church and society is needed only to decorate the façade of our society and that in the final analysis the old policy will prevail,' he said. Before the passing of the 1990 law on religious freedom, Kharchev alleged that his attempts to implement even a previous 1929 law on religion, which allowed very limited freedom of worship, had been blocked.

At Kharchev's Moscow office, a graceful single-storey nineteenth-century building which has been spared in the race to fill Moscow with high-rise offices and apartments, I met Yevgeni Milovanov, a new assistant director of the Council for Religious Affairs. He gave me an optimistic assessment of the prospects for religious freedom in the Soviet Union.

Milovanov claimed that 3,500 religious organizations had been registered during 1989 and that ten new religious schools had been opened, for Muslims, Baptists and the Reformed Churches as well as seminaries for Catholics. The Orthodox Church was now involved in hospital nursing and prison-aid societies in the Moscow area.

'All 56 religious confessions in the Soviet Union are equal before the law,' Milovanov said comfortingly. This bland assessment hardly seemed to reflect the years of persecution suffered by all believers under Communist rule.

The 45 million Muslims in the Soviet Union have also benefited from the changes effected by President Gorbachev's *perestroika* policies. In 1990 in Soviet central Asia, over 300 abandoned mosques were re-opened for worship, millions of copies of the Koran were printed and distributed, and over 1,500 Soviet Muslims were permitted to make the pilgrimage to Mecca, the largest contingent since the Bolshevik Revolution. As with the Catholic Church, Gorbachev was using the moral influence of the *muftis* in Soviet Central Asia to help combat crime and social disintegration.

The long-promised law on freedom of conscience and worship in the Soviet Union was finally passed by the Supreme Soviet in Moscow by 341 votes to 2 at the beginning of October 1990. The new law stated:

In accordance with the right to freedom of worship each citizen shall independently determine his attitude towards religion and have the right individually or in conjunction with others to confess or not to confess any religion and express and disseminate beliefs connected with his attitude towards religion.

Parents or persons in their stead shall have the right to ensure that their children are raised in accordance with their own attitude towards religion ...

Indication on official papers of the citizen's attitude towards religions is not permitted.

The law also enacts the strict separation of Church and State.

Soon, for the first time since 1917, regular religious services began to be held in the magnificent churches belonging to the Russian Orthodox Church inside the walls of the Kremlin itself.

The feast of Christmas, 7 January 1991, was declared a public holiday by the Parliaments of Russia, the Ukraine, Georgia, Moldavia and Byelorussia. The Patriarch's midnight mass from the Church of the Epiphany inside the Kremlin was transmitted live by Soviet television, with a detailed commentary on the significance of the Orthodox liturgy. Church bells rang out again in the freezing midnight air all over Russia, some of them newly restored by the bell foundry in the Netherlands which, in the days before the Russian Revolution, had been entrusted with the maintenance of the bell towers of the major Russian churches.

Pope John Paul's apparent esteem for Mikhail Gorbachev, evident since their first meeting, was based upon a common re-assessment of the importance of the 35-nation Conference on Security and Co-operation in Europe (CSCE). Speaking during a 1989 tour of Scandinavia at the Finlandia Hall in Helsinki, where the conference's first session was held in 1975, the Pope said the CSCE had rightly put religious freedom among the foundations of peace in Europe. The Helsinki accord committed the signatories to improving their record on human rights. The Pope acknowledged that Soviet policy on religion was no longer based on Karl Marx's dictum about religion being the opiate of the people. 'The idea that religion is a form of alienation is no longer fashionable because fortunately the [Soviet] leaders have come to realize that believers constitute a powerful factor in favour of the common good,' he said.

After the overwhelming political changes in Eastern Europe at the end of 1989, the Pope felt it was even more important to stress his point. Speaking at the beginning of 1990 to over 100 foreign ambassadors permanently accredited to the Vatican, he said; 'The thirst for freedom has brought down walls and opened doors. And you will doubtless have noted that the point of departure or the meeting point was often a church. One by one candles were lit forming a chain of light, as if to reassure those who for years have had to limit their horizons to earthly ones, that they cannot remain permanently chained down.'

However, he added a word of caution: 'While welcoming developments which have enabled so many peoples to regain their identity and their dignity, we must not forget that no gains are permanent. Events since the end of the Second World War, which began exactly fifty years ago, suggest that we ought to remain vigilant. Ancient rivalries can always re-appear, conflicts between ethnic minorities can flame up anew, nationalistic feelings can be fomented.

'That is why Europe conceived as a Community of Nations, should hold fast to the principles adopted in Helsinki in 1975 at the Conference on Security and Co-operation in Europe.

'Warsaw, Moscow, Budapest, Berlin, Prague, Sofia and Bucharest . . . these capitals have become like staging posts on a long pilgrimage to freedom. We must pay homage to their peoples who at the cost of immense sacrifices have courageously undertaken this pilgrimage, and to the politicians who have helped them.

'In countries where for long years a single political party told people what to believe and how to interpret history, these peoples have shown that it is not possible to stifle the basic freedoms which give meaning to man's life: freedom of thought, conscience, religion expression and political and cultural pluralism.

'These are irreplaceable values without which we cannot build a durable common house for East and West, accessible to all and open towards the world.'

Twice the Pope borrowed Mikhail Gorbachev's favourite phrase about the common European house. And he also quoted another biblical reference once used by Gorbachev – the phrase about picking up stones, which comes from Ecclesiastes and had been used by the Soviet leader when chatting in private at the Kremlin with a French priest.

'The time has come for West Europeans, who have the advantage of having lived for long years in freedom and prosperity to help their brothers in Eastern Europe to regain the place which belongs to them in the Europe of today and tomorrow. Yes, the moment is ripe to pick up the stones of walls that have been demolished and to construct the common house together.

'Unfortunately, only too often the Western democracies have not known how to use the freedom they have gained even at the cost of hard sacrifices. The deliberate absence of all reference to morals and ethics in the running of so-called "developed" societies cannot but be cause for dismay. Side by side generous initiatives of solidarity and real care about the promotion of justice, you find counter values such as selfishness, racism and materialism. Those who are coming to freedom and democracy for the first time must not be disappointed by the "veterans".'

Ex–Soviet President Mikhail Gorbachev, in an interview given in Moscow to Western journalists a year after the failed coup of August 1991, demonstrated that he continues to share many of the Pope's ideals. What was his concept of 'true' socialism a year after the collapse of Soviet Communism? 'A concept of social justice, freedom, and equality, in the general framework of contemporary human values', Gorbachev remarked. 'In brief, we advance the cause of Christ. The search for truth, humanity, justice, spirituality, these are eternal values'.

When questioned if the Pope had been responsible, in part at least, for the cataclysmic political changes in Eastern Europe, the ex-President replied, 'I can only say what I have deduced after reading the Pope's encyclicals, after having known his sense of priestly mission, his appeals for peace and in defense of freedom. I think that his view of the world, its past and its future, helped to make a change of mentality possible for us as well'.

The Pope's travels have taken him to all the rich countries of the West, where the 'hedonism' he so deplores is rampant. The geographical location of the Vatican in Rome also brings him into close daily contact with a consumer culture which has grown ever more conspicuous during his reign. Within a generation Italians have changed from being the world's most thrifty savers to some of the worlds' most lavish spenders.

So how has Karol Wojtyla fared among the wealthy consumer cultures of the West, and how have his Churches in the United States, Canada, France, Italy, Germany, Ireland and Britain reacted to being viewed from a distinctly Polish perspective?

CHAPTER 4

Cafeteria Catholics and the Consumer Society

Thank God the age of the States of the Church, and that of State religion has come to an end. The Catholic Church is learning the hard lesson that the world cannot be changed by enacting moral laws.

Bernhard Häring, German theologian

The unexpected collapse of political divisions of the Cold War in Europe may have resolved one set of problems for the Roman Catholic Church – to use the Pope's favourite metaphor it could now breathe properly with both its 'lungs'. But it created a new difficulty: how to make the ancient Christian roots of Eastern Europe relevant to Pope John Paul's fellow Slavs, as they desperately search for new creeds to replace their failed Socialist Utopias. With Communism in its death throes, East Europeans now look westwards for new social, political and economic models to follow. Inevitably, they are attracted by the material prosperity they see in the West. But the very political developments which the Pope fostered in the Slav world have spiritual and ethical implications which he now fears.

As we have seen during his visit to Czechoslovakia in the spring of 1990, the Pope urged his bishops to 'immunize' their flock against the 'hedonism' of the supermarket culture of the West to which they are now exposed. This was wishful thinking. Christians in the West know only too well that there are no vaccines against the ethical challenges of a secular, money-grabbing society. As the English Catholic weekly the *Tablet*, edited by laymen for an overwhelmingly lay readership, wrote after that visit:

Christians in the West have learned painfully that the work of conversion of heart in this age is laborious, complicated, demanding of new and inventive approaches. There are no crisp and simple answers, no available means of immunizing the faithful, no spiritual rhetoric which brings guaranteed results . . . The black side of Western Society is only too familiar to Christians who battle against it. But there is also a bright side which is rich in moral scruple, self-sacrifice and generosity, and spiritual aspiration. There are democratic convictions and practice, the exercise and defence of freedom, economics which work.

The wealthy societies of the post-Christian west have presented Pope John Paul with a difficult challenge. Raised in poor and austere Poland, the Pope's extensive travels through the wasteful consumer societies of western Europe and North America have revealed to him a world often more distasteful than the rigidly oppressive but theoretically egalitarian society of his birth.

At Avila on the edge of the plains of Castile one bright, frosty November morning, I noticed the Pope's sense of shock when 3,000 Spanish Carmelite nuns who had just emerged from their cloisters – some for the first time in twenty years – met him at the house of their foundress, Saint Teresa of Avila. A solid phalanx of nuns sat in the front row, clad in the austere black and white habit chosen by their foundress three centuries before. But many sisters clutched brand-new Japanese tape recorders with which they were going to capture the Pope's words, for later playback in the solitude of their cells. An admonitory finger shot out. 'I see the consumer society has arrived even here,' he said, not entirely in jest.

The Pope viewed the market economy, with its consumer-gadget fetishism supplying material prosperity to only a very small proportion of human kind, as another failed God.

The model for the revamped Roman Catholic Church which emerged from the Second Vatican Council (1962–5), in which Karol Wojtyla took part as the Bishop of Kraków, was for obvious political reasons interpreted differently in liberal Western societies and in Eastern Europe. Some doubt has always existed about the extent to which Wojtyla is in true sympathy with the manner in which, according to the Council, the Catholic Church was to come to terms with the modern world. The Pope has always declared his unswerving support for the decisions of the Council ('the constant reference point of my every Pastoral'), but he has also tended to deny those new freedoms which the Council encouraged among bishops, clergy and ordinary members of the flock. The Council dropped Latin as the main language of the Catholic Church, allowing worshippers to hear the liturgy everywhere in their own languages, and in a significant symbolic change, ordered priests to turn and face their congregation as they celebrate the mass.

Catholics in countries with strongly rooted democratic traditions, such as the United States, Britain and the Netherlands, saw Vatican II as a real revolution which reversed four centuries of Rome's centralized authority. They looked forward, much too optimistically as it turned out, to their own bishops sharing with the Pope in the governance of the Church.

For many First World believers, the Vatican has still not come to terms with the concept of the equal dignity of all the People of God, as proclaimed by Vatican II. They feel the Vatican of Pope John Paul still echoes the sentiments of the arch-conservative Pope Pus X, who reigned at the beginning of the twentieth century. Incredible though it may seem to Catholics of the 1990s, Pius declared in his encyclical *Vehementer Nos*, 'The Church is an unequal society consisting of two categories of persons, the pastors and the flock. The multitudes of the faithful have no other duty than to let themselves be led, and, a docile flock, to follow their shepherds.'

The Synod of Bishops, a new consultative 'parliament' of the Roman Catholic Church, was set up in 1965 by Pope Paul VI as Vatican II drew to a close. Some two hundred delegates, representing about 6 per cent of the world's Catholic bishops, are nominated to travel to Rome every three years by national Bishops' Conferences. The original idea of the Synod was to exercise the new concept of 'collegiality' of Church government as expressed by the Council, rather than to change traditional methods of decision-making in the Roman Curia. But while the Synod was never meant to have more than an advisory role, it was intended to provide a sounding-board and a regular forum for the world's 3,100 bishops. The trouble was that 'collegiality' was never precisely defined. Did it mean the Pope was *primus inter pares* (first among equals) when sitting with the elected representatives of his worldwide executive, the bishops of his Church? Or was the Vicar of Christ never morally obliged to take the opinions of his fellow bishops into account when exercising his teaching function over the Church?

From its inception, the Synod suffered from serious procedural shortcomings. The Pope sets the agenda and Vatican officials retain complete control over preparation and procedure. The press is excluded from all debate and has to rely on inadequately prepared précis of major speeches, in addition to whatever leaks they can gather from individual participants. The decisions of the Synod are submitted to the Pope confidentially. After a long period of reflection the Pope issues his own thoughts on the subject under discussion – and these may, or equally may not, reflect the deliberations of the bishops.

The 1980 Synod on the family, Pope John Paul's first Synod, was

typical. It began with wide-ranging opinions being expressed on controversial issues including contraception, the problems of divorce and
remarriage for Catholics, and the changing role of the Christian family
in different parts of the world. But at the end of the first week, Cardinal
Ratzinger from Munich, shortly to become the Pope's chief theological
adviser, structured the agenda along much narrower lines and the
assembly broke up into small language groups for informal discussions.
From this point on, a Vatican-controlled drafting committee decided on
forty-three points to be submitted to the Pope, and produced a watered-
down 'Message' which the Synod addressed to the whole Church. In
retrospect, the Pope's apostolic exhortation *Familiaris Consortio* which
came out over a year later could easily have been written without the
Synod ever having taken place. There was no effective episcopal input.

The next Synod in 1983 examined 'Reconciliation and Penance'. The
Pope was seriously preoccupied by the decline in numbers of Catholics
confessing their sins to their priest. Had the threat of hellfire lost its
terror, or had Catholics decided unilaterally to downgrade the gravity
of their mortal sins? Bishops from the Third World (who make up more
than half the members of the Synod) were in favour of a rite of general
absolution simply because it was impossible for a visiting missionary
priest to hear hundreds of thousands of individual confessions. A bishop
from the Sudan complained that while Pope John XXIII had granted
him permission in his vast African territory for collective absolution,
this had now been withdrawn. Cardinal Ratzinger, by now in charge of
the Vatican's Congregation for the Doctrine of the Faith and hence the
Pope's chief theological adviser, again said no. This would be giving
way to 'depersonalization and collectivization'. It was a curious argument: were the huge crowds attending the Pope's masses as he progressed
around the world also 'depersonalized' as they approached the
Eucharist?

Asian, African and Latin American bishops brought with them to
Rome a new category of sin, 'social' or 'structural' sin. Archbishop
Henry D'Souza from India said Asia was a victim of 'structural sin'.
The continent had been pauperized by the multi-nationals, international
banks and colonial trading patterns. Cardinal Paolo Evaristo Arns, Archbishop of São Paolo in Brazil, the most populous city in the southern
hemisphere, also raised the question: who is responsible for confessing
the economic sins committed against the Third World?

On the matter of reconciliation, the Bishop of Helsinki, Paul
Verschuren, recommended that the Vatican should attend to the un-

reconciled within its own ranks, those who divorced and remarried, the priests who had left their ministry, and the theologians who had come into conflict with Cardinal Ratzinger's Congregation for the Doctrine of the Faith, the former Holy office.

None of these important points about shriving the sins of the modern world found their way into the Vatican-piloted final recommendations to the Pope.

The next Synod, which took place in 1985 was a specially convened 'extraordinary Synod' called at short notice by the Pope to 'celebrate' the twentieth anniversary of the end of the Second Vatican Council. Addressing the College of Cardinals, the Pope made it clear that his views about the relative roles of the Pope and his cardinals and bishops in the running of the Church government were more in line with those of its sixteenth-century founder, Pope Sixtus V, than with the bishops of the Second Vatican Council who had stressed the importance of power sharing.

The Pope said the Roman Curia received its power directly from him, and its authority depended on the identity of its views with his own. He emphasized the cardinals' duty of personal obedience and dismissed as erroneous the notion that the central government of the Church acts as a sort of parallel power, or as filter, for the Pope's views.

The subject chosen by the Pope for the next session of the Synod in 1987 was of more than passing interest for ordinary Church members: the role of the laity, the vast silent majority of ordinary believers, and their relationship with Church authority. One key problem was the Church's traditionally misogynist attitude towards women. Catholic women's groups in the United States and other Western countries had for years complained without result about male dominance within the Church. This discrimination was rooted in the questionable proposition that as Jesus Christ and his disciples were males, so only males can be ordained as priests.

Archbishop Rembert Weakland of Milwaukee spoke on behalf of women in the Church: 'Women ask to be treated in a way that is not condescending or paternalistic. Women wish to be treated in the way that Jesus treated women: with trust and respect. Non-ordination to the priesthood must not be seen as a manifestation of baptismal inferiority.'

He proposed the immediate opening up of jobs in the Roman Curia and the Vatican's diplomatic service to women, and the rejection of sexually discriminatory language in all Vatican documents. Only a handful of women, such as Edith Cicerchia, head administrator of the Vatican museums, hold executive jobs inside the vatican – most women employees of the Holy See hold secretarial or menial posts.

An engaging African Cardinal from Nigeria, Francis Arinze, who heads the Vatican's Secretariat for relations with non-Christians, pointed out that fruitful dialogue between Christians and followers of Hinduism and Islam, who have no clergy as such, must ultimately depend on contacts between lay people not clerics otherwise non-Christian believers might get the impression that only clerics are able to lead the Christian life to the full.

Once again the differing preoccupations and the political divisions of the Church in the First and Third Worlds were a topic for general debate.

For the understaffed Church in the Third World, separating the sheep from the shepherds is a futile task; there are simply not enough shepherds. Out of a worldwide total of some 300,000 Catholic parishes and communities, less than half now have a resident priest to celebrate Sunday mass and minister to them. Yet a recent Vatican directive forbids laymen and women to preach at mass. The question now asked is to what extent can lay people, men and women, fulfil the office previously reserved exclusively to ordained males? Not very much, according to the views imposed by Pope John Paul in 1990 at the Synod he called to discuss the anticipated worsening of the crisis in priestly vocations.

As this century draws to a close, there has been a dramatic decline in the number of young men studying to become priests in the very countries where Catholicism was once strongest. When the Pope visited Lyons in France in 1986, on what was basically a recruiting mission, I noticed that the entire student body of future priests, in a country once described as the 'Elder Sister of the Church', scarcely filled the marquee in which they had gathered to hear the Pope's talk. This was in the small village of Ars, whose mid-nineteenth-century local parish priest, the Curé of Ars, is now held up to the rest of the world as the model of modest priestly virtue.

According to *L'Osservatore Romano*, between 1970 and 1985 the number of young men studying in American seminaries dropped by 44 per cent. By the turn of the century, there will be only half as many priests in the United States as during the pontificate of Paul VI. And their average age will be sixty-five.

The search for new vocations led the archdiocese of Detroit, which has to minister to a population of 1.5 million Catholics, to try TV advertising. A handsome young all-American crew-cut priest appears on the screen with the slogan, 'The work is hard, but the reward is infinite!' In another TV spot, an elderly woman takes a smiling priest by the arm with the caption, 'My son! the father!' The advertising campaign had no ascertainable result.

The shortage of priests, coupled with the high cost of keeping open huge under-used churches in the centre of Detroit, led to a decision to close more than one-third of the city's 112 Catholic churches in 1988. Closures are also likely in other eastern American city centres where there are insufficient new Hispanic parishioners to replace Catholics of European origin who have migrated to the suburbs. Chicago has plans to disband twenty-five city parishes.

After the 1987 Synod, which discussed the future relationship of the Roman Catholic Church's sheep and shepherds, I asked Archbishop Weakland for his personal reactions to the proceedings. I came to know him in the 1970s when he was living in Rome, and was Abbot General of his religious order, the Benedictines. So he had useful points of comparison with the pre-Wojtyla Vatican.

'The great disappointment for me at this Synod was that I found much less tolerance than at the 1974 Synod, the last I attended. That Synod also had a little bit more excitement about helping each other. I found the Third World nations facing new problems and more uptight about persecution, about their inability to develop. I found them a little less eager to listen to First World problems. We didn't get to know each other well enough. I should have liked to have had all 230 of us members of the Synod living in the same building, where we would pray together, eat together, recreate together and then we would have been able to discuss together. It was all too formal, we lived in different parts of Rome and when the meetings were over we rushed home. I don't think we were able to create the mutual trust you need for any kind of discussion . . .

'If you were to ask me what was the greatest awareness I received out of this Synod I would say that the Church is no longer identified with Western culture. I felt in a minority at the Synod. If you look at the numbers of people present, the dominant forces are the Africans and the Spanish speakers. Those are the two big blocs. That poses many questions. Some of the hypersensitivity over dissent and the trend towards orthodoxy in the church is an attempt to maintain a unity in the light of all that diversity. I'm sure the Pope's thought during his travels is to try and hold it all together. The more diversified the Church gets, the more need you have for a point of unity. I don't think that point should converge in a single person. I think that's very dangerous. We happen to have a Pope who is multilingual and able to handle that kind of travel. But I don't think one should expect that's what a Pope should always do.

'I find the greatest danger of the moment is how pastorally I can prepare people in Milwaukee for that church. I don't think we are ready for it. I come home having had that experience in Rome – the only representative from my diocese to have been present at the Synod – and it is difficult for us Americans to realize that the issues that concern us will not have an answer because they are not the issues of Africa or Asia. That is hard.

'The women's issue is the one that most people notice most. The one I noticed most is the political question. Each nation began by describing the role of their laity in their culture and in their present national situation. It is one thing to talk about laity and politics in a country like the United States with its democratic background. Our problems are how you relate to a constituency and how you relate to laws that may not be in consonance with Catholic moral teaching. We have Catholics in every political party. The European situation is similar except they have Catholic parties. That complicates things. But to most Africans all this makes no sense at all. Their problem is that if you have a Muslim government in which the Head of State is also the one who does the praying, what does a Catholic do? Do you get into that mess, or do you stay out of it? It's a totally different world. We tend to separate the military from politics; for them the military and politics are inseparably linked. The military coup is the normal way you change government. It is when you get into that situation, or the Asian situation where Catholics are often less than one per cent of the population, that decisions become difficult. Tell an Asian Catholic he has got to become a great politician and it makes no sense. Because of the cultural diversity, I found that section not too helpful for us.

'But I raised the larger issue. Either you have to have more Synods involving more people to get that mix more often, or you have think of ways of bringing together more parts of the Church. After our economic pastoral was issued it would have been wonderful to meet with bishops from Korea, Japan, Singapore and Djakarta to talk about capitalism so that we begin to take themes and work on them together on a more international basis. As the Canadian bishops were leaving this Synod they said we must get together more often. We do meet regularly once a year with officials of the South American Bishops' Conference, but it's an unstructured contact.'

American Catholics, whether they wear clerical collars, monkish garb or are simple sheep, tend to see their faith in a quite different perspective to that of John Paul. Although the American Catholic Church began as a poor immigrant Church, predominantly Irish, Polish and Italian, membership has moved upwards socially over the last few decades. Today it perceives itself as a better educated community of believers than it has ever been before. For example, although the number of American nuns may have declined by almost a half since 1960, 90 per cent of those still keeping their vows hold master's degrees or post-graduate qualifications.

There are almost three hundred active bishops in the United States, and the American National Bishops' Conference has become a sounding board for American Catholics, who believe, unlike the Vatican, in open debate as a means of resolving difficult questions.

Many American Catholics simply cannot understand why experiment and debate are so frowned upon in Rome. They want the reasons for priestly celibacy to be re-examined; they want more participation in decision making by women, blacks and Hispanics.

The Pope provoked controversy in 1986 when he disciplined two prominent and respected American churchmen, the theologian Charles Curran, a teacher at the country's leading Catholic university in Washington, and Archbishop Raymond Hunthausen, head of the Seattle diocese on the west coast. Curran had his licence to teach revoked by the Vatican for what Rome considered unorthodox teaching on sexual morality. Archbishop Hunthausen a well-known opponent of nuclear weapons, was forced to accept a deputy appointed by the Pope to deal with questions he was deemed unfit to decide on – including marriage annulments and relations with the local homosexual community.

In Europe, attitudes are evolving in the same direction. Just over a year after John Paul's election, the renowned German priest and theologian Hans Küng had his official teaching career suddenly brought to an end by an edict issued from the Holy Office bearing the personal approval of the Pope. His 'crime' was to have brought into discussion the doctrine of Papal Infallibility, which was declared part of the integral teaching of the Church at the First Vatican Council held in 1870.

The Holy Office was renamed the 'Congregation for the Doctrine of the Faith' as part of the reforms of the Second Vatican Council back in 1965. It was originally known as the Holy Inquisition, founded in the sixteenth century to fight heresy after the Reformation had caused such damage to the Catholic Church, and perhaps best known for its trial and condemnation of Galileo for having questioned the traditional Roman view of the universe. This body now has a procedure for investigating suspected deviation from Church doctrine that is supposed to be far removed from the excesses of the Inquisition. However, Hans Küng refused to obey various summonses to Rome. He felt it was an infringement of his basic human rights as a teacher, and sensed that academic discussion did not really interest Rome; what they wanted was a loyalty test. Küng felt that any progress towards Christian unity – not only with the Anglicans and the Reformed Churches but also with the Orthodox – depends on a basic re-examination of the Catholic doctrine of the Pope's infallibility. He also held that theology was not just a matter for ecclesiastical specialists, but was of relevance to ordinary believers as well. He accused the Vatican of 'totalitarian suppression of conscience', and in turn the Vatican found him guilty of 'causing a disturbance' in the minds of the faithful.

At the same time another Catholic theologian, Edward Schillebeeckx from Belgium, was being subjected to rigorous investigation at the Holy Office for his book *Jesus – An Experiment in Christology*. This openminded theology teacher had been summoned to Rome no less than three times to explain himself to Cardinal Ratzinger, and had publicly expressed his resentment at being treated like a naughty schoolboy by the Vatican. His basic sin, in Rome's view, was his refusal to conform to old ways of interpreting the scriptures.

As he put it himself, 'I do not begrudge any believer the right to describe and live out his belief in accordance with the old models of experience, culture and ideas. But this attitude isolates the Church's faith from any future and divests it of any real missionary power to carry conviction with contemporaries for whom the Gospel is – here and now – intended.'

Pope John Paul's views on theology were deeply coloured by those of Cardinal Stefan Wyszynski, the Primate of Poland who had been responsible for propelling the young Archbishop from Kraków on to the world stage. Wyszynski had said in 1972, 'We want a Polish theology for Poland.' He believed that the modern Western theologians had emptied the churches in the West, and he declared bluntly he did not want to see the same happen in Poland. In a like-minded lecture to Polish theologians given the previous year, Cardinal Wojtyla (as he then was) defined the proper task of the theologian in extremely narrow terms, 'to guard, defend, and teach the sacred body of revelation in strict subordination to the Pope and his bishops'.

Bernhard Häring, one of the Roman Catholic Church's most eminent contemporary theologians, who taught moral theology at a papal university in Rome for over thirty years before retiring to a monastery in Bavaria, compared the treatment he received from the Holy Office to that he had suffered under Hitler. In a letter to Cardinal Seper, Cardinal Ratzinger's immediate predecessor, he declared that he would rather find himself back in the dock in one of Hitler's courts (as happened four times during the Second World War) than be called to explain himself again in Rome before the Inquisition of the Holy Office.

'The Hitler trials were certainly more dangerous, but they were not an offence to my honour, while those of the Holy Office were a grave offence and also dishonoured the two "great moralists" who drew up the accusations and whose names were never officially revealed to me.

'The minimum reform I ask for is transparency; that the accused should appear before his accusers, that he can choose his own defence counsel. And a theologian who is expressing his basic consent to church doctrine should not be put on trial over secondary matters. Dissent upon what is a matter of opinion cannot be a crime. The best reform would be to interrupt the links which bind the Congregation for the Doctrine of the Faith to the old Inquisition, and let the Church live for a few years without this incubus hanging over it. It could then start all over again with real experts in spreading the gospel message, men and women living in the real world, who are not nominated for life.'

Häring tried to lift Catholic theology out of the mechanistic value system it applied to human sexual conduct in favour of one which stressed personal responsibility. He warned priests never to get mixed up in conjugal ethics or to instruct couples on how many children to have and when. In his book *Faith, History, Morals* Häring suggested that the Holy Office in Rome should pause for reflection and take a sabbatical for a few years:

The Church could well go on living without such an institution. Look at the Orthodox church which has kept its spirituality and faith without having any similar body. Amnesty International should also have a look inside the Vatican. The Holy Office is a poisoned lake where healthy fish cannot swim. It is a combination of ignorance and arrogance, run by ecclesiastics who are career terrorists.

Häring recommended one of the Pope's chief theological advisers, Bishop

Carlo Caffarra, who had attacked him over his attitude to *Humanae Vitae*, to go and see a psychiatrist.

At the time that he was under attack by the Holy office the Swiss theologian was fighting against cancer of the throat. While the experts of the Holy Office were scanning his writing for theological error, Häring was undergoing seven major operations, which resulted in the complete loss of his voice. (Today he speaks only with the help of a special device inserted in the oesophagus.)

'The most terrible thing,' he said, 'was that they never stopped persecuting me even when they knew I was near death. That was shameful.'

In a moving personal appeal to the Pope, Father Häring wrote in 1988 to Wojtyla asking him to consider carefully the impact of his absolute continuing ban upon artificial birth control.

'The Pope's teaching office', he wrote, 'should not become a battle cry of the Church's intransigent hussars, and as a result become for many others an incomprehensible myth.'

The Pope did not reply.

One of the most significant protests against Pope John Paul's philosophy and style of Church government came at the end of January 1989, just after the tenth anniversary of his election. This was in the form of a strongly worded document, issued in Cologne but drawn up in Tübingen, Cardinal Ratzinger's old university. Eleven out of seventeen leading Tübingen professors signed, led by Norbert Greinacher, Dean of the Theology Faculty and Dietmar Mieth, Professor of Ethics. Altogether the document bore the signatures of 163 theology teachers from Catholic universities all over German-speaking Europe. The signatories came from East and West Germany, Switzerland, Austria and the Netherlands. They included Hans Küng and Edward Schillebeeckx.

The choice of Cologne was significant. Cologne is the world's second wealthiest Catholic archdiocese after Chicago. The Cologne Cardinal administers an annual budget of over 500 million dollars – almost four times the size of the total Vatican budget. There had been a standoff lasting many months between the Pope and the local cathedral chapter over the controversial appointment of a successor to the late Cardinal Hoffner. The Pope had chosen Cardinal Joachim Meissner, former Archbishop of East and West Berlin, who had straddled the two political Germanies through the last years of the Cold War from his diocesan headquarters in East Berlin. John Paul had pushed his nominee through, in the face of strong opposition from his Cologne flock.

The Cologne protest – entitled 'Against bans: for an open-style

Catholicism' – found fault with the Pope under three headings: first, the manner in which he appointed bishops without sufficiently taking into account local feelings, the signatories said he was 'suffocating' the Second Vatican Council's call for greater co-operation between the Pope and local bishops, and was overstepping his powers; second, the appointment to theology teaching posts in Catholic universities according to a subjective assessment of reliability by Rome, which was not necessarily related to academic ability; and, third, the Pope's attitude towards contraception.

The Cologne declaration complained that the Pope had failed to consider the degree to which his various statements were to be considered official Church doctrine. He had linked his teaching on birth control with such fundamental articles of faith as the divinity of God and salvation through Jesus Christ. As a result, critics of papal teaching were now being indiscriminately charged with 'attacking fundamental pillars of Christian doctrine'. Catholics should be given the right to make up their own minds. The dignity of the papal teaching office was being damaged by bans on thinking and education. The theologians regretted what they called John Paul's 'intense fixation' with the problem area of contraception.

The Pope's reaction was to ignore the criticism. His spokesman dismissed the Cologne document as a 'local matter' for the German bishops. Cardinal Meissner went on West German TV to defend the way in which the Pope had appointed him. But the West German media was hostile to the Pope. 'The declaration of the theologians shows that for many faithful Catholics, the final limit has been reached,' ZDF television said. 'The criticism directly touches sore points.' ZDF concluded, 'The Pope should be careful to prevent too many Catholics from walking out on him.'

Saarbrücker Zeitung, a daily newspaper, commented, 'The rebellion of the theologians was only a question of time. Rome cannot be surprised by it. The Universal Church cannot be run according to Polish Catholic standards.'

Within a few weeks 130 eminent French-speaking theologians had written to Rome adding their support to the stand taken by their German-speaking colleagues. They were joined by 25 Spanish speakers and 52 more teachers from the Catholic university at Louvain in Belgium.

Three months later, another group of over 60 Italian theologians joined in the protest against John Paul's authoritarian attitudes. They told the Pope in an open letter that they felt uneasy at the way the

Vatican was dealing with matters of discipline and teaching. 'We theologians do not believe that it is our job simply to follow Church teaching. We are also at the service of the Church when we formulate new questions arising from new situations.' The Italian theologians also said they did not think the Vatican was doing enough to spread the new concept of a more open style of Church government envisaged by the Second Vatican Council, and criticized the limits placed upon national Bishops' Conferences and the procedure for the nomination of bishops who blindly follow the Pope's orders.

Pope John Paul's chief political instrument in imposing his views on the Catholic Church has been the appointment of bishops who are docile, totally in accordance with Roman thinking, and who are not prone to asking awkward questions.

The American theologian Charles Curran has been critical about this. 'The Pope is the head of the Church as well as its symbol of unity, but the Pope can be wrong,' Curran said. He believes that the ideal of 'collegiality' among the world's bishops, including the Pope as Bishop of Rome, is meaningless until 'individual bishops can publicly express disagreement with the Pope on certain issues, even those belonging to non-infallible Church teaching on faith and morals'.

Curran made these remarks in a lecture in 1986 which he entitled 'Being Catholic and Being American'. The dilemma facing many loyal American Catholics in the last quarter of the twentieth century is how to remain authentically Roman and at the same time feel distinctively American.

The chairman of the American National Bishops' Conference, Archbishop Joseph Bernardin of Chicago, writing for his local Catholic magazine, acknowledged the difficulty in reconciling these opposite poles of loyalty. He said the Pope had a duty to 'respect and encourage a proper sense of diversity' within the Catholic Church. Vatican attempts to impose theological orthodoxy had affected morale adversely, he admitted. Yet he felt bound to qualify his criticism by adding that diversity could sometimes have a negative impact. 'We are not and cannot be Lone Rangers.'

In 1986 Charles Curran was sacked from his teaching post at the Catholic University of America on Cardinal Ratzinger's orders. He had failed to follow Rome's line in his lectures on some aspects of sexual morality. The American courts refused to re-instate him, on the grounds that the Vatican had the right to lay down its conditions of employment at its own universities anywhere in the world.

During the 1980s the Pope used his faithful Vatican eye Archbishop Pio Laghi, as Ambassador or Nuncio in Washington, to vet all recommendations for new American bishops' appointments. He can now be sure that his hierarchy in the United States will in future be even more obedient. The current leaders of the highest profile American dioceses – Boston, New York, Chicago and Los Angeles – were all promoted by him. When he called thirty American bishops to Rome in the tenth year of his pontificate for joint discussions and reflection, he was already preaching to the converted. Two-thirds of them were his own appointees.

It is unusual for a Pope to appoint all his own bishops. In the early days of the Church, bishops were often elected by their congregation. Fifteen centuries ago, Ambrose of Milan, for example, who was to prove one of the most influential bishops of all time, had not even been baptised when he was chosen as spiritual leader by his fellow believers. Within a week he was both baptised and consecrated bishop. Bishops were normally elected by cathedral chapters, or nominated by kings or emperors. Until the nineteenth century the Pope usually appointed only those bishops within his temporal domain, the Papal States of central Italy, and was thus just like any other sovereign ruler.

It was the United States which indirectly caused the Vatican to change its practice. The first Catholic Bishop of the United States, John Carroll, was elected leader of his Church by his fellow clergymen in 1789. Pope Pius VI agreed to leave the choice to them in accordance with custom. Yet the newly independent Americans had no ancient cathedral chapters to elect their bishops. Neither could they hand over the right of appointment to the President of the United States, because of the separation of Church and state enshrined in the United States Constitution. So the Pope began to make his own appointments, imposing Irish bishops instead of the Frenchmen that many American Catholics would have preferred.

Later the Vatican justified making episcopal appointments elsewhere on the grounds of defending the Church's freedom against interfering governments. France was a case in point. From Napoleon to General de Gaulle, the French government always took a keen interest in episcopal appointments.

Over one half of the current members of the American National Bishops' Conference are now John Paul's appointments. The American bishops have given strong backing to the Pope's stance on important contemporary ethical issues. They condemned nuclear arms, while accepting the concept of a limited nuclear deterrent. They criticized the raging poverty that exists side by side with affluence in the United States, where 35 million Americans live below the poverty line. They condemned the 'selfishness and flagrant consumerism' of many former immigrants from Europe, who have become affluent US citizens yet fail to provide for the basic needs of new waves of immigrants of different ethnic origin.

Notwithstanding this unity, some American bishops did stand up to the Pope during his 1987 visit to Los Angeles. Tactfully yet firmly, they tried to explain to him how Americans think.

As Cardinal Bernardin told the Pope, 'It is important to know that many Americans, given the freedom they have enjoyed for more than two centuries, almost instinctively react negatively when they are told they must do something. As a result the impression is sometimes given that there is a certain rebelliousness in many American Catholics, that they want to "go it alone".

'When the Holy See re-affirms a teaching which has been part of our heritage for centuries, or applies it to today's new realities, it is sometimes accused of retrogression, or making new and unreasonable impositions upon people.

'When someone questions how a truth might be better articulated or or lived today, he or she is sometimes accused [by the Vatican] of rejecting the truth itself or portrayed as being in conflict with the Church's teaching authority. As a result, both sides are locked into what seem to be adversarial positions. Genuine dialogue becomes almost impossible. We must be able to speak to one another in complete candor, without fear.'

Archbishop John R. Quinn of San Francisco told the Pope, 'We cannot fulfil our task simply by an uncritical application of solutions designed in past ages for problems which have qualitatively changed or which did not exist in the past.'

But it was Archbishop Weakland who pinpointed the dilemma that Pope John Paul has to resolve in his universal church. Archbishop Weakland was like the Pope a worldwide traveller, and used to pay regular visits to religious communities overseas when he was Abbot General of the Benedictine order.

'The faithful are now more inclined to look at the intrinsic worth of an argument proposed by the teachers in the Church than to accept it on the basis of the authority itself. Since so often that teaching touches areas where many of the faithful have professional competence – from medical-moral issues to economic ones, for example – they wish to be able to contribute through their own professional skills to solving the issues. This demands a new kind of collaboration and a wider range of consultation on the part of the teaching office of the church.

'Moreover in the political arena, Catholics in the USA are jealous of their freedom and deeply resent being told how to vote on an issue or for which candidate to vote. In all these cases an authoritarian style is counterproductive and such authority for the most part then ignored.'

The Pope was unmoved. 'It is sometimes claimed that dissent is totally compatible with being a "good Catholic" and poses no obstacle ito the reception of the sacraments. This is a grave error.' he replied. 'Dissent from Church doctrine remains what it is, dissent; as such it may not be proposed or received on an equal footing with the Church's authentic teaching.'

The Pope will evidently concede nothing to American Catholics. But to what extent is he correctly reading the 'signs of the times'?

A newspaper poll conducted among over 300 Massachusetts Catholics two years after this 'face to face' between the Pope and his American bishops, appeared to show that he had failed to convince his US followers that they cannot be 'cafeteria' Catholics, free to pick and choose their beliefs as they please.

A majority of those polled indicated that they were at odds with the Church's position on birth control, the ordination of women as priests and marriage and divorce. Yet 50 per cent of those interviewed indicated that they attended Church at least once a week. Among key findings of the survey were:

71 per cent of those polled said that they should be able to dissent from Church teachings and still be considered good Catholics.

56 per cent opposed the Church's stand against making sex education and birth control available to high-school students.

54 per cent opposed the Church's position against the ordination of women.

68 per cent disagreed with the Church's stand against using artificial birth control.

Cardinal Bernard F. Law of Boston commented, 'The Pope's teaching authority doesn't rest on whether or not people agree with him. Therefore, whatever a poll might show has no relevance to his teaching responsibility and the message that he teaches.'

In March 1989 the Pope invited thirty-five American bishop's to Rome for a 'friendly encounter'. The official theme, as expressed in Vaticanese, was 'Evangelization in the Context of the Culture and Society of the

United States of America with Particular Emphasis on the Role of the Bishop as Teacher of the Faith'.

This turned out to be another Wojtyla propaganda exercise. No progress was made on the most controversial question: the proper role of national Bishops' Conferences. When the Vatican sent round a questionnaire to test local feelings among Bishops' Conferences around the world in 1988, the Americans had returned the draft to Rome as being 'unsuitable for discussion'. They saw no point in accepting a Roman veto as a starting point for a dialogue.

Archbishop John L. May from Saint Louis, President of the American Conference, bluntly told the assembled Vatican dignitaries clustered around the Pope that Americans would not put up with an authoritarian approach from Rome. 'Authoritarianism is suspect in any area of learning or culture. Individual freedom is prized supremely. Religious doctrine and moral teaching are widely judged by these criteria. To assert that there is a Church teaching with authority binding and loosing for eternity is truly a sign of contradiction to many Americans who consider the divine right of bishops as outmoded as the divine right of kings.'

The difficulties that the application of the Pope's doctrine can produce in American politics became evident in 1990, in an article by Cardinal John O'Connor of New York on the abortion issue. The question was: can American Catholic politicians legitimately oppose women's legal right to abortion on a personal private level, and at the same time uphold it as part of their duty as elected office holders to help poor women? Some politicians, such as New York State's Governor Mario Cuomo, feel that in conscience they can. The Cardinal, however, not only banned Cuomo and like-minded politicians from speaking on Church premises, but went so far as to threaten them implicitly with excommunication. American non-Catholic opinion found the political interference by the Cardinal quite unacceptable. As the *New York Times* commented:

The logic of what the Cardinal says is that if these Catholic politicians are so bad as to be in danger of being denied the sacraments of their Church, then other Catholics should not vote for them. That would touch all Americans. Some of the best and most important elected officials in America fall within the Cardinal's definition. Catholics make up about 25 per cent of the population. If a substantial number of them are persuaded to vote against the Cardinal's targets, the politicians could be denied office. All Americans could be losers if the Cardinal's religious authority became the Cardinal's political clout.

Pope John Paul is determined to leave his imprint upon local churches by filling Bishops' Conferences with men of his own stamp. He chose Jean-Marie Lustiger, born in France of Polish Jewish parents, one of whom died at Auschwitz, to lead the Church in France. Lustiger was propelled, within the space of a few years, from his parish in Paris to become Cardinal Archbishop and Primate of the French Church.

In the Netherlands, many Dutch Catholics opposed the Pope's solution for what was, in his estimation, an indisciplined Church – the nomination of a series of 'safe' new bishops. When the Pope visited Den Bosch during his Benelux tour in 1985 I was surprised to see the streets of the Dutch city almost deserted. This was a telling protest against his nomination of a new local bishop, someone who had spent most of his professional life in an office at the headquarters of a religious order, the Salesians, in Rome.

John Paul was embarrassed. He had written:

In all sincerity, the Pope attempts to understand the life of the Church in the appointment of every bishop. He gathers information and advice in accordance with ecclesiastical law and custom. You will understand that opinions are sometimes divided. In the last analysis, the Pope has to take the decision. Must the Pope explain his choice? Discretion does not permit him to do so.

At the last minute he struck out the final two sentences from his prepared text.

Co-ordination of policy between the Pope and his bishops is increasingly carried on at a personal level. The Pope's foreign visits always include a meeting with the host country's entire episcopal body. And once every five years, each Catholic bishop has to pay what is called an *ad limina* (to the threshold of Peter) visit to the Vatican, where he reports to the Pope on the state of his diocese. Normally the visit is made in a group from the same country in order to save time. It usually includes an informal luncheon in the Pope's private apartments in addition to the formal sessions.

The Pope's controversial decision to invite Kurt Waldheim, the President of Austria, on an official visit to the Vatican in 1987 was made while the Austrian bishops were in Rome on their *ad limina* visit. Not only did the Pope fail to consult his bishops about the invitation – which raised an international storm of protest from Jews because of questions over Waldheim's Nazi past – but he even delivered a pointed homily to them about his absolute right to appoint whomever he liked to local hierarchies.

His appointment of an ultra-conservative Benedictine monk, Hans

Groer, to succeed the retiring Cardinal Archbishop of Vienna, Franz-Josef Koenig, had been criticized by some Austrian Catholics. 'You must not allow any doubts to arise about the right of the Pope freely to appoint bishops,' Pope John Paul told his Austrian brothers in Christ.

In Switzerland, the Pope's appointment of Wolfgang Haas, an unpopular and ultra-conservative prelate, as auxiliary Bishop in Chur, the country's second largest diocese, was contested by a hundred protesters at his consecration. They formed a human carpet in front of the cathedral's main portal and the celebrants had to step over them to enter the building. The local press strongly criticized the Pope's veto of the procedure for the election of the local bishop by the cathedral chapter. At Fribourg, the largest Roman Catholic university in Switzerland, a funeral cortège of students accompanied a coffin marked 'Second Vatican Council'. In 1991 the Pope called all his Swiss bishops to Rome to try to put an end to the continuing row over Haas's appointment. The meeting resolved nothing.

It is difficult to estimate what impact the years of Pope John Paul's rule have had upon Church membership. Vatican statistics show the anticipated increase of numbers, due to rapid demographic growth in Third World countries. These will soon contain more than half the world's Roman Catholics. The statistics also reveal a decline in membership in the formerly Christian West due to persistently falling birth rates. But, from the Vatican point of view, the really vital statistics concern the numbers of its future priesthood.

Pope John Paul believes he can marshal the battalions of his Church and obtain obedience through a barrage of instructions from the Vatican which lay down rigid Church guidelines.

The argument used by Cardinal Ratzinger, the chief executor of the Pope's moral directives, can be paraphrased as follows. Mankind's future is under threat. Because of this, Universal Church must deal with threats to life as well as to men's souls. And therefore, the papal brief extends beyond Church dogma to include cultural, social and political matters.

This is in effect a totally new interpretation of the Papacy's function. Cardinal Ratzinger has reversed two fundamental decisions of Vatican II – the independence of national Bishops' Conferences and the freedom of Catholic theologians to carry out research not only on past issues, but on matters of current concern.

Wayward or suspect theologians and priests are obliged to swear a new oath of fidelity. Dissent is not allowable, whatever the extenuating circumstances. Either you subscribe to the Church's teaching, or you do not. There are to be no shadowy areas.

The new catch-all oath of fidelity is to be sworn by all parish priests, rectors and professors of theology in seminaries and rectors and professors of theology in seminaries and rectors of Catholic universities, as well as by all university teachers of subjects dealing with faith and morals. It took effect from 1 March 1989, and contains these words:

I firmly embrace and retain all and everything which is definitely proposed in doctrine about faith or morals by the Church.

In addition I adhere by religious assent of the will and intellect to the teachings which either the Roman Pontiff or the College of Bishops declare when they excercise the authentic magisterium, even if they do not intend to proclaim them by a definitive act.

Pope John Paul decided that 'Cafeteria Catholicism' should also be fought by the introduction of a new compendium of Catholic doctrine – a universal catechism which has been in preparation at the Vatican since 1985. Several countries had experimented with interpretations of Catholic belief felt to be more suitable for teaching the faith to their better-educated congregations: notably the French bishops with a publication entitled *Pierres Vivantes* (Living Stones) in 1981, which attempted to encourage young believers to explore for themselves the structure of the Church as a living organism, rather than a dead body of knowledge to be learned by rote.

The Vatican draft catechism, circulated for comment in 1990, shows no signs of learning from such experiments. It has been attacked by bishops in many parts of the world for being too cumbersome, too exhaustive and too one-sided.

A French Jesuit, Paul Valadier, put it this way:

Rather than reflecting a true concern for doctrine, does not this pressure for uniformity spring from an unthinking panic [at the Vatican]?

This anti-psychological reaction seems strangely to overlook the fact that the Christian religion is above all a 'path'. It is misrepresented as a body of knowledge to be acquired rather than a way of life to be experienced.

Do the authors believe that the present-day believer lives in a cocoon, shut off from the spirit of the times? Instead of confining believers to a doctrinal straitjacket, would it not be better to forearm them against doubt by introducing them to the different ways of reading available to them? Far from enabling them to acquire an adult faith in the world as we know it, the course taken now is likely to produce insecure or credulous souls clinging to faith for faith's sake. Many will ask themselves whether it is not a sign of weakness in a religion to be unwilling to discuss either its philosophical basis or its historical roots; the result may well be to breed generations of sceptics and disillusioned believers.

The latest word from the Vatican on dissent is an 'instruction' from Cardinal Ratzinger to the world's Catholic theologians. If they cannot agree with Rome, then they should in conscience keep quiet or, in the more euphemistic words of the Congregation for the Doctrine of the Faith, 'suffer for the truth in silence and in prayer'. What they must not do is use the media to publicize the fact that they are at loggerheads with the Pope. Public opinion, in the eyes of Cardinal Ratzinger, has no independent right to criticize. The mass media 'manipulates' what Rome decrees.

The document extended the scope of 'infallible' papal teaching to include any moral doctrine. Paraphrasing the 1968 encyclical *Humanae Vitae*, Paul VI's ban on artificial birth control, Cardinal Ratzinger wrote that 'the competence of the magisterium [the teaching authority of the Church] also extends to that which concerns the natural law'.

The Church cannot be run like a political democracy. 'Standards of conduct appropriate to civil society or the workings of a democracy cannot be purely and simply applied to the Church.' The punishment of dissident theologians is part of Rome's duty to defend its teaching from 'a particular dangerous opinion'.

And 'to speak in this instance of a violation of human rights is out of place'. Not all the ideas which circulate among Roman Catholics are compatible with the Faith. 'Nobody is to be forced to embrace the Faith against his will.'

Opposition to Pope John Paul in the prosperous West has come not only from those who consider him too authoritarian, but also from those who consider him not to have been authoritarian enough. Some consider him to have strayed from traditional Church doctrine. The rebel Catholic Archbishop Marcel Lefebvre, a former French missionary priest who founded a society to preserve the Latin mass and other forms of Catholic worship abandoned by the Second Vatican Council, was formally excommunicated by the Pope in June 1988. At the age of eighty-two, Lefebvre threw down the gauntlet against Rome and ordained four new bishops from among his followers.

It was the first official schism in the Roman Catholic Church this century.

Archbishop Lefebvre had accused the Pope of giving way to 'false ecumenism' by holding a dialogue with Protestant and non-Christian spiritual leaders. He had already been suspended from his priestly duties by Pope Paul VI in 1976, but continued to ordain new priests. The Archbishop claimed supporters in thirty countries around the world, but his traditionalist breakaway movement could not really stand comparison with previous Church schisms, such as the split between the Eastern and Western Churches in 1054 or the Protestant Reformation in the sixteenth century.

Archbishop Lefebvre had neither the massive support nor the charismatic personality that could significantly endanger Rome's authority. The Archbishop's headquarters were a seminary in a Swiss mountain valley at Econe, near Chur, the Fraternity of Saint Pius X – named after the early twentieth-century Pope who had combated the 'modernism' of his time, – I was present here when Lefebvre incurred the ultimate penalty of excommunication. The white-haired prelate, surrounded by his incense-swinging acolytes, ordained his breakaway bishops in a marquee before a congregation of about 5,000 supporters, many of whom had come across the border for the day from France. The resolute way in which John Paul dealt with the crisis may simply have been due to a correct assessment that this mini-rebellion of right-wing Catholics, nostalgic for a pre-Vatican II Church, presented no major threat to Church unity.

When Archbishop Lefebvre died of cancer, still unrepentant, three years later, the Pope issued a statement saying that he had hoped until the last moment for a gesture of repentance, and had been ready to lift the excommunication decree if there had been any sign from the rebel Archbishop.

John Paul's approach was, as ever, robust and decisive, offering a way out only if his opponent underwent a change of heart. The iron fist had no real need of velvet gloves.

CHAPTER 5

Other Believers

Fault, where it exists, must be recognized, on whichever side it occurred.
Pope John Paul II describing the need for a re-examination of the causes
of the Protestant Reformation, on the occasion of the 500th anniversary of
the birth of Martin Luther, October 1983

In the thirteenth year of Pope John Paul II's reign, the year of the Gulf
War, there was an unusual addition to Rome's 900 churches. The building has rich political significance. It is Italy's first major mosque, a
gleaming marble mixture of modern and traditional Islamic architecture,
which rises in a woodland setting by the banks of the river Tiber,
three miles upstream from Saint Peter's basilica. The Rome mosque was
designed by one of Italy's leading architects, Paolo Portoghesi, and by
an Iraqi architect who practises in Britain, Sami Mousawi. The cost,
50 million dollars, has been borne mainly by the Saudi royal family. Big
enough to hold 4,000 worshippers, the mosque is the largest in Western
Europe and the complex contains an Islamic library and cultural centre.
The central cupola is flanked by twenty smaller domes and half-domes.
Inside, towering pillars open up like fingers to support a sky-blue ceiling.
The exact orientation of the mosque towards the Holy City of Mecca
was decided with the help of a computer survey carried out by the
universities of Rome and Manchester.

For centuries the idea that a mosque could be built almost within
sight of the Vatican would have been unthinkable. The Fascist dictator
Benito Mussolini when approached in the 1930s by Muslims living in
the short-lived Italian African Empire for permission to erect a mosque
in Rome replied sarcastically that when a Catholic Church was erected
in Mecca he would consider the matter.

Work on the mosque began in 1983 on a low-lying site donated by
the Rome city authorities. A hilltop location was vetoed by the Vatican
on the grounds that the minaret might have soared above the cupola of
Saint Peter's, and so dominate the famous Rome skyline. The city plan-

ning authorities initially refused permission for a minaret higher than the standard twenty-five-metre limit on all new buildings in and around Rome. But at the last minute, under pressure from Arab governments, the authorities gave way and agreed to increase the minaret to forty metres, the height of a typical Roman campanile.

The Vatican believes the new Imam of the Rome mosque (who holds no official status within the Islamic world) might provide a useful interlocutor in the difficult search for international dialogue with Muslims. The lack of a comparable hierarchy in the Islamic religion is cited by the Vatican as one of the main impediments to a better understanding between the two religions. This has become ever more crucial as the Catholic Church steadily cedes its position to Islam as the world's leading faith. Already Asia and Africa are predominantly Muslim. By the year 2,000, Vatican statisticians estimate, there will be 1,200 million followers of Islam worldwide, against 1,144 million Catholics. In the Islamic world the Pope's flock is under pressure where it is not being gradually squeezed out.

These developments lay behind the Pope's public and often seemingly pro-Arab stance in his attempts to halt the war in the Gulf. Although strikingly unsuccessful, during the war he was to make no fewer than fifty-five separate calls on the combatants to end the fighting. In an openly anti-Bush editorial the Vatican newspaper criticized as 'primitive' the American decision to mount a ground offensive following the month of intensive air operations against Iraqi forces, and instead supported the Soviet peace initiative.

Speaking to over 100 foreign ambassadors to the Holy See at the Vatican on the eve of the outbreak of hostilities, the Pope had explained his well-founded fears: 'These lands [of the Middle East], cradle of the three great monotheistic religions, ought to be the place where respect for man, reconciliation and peace are evident. Alas, dialogue between these spiritual families is often lacking. Christian minorities are, at most, tolerated. Sometimes even the symbol of the Cross is forbidden. This is a flagrant violation of human rights and international law. In our world where it is rare for the population of a country to belong to a single ethnic group or religion, it is a basic requirement for domestic and international peace that respect for people's consciences should be an absolute rule.'

Some of those present could not fail to notice how radically Catholic doctrine had changed; a nineteenth-century Pope had condemned freedom of religious belief for 'corrupting peoples' habits and souls'.

John Paul went on to criticize the presence of weapons and armies of 'terrifying proportions' in the Middle East. He had already denounced American war plans as 'an adventure without return' in his December 1990 Christmas Day message. Now, while supporting the United Nations' condemnation of Iraq's military occupation of Kuwait the previous August ('the law of the strongest cannot be imposed on the weakest'), the Pope cast strong doubt upon what, until his pontificate, had been the traditional Christian teaching on the requirements for waging a just war. It was Saint Augustine of Hippo who had first outlined these conditions in the fourth century AD. His theory was interpreted by the mediaeval theologian Saint Thomas Aquinas in these terms: 1) war must be an act of last resort; 2) it must have legitimate authority for its declaration; 3) it must have a right intention underlying it; 4) the means used must be proportionate to the intended objective; and 5) it must have a fair chance of success.

Pope John Paul's doctrine on the just war, however, appeared to rule out altogether under condition (4) the use of high technology modern warfare and its weapons of mass destruction.

'Recourse to force on behalf of a just cause is only allowable if it is proportional to the result that one wishes to obtain, and if one weighs the consequences that military action, made ever more devastating by modern technology, can have for the survival of populations and of the planet itself.

'The needs of humanity today require us to proceed resolutely towards the absolute banning of war and the cultivation of peace as a supreme good to which all programmes and strategies must be subordinated,' he said in his speech to diplomats at the Vatican.

The Pope then praised the United Nations, recalling the words of the UN founding charter about preserving future generations from the plague of war, and called American plans to go to war in order to restore political independence to Kuwait a 'tragic adventure'. 'The true friends of peace know that this above all is the time for dialogue and negotiation, for the pre-eminence of international law. Peace is still possible; war would represent a step backwards for the whole of humanity.'

Inevitably, the Pope's concern with peace is linked with questions of justice, and just as inevitably, however much he may publicly deny it, this brings him into the sphere of politics. The redressing of political and economic injustices has been established as a legitimate area of papal interest.

The Pope sent separate last-minute peace appeals to President Bush and to Saddam Hussein on 16 January, the day before the Americans decided on military action. President Bush replied that he was intent on setting up a new world order in the Middle East, an idea which failed to convince Pope John Paul, who foresaw only greater disorder as the consequence of war. Saddam Hussein replied in his usual Messianic vein. His message was conveyed to Rome, it was noted, by the newly appointed Soviet Ambassador to the Vatican, Yuri Karlov, normal channels of diplomatic communication with Baghdad having been interrupted. (Indeed, the Papal Nuncio there, Marian Oles, a Pole, ironically had had his office windows blown out by an American bomb.) Mr Karlov also kept the Pope closely briefed on Mikhail Gorbachev's diplomatic peace offensive during the period before the ground attack began.

While the bombing of Baghdad continued, the Pope decided to summon to Rome leaders of his Church from all the major combatant countries, Arab and Western, to discuss what role the Vatican might play in re-establishing peace in the region once a cease-fire was declared. From the Middle East the Pope invited all seven patriarchs of churches in communion with Rome. The patriarchs represent a thinly spread Christian flock of just under 5 million Catholics, who cohabit uneasily in Arab lands with 200 million Muslims. From Baghdad came the head of the Chaldean Church of Babylon, an Iraqi; from Beirut, the leader of the Maronites; also from Lebanon, the leader of the Armenian Catholics; from Damascus, the Patriarch of the Arabic-speaking Melkites; from Jerusalem, Michel Sabbah, a Palestinian born in Nazareth, the first Arab to be appointed Latin Patriarch of Jerusalem, a title dating back to the time of the Crusades; and from Alexandria, the head of the Coptic Catholics. From North Africa came the Archbishop of Algiers, a Frenchman.

The heads of local Bishops' Conferences represented Western Catholics from the main coalition countries – the United States, Britain, France and Italy. The Pope had taken care to distance himself from local pacifists and left-wingers in Italy, who had seized on his anti-war statements during the fighting. On a Sunday parish visit in Rome during the Gulf War, the Pope spelt out his policy – peace, yes, but not peace at any price, only peace with justice. The Church was not composed of political pacifists, he said.

In his opening remarks to the Vatican meeting, which turned out to be the first international gathering to discuss the postwar Gulf situation, the Pope, normally reluctant to name individual countries when he casts moral blame, harshly criticized Saudi Arabia for failing to allow freedom of worship for non-Muslims. He catalogued the political problems whose solution, he said, was a pre-condition to a general Middle East settlement, as follows: a settlement in Iraq, a homeland for the Palestinians, secure frontiers for Israel, an accord between Greeks and Turks over Cyprus, the regulation of arms sales and regional disarmament.

'There is no religious war taking place,' the Pope insisted, although he recognized the small size and weak means of Catholic communities of the region. The heads of these communities disagreed with him. They insisted that in their part of the world many Muslims had indeed interpreted the war as a battle between Muslims and Christians, notwithstanding the fact that fourteen Arab countries had sided with coalition forces against Saddam Hussein.

The leader of the Catholic Church in North Africa, Archbishop Henri Teissier from Algiers, the only European among Catholic Church leaders who had travelled to Rome from Arab lands, said the conflict had reinforced Arab resentment at the way the West looked down on them as second-class citizens. 'They have understood that the value of an Arab is not the same as that of a European. This attitude must be changed so that everyone enjoys respect.'

His Beatitude Nasrallah-Pierre Sfeir, Patriarch of Antioch and leader of the Maronite Church, the largest of the Eastern Catholic Churches with over 2 million members living in Lebanon, Syria, Egypt, Cyprus and Israel, as well as a diaspora in North and South America and Australia, re-inforced the point. 'Muslims feel that Western forces came arrogantly and boastingly to deprive Islamic peoples of their wealth rather than to liberate Kuwait,' he said. The Patriarch complained of double standards adopted by the international community over Security Council resolutions on the Middle East. In the case of Kuwait, action had been taken very rapidly, while resolutions concerning Lebanon and the Palestinians had for years remained unenforced.

But the Patriarch held out hope of peaceful cohabitation at a human level, if not in doctrinal terms, between Christians and Muslims. 'Do I need to recall that Muslims also believe in one God and venerate Christ and his Mother? They hold the Christian religion in esteem, although they say it is impossible to practise Christianity as its precepts are beyond human capability.'

The Patriarch recalled that for 1,300 years Maronite Christians had had the 'rich but difficult' experience of living among Muslims. He warned the Pope that if religious dialogue between Christians and

Muslims were to fail in Lebanon, whose fragile democracy had been the only partial success story in the region, then there was no hope for it elsewhere in the Middle East.

The Pope concurred. Unrealistic as it seemed during the worst days of bloodshed in Beirut, he had always held to his belief that his own presence in Lebanon might somehow help to inspire peace in that troubled country. 'The Church desires to show the world that Lebanon is more than a country: it is a message of freedom and an example of pluralism for East and West,' he wrote to all the bishops of the Catholic Church in 1989, announcing his intention to travel one day to Beirut.

Pope John Paul's first personal contact with the Arab world had been a brief stopover in Casablanca, Morocco, at the end of an African tour in 1985. Would he ever go to Mecca, I remember asking him on the plane as we flew over the Sahara desert. He reminded me of what Pope Pius XII once told a questioner about his readiness to negotiate with Stalin, 'I would negotiate with the devil if I could save one soul!'

That day King Hassan brought ordinary life to a halt in the teeming city of Casablanca in order to give what he considered a proper and dignified welcome to his guest. On the way into town from the airport, a group of Arab horsemen was despatched by the King to perform the traditional desert dweller's greeting for the Pope – a hair-raising gallop followed by a fusillade of rifle shots into the air. Later at the sports stadium before a crowd trucked in from towns and villages at the King's order, the Commander of the Islamic Faith, who claims direct descent from the Prophet Mohammed, sat beside the Pope in an identical chair, to symbolize their equality. This first formal contact with the Arab world was an experiment, the Pope admitted to us.

In his homily, addressed to Moroccan youth, the Pope mentioned God sixty times and Jesus Christ only three times, in deference to Muslim beliefs. The Pope said it was time for Christians and Mulsims to recognize the religious values they have in common. In the past, he said, followers of the Prophet and of Christ had failed to understand one another and had become embroiled in argument and wars. It was time to change these habits, he suggested.

In subsequent African journeys in the poverty and drought-stricken Sahel, in Mali, Niger and Chad, the Pope was to meet other local Muslim leaders, but no significant response was ever noted to these small gestures of friendship offered by the Holy See.

A part of the world that Pope John Paul never visited as Roman pontiff was, paradoxically, the very place where the Christian religion was born, the Holy Land. It was to Israel and Jordan and the 'Holy Places' in East and West Jerusalem that his predecessor Paul VI had paid his first foreign visit in 1964, which was the first papal journey outside Italy in modern times. Yet despite his frequently expressed desire to visit Lebanon during its long civil war, and his suggestion at the end of the Gulf War that he should visit Jerusalem (which was quickly forgotten as the Vatican's conditions for the visit were clearly unacceptable to Israel), security and political considerations prevented Pope John Paul from ever following as a pilgrim in the footsteps of Jesus Christ.

Yet politics and religion remain inextricably intermingled in this unstable area of religious and national conflict. More than forty years after the setting up of the Jewish State, the Vatican still has no diplomatic relations with Israel and no intention of sending a permanent envoy to Tel Aviv. The Israeli Prime Minister, Yitzhak Shamir, was one of the very few foreign heads of government who paid official visits to Italy during the reign of John Paul, to deliberately exclude a papal audience from his Roman itinerary.

The first Iraqi Scud missile attacks against Israel at the beginning of the Gulf War did, it is true, draw some public words of support from the Pope, on Israel's right to secure frontiers. Catholic pilgrims were startled one Sunday to see a large group of several hundred Roman Jews gather for the traditional noon blessing in Saint Peter's Square, and wave the Israeli flag to plead for official recognition. It was to no avail.

The Christian presence in the area where Jesus Christ was born is fast disappearing. The Israeli-Palestine conflict has forced tens of thousands of Palestinian Christians, who used to form the backbone of the Christian presence in the Holy Land, to migrate. The Christian portion of the Arab population of Jerusalem, for example, has declined from one-half in 1949 to less than one-tenth in the 1990s.

Pietro Rossano, an Italian Bishop who is in charge of the Vatican's relations with world Jewry, says Arab Christians in Israel are having their rights constantly eroded by the authorities in Tel Aviv:

For many centuries, under Ottoman Turkish rule, Arab Christians acquired property rights and privileges. The Jewish immigration is now besieging the remaining pockets of Christian population, who see their very survival at risk. The arrival of more and more Jews particularly from the Soviet Union tends to submerge the old communities. The Christian presence is diminishing rapidly.

There are also consistent Christian communities in Syria, Iraq and Egypt.

The Holy See is not a State, but a supranational entity protecting communities located in the most diverse cultural and constitutional contexts. The Vatican cannot fail to take these populations into account and cannot, for example, establish diplomatic relations with Israel, going above their heads.

This sort of argument fails to convince the Israelis that the Pope is being even-handed in the dispute between Jews and Arabs. Israelis take little comfort from the explanation the Vatican offers that Tel Aviv is not the only Middle East capital without a Vatican Nuncio since the Holy See has no official relations with either Jordan or Saudi Arabia.

In modern times, the Roman Catholic Church in the Middle East has been wedded to Palestinian Arab culture. Nine out of ten Christian believers in the region are of Arab race, language and culture. Rome is bound to have a steadily decreasing say in local affairs unless the departure of Christian Arabs is halted. By the twenty-first century, the role of the Catholic Church in the Middle East risks being limited to that of museum and church curator, guardian of the stones sacred to Christians in the rest of the world.

Inside Israel Christians obedient to Rome are in a minority three times over: first as Arabs among Jews, then as Christian Arabs among Muslim Arabs, and finally as a minority within local Christian society, that rich mosaic of Greek Catholics, Greek and Russian Orthodox, Armenians, Copts, Maronites, Syrians and Anglicans, to name only a few of the divisions of Christendom present in the Holy Land.

When Pope John Paul decided to send delegates from Rome to the General Assembly of the Middle East Council of Churches meeting in Cyprus in 1990, it was the first time since the Council of Chalcedon in AD 451 that representatives from all the Churches of Christendom had gathered together for official discussions on Church unity.

After the capture of Byzantine by the Turks, it fell to the Greek Orthodox Church to provide the continuity of the Christian presence in the Holy Land. Most other Christian groups present today, including the Catholics, did not arrive until the nineteenth century. Before then Catholic interests had been looked after by Franciscan monks, who had remained behind after the last of the Crusades some six centuries ago.

It was Pope Pius XI who set up the Latin Patriarchate of Jerusalem in 1847. The post was traditionally filled by an Italian, until Pope John Paul II appointed the first Palestinian as Bishop and Patriarch of Jerusalem in 1988. He was Michel Sabbah, former rector of the Catholic University in Bethlehem. This university had been created in 1973, when the Vatican realized – somewhat tardily – that it was not enough to care for stones and shrines in the Holy Land. Something had to be done about educating a new Palestinian Christian élite, despite the tensions this was bound to cause with Israel.

John Paul has supported the cause of the Palestinian people more than any of his recent predecessors. Speaking during a visit in October 1980 to Otranto near Bari, the nearest port on the Italian peninsula to the Middle East, the Pope pointed an accusing finger at the Israelis for causing the Palestinians' present plight. Then in 1982, and again in 1988, he received the Palestine Liberation Organization leader Yasser Arafat at the Vatican – each time to shocked criticism from Israel and world Jewry.

The Israeli government did not mince its words.

The [Catholic] Church which did not say a word about the massacre of Jews for six years in Europe, and has not had much to say about the killing of Christians in Lebanon, is now ready to meet a man who committed the killings in Lebanon and who wants the destruction of Israel in order to complete the work carried out by the Nazis in Germany. If John Paul meets Arafat, it is indicative of a certain moral standard...

The Vatican responded with a tart communiqué criticizing Tel Aviv's tone and pointing out that Pope John Paul, who had lived in Kraków as a witness of the Holocaust, had frequently denounced Nazi genocides not only against the Jews, but also against his own Polish people and against the gipsy nation.

John Paul's three guiding principles towards the Israeli-Palestinian conflict are: first, a categorical condemnation of terrorism or reprisals as a way of resolving the conflict; second, strong support for the Palestinians' right to their own homeland; and, third, *de facto* acknowledgement of the existence of the Jewish State and its right to secure borders. Above all, as he stressed in a general comment on the Middle East crisis after the Israeli invasion of southern Lebanon, 'There can be no true peace without justice, and there cannot be justice unless the rights of all peoples involved are recognized.'

The issue which brought the Pope into apparent deadlock with the Israelis was a declaration by the Knesset in 1980 that the city of Jerusalem is the 'eternal and indivisible capital' of the Jewish State. The Pope's aim has been to try to salvage for posterity the Holy See's historical and cultural patrimony, those parts of the city sacred to Christians. But because Jerusalem is also a place sacred to Jews and Muslims, the situation appears complicated beyond any reasonable hope of compromise. According to Jewish law, when a Jew prays he must do so facing the direction of the 'City of Eternity', just as Muslims face Mecca. Jerusalem symbolizes the link between the temporal and the spiritual in the Jewish faith. But there is, of course, an overlap between some Jewish and Muslim shrines. For example, the Dome of the Rock and the Aqsa mosque, whence the Prophet is believed by Muslims to have ascended to the Seventh Heaven after riding to the Holy City on a winged steed from Mecca, are built over the site of the second Jewish Temple.

The Vatican's view is that the city of Jerusalem ought to be placed under a special international regime. This would be guaranteed by powers outside the region and would exist to protect the interests of members of all three monotheistic religions in their various Holy Places. Yet since 1949 the Israelis have never let up in their efforts to consolidate their unilateral control over the city. And the Arabs too are opposed to the internationalization of Jerusalem: for them the city is an integral part and parcel of Palestine, and its destiny cannot be separated from the problem of finding a home for the Palestinian people.

In April 1984 Pope John Paul took the Holy See's position on Jerusalem forward slightly when he suggested in an Apostolic Letter that the Holy City should become the pivot for a general settlement of the Israeli-Palestinian conflict. Jerusalem, he proposed, might become the unifying and pacifying element between Arabs and Israelis, between Christians, Muslims and Jews. He reminded the warring parties that religion could and should play a constructive role in resolving their conflicts.

At the beginning of his letter, the Pope recalled the visit of his predecessor Paul VI to Jerusalem in 1964. But, he added, he himself could not under present conditions repeat the journey. It was difficult to imagine the relatively carefree days of 1964 when a burly young American prelate, Paul Marcinkus, was selected by Paul VI to negotiate all the official papal travel arrangements with the Israeli and Jordanian authorities and to double up as papal bodyguard as well.

The establishment of diplomatic relations with the Holy See has been requested by Israel many times: the Pope's answer has always been negative. The Vatican chooses to distinguish between religious *rapprochement* with the Jews which began with the Second Vatican Council Statement *Nostra Aetate* (the first unequivocal statement from Rome repudiating collective Jewish guilt for the death of Jesus Christ), and relations with the Jewish State, seen in Rome as a purely diplomatic and political question.

The Roman Catholic Church's history of relations with the Jews is not edifying. Anti-semitism was enshrined in the Catholic liturgy for

Holy Week for centuries. Until 1966 a prayer used to be said for 'the perfidious Jew', an allusion to the denial by the Jewish people that Jesus Christ is the Messiah. In many Catholic European cities Jews were forced to live in ghettos (an Italian word which came into general use in the sixteenth century) for their own security. The Holy Week prayers denigrating the Jews for their treachery against Christ sometimes triggered attacks on individual Jews and pogroms within Jewish ghettos.

Perhaps the high point of John Paul's relations with the Jews was his visit to the Rome synagogue in April 1986, the first time that a Pope had ever attended a Jewish religious service. He referred affectionately to the Jews as 'our respected elder brothers'.

However, his decision the following year to invite the President of Austria, Kurt Waldheim, on a solemn State visit to the Vatican cast serious doubt upon any real commitment to improving the historically poor relations between Catholics and Jews. The visit provoked bitter protests from North American and European Jews. It was alleged that President Waldheim, former Secretary-General of the United Nations, had as a serving officer in the German Wehrmacht participated in the deportation of Jews in the Balkans during the Second World War. Waldheim denied he had been party to any Nazi war crimes. Jews found it intolerable that the Pope should be the first foreign Head of State to give public recognition to Waldheim, given that the Austrian President was being boycotted by most other states including America, which had gone so far as to forbid him entry.

Cardinal Albert Decourtray, Archbishop of Lyons and head of the Catholic Church in France, said after a meeting with the Chief Rabbi of Lyons, Richard Werthenschlag, 'I experienced a certain suffering on hearing that the Pope was going to receive Mr Waldheim. I am still trying to understand the reasons for the visit that I must say I have not understood.'

Later he issued a joint statement with the Cardinal Archbishop of Paris, Jean-Marie Lustiger, who is of Polish extraction and whose parents were Jews:

We all carry in our memories and in our flesh the mark of Nazi madness. For the international community and its leaders this has always posed a moral problem, of which the Waldeim affair is the most recent manifestation. Pope John Paul has shown in all his actions that political motives must not take precedence over moral demands. It is by meeting the Austrian people and its leaders that this problem can be dealt with.

In the United States, where reaction against Waldheim's visit was perhaps strongest because of the powerful Jewish lobby, Cardinal Law of Boston defended the Pope's right to receive at the Vatican whomsoever he wished. 'From the beginning of modern diplomacy,' the Cardinal explained, 'the Papacy has followed a policy of receiving Heads of State or their emissaries even when the Holy See was in disagreement with that State's policies.'

A dispute had raged for years over a convent established by fourteen Polish Carmelite nuns inside the former concentration camp at Auschwitz, understandably regarded by Jews as a shrine to the millions of their faith who perished there. The Vatican, Jewish leaders and local Polish Church officials eventually reached an amicable solution. After ugly scenes of violence at Auschwitz involving radical Jews and Polish workers, an agreement to move the nuns to new premises outside the former concentration-camp site and build an inter-faith centre of worship was finally implemented.

At the Pope's behest in 1990, to mark the twenty-fifth anniversary of the *Nostra Aetate* Second Vatican Council pronouncement on relations with non-Christian religions, a strong statement by the Polish bishops on relations between Catholics and Jews was read out in all Polish churches. The pastoral letter expressed blanket regret for 'all incidents of anti-Semitism which were committed at any time upon Polish soil', and also expressed sorrow for 'all injustices and harm done to Jews'. Sir Sigmund Sternberg, chairman of the executive committee of the International Council of Christians and Jews, said he regarded the new statement as a breakthrough in Catholic-Jewish relations. But the feeling remains among international Jewry that Rome cannot claim to be acting entirely in good faith towards the Jews until it grants full diplomatic recognition to Israel. Jews feel that Catholics fail to recognize the close connection between the religious and political significance of the creation at last of their own homeland. One of the early drafts of *Nostra Aetate* had stated specifically:

Jews have indicated in a thousand ways their attachment to the land promised to their ancestors from the days of Abraham. It could seem that Christians, whatever the difficulties they may experience, must attempt to understand and respect the religious significance of this link between the people and the land. The existence of the State of Israel should not be separated from this perspective, which does not in itself imply any judgement on historical occurrences or on decisions of a purely political order.

Despite Pope John Paul's obsession with the indivisible nature of Europe's Christian traditions, overall progress towards re-uniting divided Christians, Anglicans, Lutherans and the Orthodox has been painfully slow during his pontificate.

It must be said that the traditional concept of the role of the Bishop of Rome as Supreme Pastor of an uncompromisingly exclusive Catholic Church did change significantly during the hundred years that elapsed between the holding of the first and second Vatican Councils. At the time of Vatican I in 1869, the Roman pontiff was seen as head of a movement that was still modelled upon the ancient Roman Empire – one vast Church, under a single leader, divided into various provinces whose bishops were virtually delegates of the Pope and received all their powers from him.

Vatican II produced a very different picture of the Universal Church; it was now perceived as a community of individual churches, each one of which was the true Church in its own geographical setting, but which together formed the Universal Church. The chief pastor of each of these individual churches was perceived as the 'Vicar of Christ' for his own following. The local head of the Church, it was now believed, received his mandate to teach and govern not from the Pope but from Christ himself, at the moment when he was ordained Bishop.

Pope Paul VI realized that the papal office constitutes an obstacle for many Christians in their search for unity. None the less, the Anglicans have gone a long way towards accepting the primacy of the Pope since starting an official dialogue with the Roman Catholic Church in 1970.

The reasons why the Anglicans originally split away from Rome in the sixteenth century were political as much as they were religious. Unlike the Protestant churches of the Reformation, the Anglicans retained the episcopal structure of the Roman Catholic Church. Today the Anglican communion consists of a loose confederation of national or regional churches, and is not closed to the idea of recognizing in the Papacy the focus of the whole Christian world. Yet talks between the Vatican and the 75-million-strong Anglican communion have foundered over the issue of the ordination of women priests. This is despite the Pope's successful visit to Britain in 1982 and the Archbishop of Canterbury's cordial return visit to Rome in 1989.

The first-ever papal visit to Britain, in 1982, took place in dramatic circumstances – at the height of the war between Britain and Argentina over the Falkland Islands. The visit was almost cancelled at the last minute on the advice of some of the Pope's top advisers, but the forceful intervention of Cardinal Basil Hume, leader of English Catholics, saved the situation. He managed to convince two fellow cardinals from Argentina to travel to Rome and arrange that, immediately following his tour of England, Scotland and Wales, the Pope would make a quick face-saving visit to Buenos Aires and so safeguard the political impartiality of the Papacy.

In Britain there were two highlights of the Pope's visit. At the airport mass in Coventry he spoke to the biggest gathering of British Catholics in history. His speech in the reconstructed city, bombed by the Germans during the Second World War, seemed to invalidate the theory of the just war. It was particularly poignant as it came after the loss of HMS *Coventry* in action in the south Atlantic.

'Today, the scale and the horror of modern warfare – whether nuclear or not – makes it totally unacceptable as a means of settling differences between nations,' he said. 'War should belong to the tragic past, to history, it should find no place on humanity's agenda for the future.'

The other great set piece was a solemn joint Anglican and Catholic prayer service in Canterbury Cathedral, where the Pope and the Archbishop of Canterbury, Dr Robert Runcie, renewed their baptismal vows. At Canterbury the Pope was engaged in a dialogue with priests of the Church of England who, under a decree of his predecessor Leo XIII a century before, were not true priests because they were not ordained correctly according to the Roman rite.

Yet the Bishop of Rome accepted equality of status with his fellow Bishop of Canterbury as they processed side by side up the nave of the great Gothic cathedral where Thomas Becket was murdered. In deference to Dr Runcie the Pope appeared without his crozier or any symbol of his supreme office. The Archbishop of Canterbury elegantly expressed the hopes – and also the limits – of this undoubtedly moving ceremony: 'If we can lift our eyes beyond the historic quarrels which have disfigured Christ's Church and wasted so much Christian energy, then we shall enter into a faith worthy of celebration,' he said.

The two prelates signed a joint declaration expressing satisfaction at the conclusion of the work of the first Anglican-Roman Catholic commission of theologians (ARCIC) who had been labouring for twelve years to define and to narrow doctrinal differences. As an act of good faith, the Pope and the Archbishop agreed to set up yet another commission to prepare for mutual recognition of Anglican and Catholic ministries and even for the eventual restoration of full communion between the two churches. But this was over-optimistic, as became clear during Dr Runcie's return visit to Rome seven years later. By this time the new set of talks had become seriously hampered by the divisions which arose within the Anglican Church over the decision by some members of the Anglican communion to allow the ordination of women priests.

At the Pope's request the Vatican had arranged the most cordial of receptions for Dr Runcie's visit. No less than six meetings were organized between the two men during the four days that the Archbishop of Canterbury spent in Rome. The Roman Curia organized a drinks party in an elegant hunting lodge built by the pleasure-loving Pope Paul IV in the Vatican gardens, which now houses the Pontifical Institute of Science; solemn vespers were celebrated by the Pope in the church of Saint Gregory from which the first Archbishop of Canterbury, Saint Augustine, had set out from Rome fourteen centuries before to carry the Christian faith to England; the Archbishop attended an open-air papal mass in Saint Peter's Square; and there were talks in the Pope's library followed by a final informal lunch in the private apartments.

The point in dispute, however, remained the same: the primacy over all Christians claimed by the Pope, and the validity of Anglican Holy Orders, especially for women. On primacy, Dr Runcie suggested a formula which would emphasize both the unity of all Christians and the diversity of the worldwide Anglican communion. The Archbishop should have read carefully the all-embracing definition of the Pope's primacy enshrined in the Catholic Church's revised Code of Canon Law. There the Pope's primacy over all Christians is defined as 'supreme, full, immediate and universal'. There is no way in which this concept could be watered down to accommodate the semi-independence and flexibility of the various component churches of the Anglican confession.

In private Dr Runcie explained to Pope John Paul some of the political as well as the theological complexities of the history of the Anglican Church, and its relationship to the monarchy. He told me afterwards that the Pope had not appeared to fully understand the unusual relationship between the British Crown, the Prime Minister and the Archbishop of Canterbury. At the end of their Rome meeting the Pope and the Archbishop publicly expressed their agreement on the erosion of religious faith in Europe and the material greed of society.

However, to a Slav Pope preoccupied by events in his native Eastern Europe, and bearing the heavy responsibility of dealing with Islam and the young churches of the Third World, the Anglican problem must have seemed peripheral. And as he noted gloomily, despite a new 'intensity' in relations between Rome and Canterbury, the differences separating the two Churches had been brought into focus.

Many British Catholics decided not to wait for Rome to dismantle the barriers which isolated them from their fellow Christians for four centuries, and enthusiastically welcomed the close relationship which had developed between Dr Runcie and Cardinal Hume. Catholics and Anglicans may not yet share communion at the same altar, but they do share the same preoccupations about the shameful persisting divisions among Christians which theologians and their own Church leaders find themselves unable to resolve. In other European countries as well, particularly in the Netherlands, the claims of primacy over all other religious leaders made by the Pope are seen as useless historical relics. Many European Catholics long for the day when one of Pope John Paul's successors as Bishop of Rome will have the courage to break down the theological barriers which Christians have created among themselves. These Catholics find it difficult to accept that sharing the communion table with other Christians can only be the goal of unity and not one of the visible steps towards achieving that unity. They understand the doctrinal separations of Christendom, but they find that these divisions make less and less sense for twentieth-century Christians.

John Paul's visit in the summer of 1989 to the post-Christian societies of Scandinavia differed from his other European journeys. In the cold northern fringes of Europe Catholics are a tiny minority, less than one per cent of a thinly distributed and widely scattered population. For example, in the Norwegian diocese of Tromsö, north of the Arctic Circle, a total of 783 Catholics are spread out along a coastline more than 600 miles long. Scandinavian Catholics are mainly migrants, not rooted in the local culture which is strongly Lutheran. The Pope was certainly breaking new ground here – the last visit to this part of Europe by a papal legate was in the middle of the twelfth century. Nicholas Breakspeare, the first and only English Pope, went on a diplomatic mission as far as modern Trondheim just before his election as Pope Hadrian IV. He set up there what was at the time one of the largest archdioceses in Europe, embracing northern Russia, northern Europe, Greenland and parts of Britain.

For centuries after the Lutheran Reformation, conversion to Catholicism in Scandinavia was regarded as treasonable. In modern times the Nordic countries have moved further away from the practice of the Christian religion as taught by the Catholic Church. In all five countries – Sweden, Norway, Finland, Denmark and Iceland – abortion is available on demand, the use of contraceptives is universal and marriage is crumbling as an institution. 'If I look at Swedish society,' said Bishop William Kenney, who ministers to about 135,000 Swedish Catholics, 'it has probably lost a conscious belief in God, although it still has many factors which express values that Christians can share.'

The number of abortions in relation to live births in Norway and Sweden is about one-third; and about one-third of the children in Scandinavia are born outside marriage. It is ironic that it is Scandinavia's relatively large homosexual communities who seem most to feel the need for Church or State to bless their relationships. Some Danish and Swedish pastors offer informal 'marriage' ceremonies to homosexual couples and in Denmark such partnerships are now given by law the same housing, pension and immigration rights as heterosexual couples.

Conscious that the sort of denunciations of contraception and abortion that he used in Latin America or Africa would have little effect in Norway, the Pope decided to concentrate instead upon ecumenical matters and the Nordic countries' excellent human rights record. However, in one of his final speeches in Denmark before returning to Rome, he could not resist condemning Scandinavian society's liberal views on sex and its easy acceptance of abortion and divorce.

The Pope was uncompromising with Norway's Lutheran bishops when they asked him to regard their Church as an equal of Rome. Bishop Andreas Aarflot said many Scandinavians believed that Rome was moving away from the isolation and self-sufficiency which had been its hallmark since the Reformation, but that much more needed to be done.

Although the Pope agreed that the quest for unity was 'part of the Church's life', he said that Catholics and Protestants could not yet proclaim a common faith in the Eucharist and in the Church because they did not share full communion.

Nordic Lutherans expressed a low opinion of the Pope's real ecumenical commitment. 'In the decade of this Pope's office the movement towards Church unity has stopped,' said Bishop Per Loenning of Norway. Seven out of his country's eleven Lutheran bishops boycotted an ecumenical service led by the Pope in Trondheim cathedral. In Iceland, where there are only 2,000 Catholics among a population of a quarter of a million, women pastors of the local Lutheran church boycotted the Pope's mass in protest at his refusal to consider the admission of women to the Catholic priesthood.

However, after a prayer service in the twelfth-century cathedral at

Roskilde in Denmark, the hallowed burial place of Danish kings where the local Bishop had refused to allow the Pope to speak for fear of 'confusing and troubling' his Protestant congregation, the Pope said that Rome was ready for dialogue. But he refused to issue an apology to the Lutherans for the way in which the Church had treated Martin Luther, or to cancel the excommunication decree passed against the Reformer 468 years before. He explained that such a juridical act was impossible and also unnecessary. The excommunication decree had expired with the reformer's death. The Pope praised Luther for his 'profound faith' and explained that some of the German theologian's teachings on reform and renewal had long been accepted by Rome. 'Today we need a common re-assessment of the many questions raised by Luther and his message. A re-assessment on the Catholic side has already begun,' he said optimistically.

This was certainly a more generous approach to the priest from Wittenberg than Pope John Paul had shown on the 500th anniversary of Luther's birth in 1983. In a studiously even-handed letter written to Cardinal Willebrands, head of the Vatican's Secretariat for Christian Unity, the Pope had admitted on that occasion that the Catholic Church of Luther's day had shown scant understanding of the Reformer's vision of God, but he had also castigated Luther for failing to understand 'true' Catholicism. He did not clarify that distinction.

During his stopover in Reykjavik, the Pope more realistically stressed the impossibility of a rapid re-unification among the different Christian churches. 'We cannot ourselves heal the wounds of the division and restore unity among Christians. This could only be a gift of God,' he said.

While visiting Prague in 1990 Pope John Paul expressed understanding for the Czech priest and religious reformer Jan Hus, a precursor of the Reformation. Hus had been convicted and burnt at the stake for heresy in 1415, after being shamefully tricked into attending a church gathering with a false promise of safe conduct. It could not be denied that Jan Hus had 'personal integrity of life and a commitment to the instruction and moral life of the Czech nation', the Pope said. But having acknowledged Hus for local political reasons, he let the matter drop.

John Paul's most idiosyncratic and colourful gesture towards religious unity took place in 1986, in the small Umbrian town of Assisi, birthplace and shrine of Saint Francis. The Pope invited 150 religious leaders not only from all the various branches of Christendom, but from many other faiths as well, including Buddhists and Shintoists from Asia and worshippers of the forest spirits from Africa. All came to central Italy to fast for a day and to pray with him for world peace, each in their own fashion. The Pope appealed for a twenty-four-hour truce to be observed in all countries at war at that moment, including the Lebanon and El Salvador.

The idea was attacked by right-wing Catholics as a particularly dangerous and insidious example of 'syncretism', a pejorative word in ecclesiastical jargon meaning the reduction of all religions to their lowest common denominator. The idea is abhorrent to those who claim that the Roman Catholic Church has a monopoly upon religious revelation, interpretation and truth.

The ceremony began in the Porziuncola, the tiny Romanesque church in the valley below the great monastery where the saint now lies buried and where the Italian painter Giotto created his great series of frescoes of Francis's life. It was in the Porziuncola, now enclosed within another much larger church built several hundred years later, that Saint Francis died in the early thirteenth century aged forty-five.

Francis would have been surprised to see the procession of dignitaries from around the world mobilized in his name by Pope John Paul. They included the Archbishop of Canterbury, the Dalai Lama from Tibet, Mother Teresa of Calcutta, and the Italian Prime Minister Giulio Andreotti, a devout Catholic. Also present were saffron- and white-robed Buddhist monks, grave Lutherans, Japanese Shintoists, Jewish Rabbis, bearded Muslims, turbaned Sikhs, barefoot African animists whom the Pope had first met during a visit to Togo, and Eastern Orthodox Christian Patriarchs wearing flowing white headgear. Other 'religious families', as the Peace Day organizers quaintly called their guests, included Jains from India, Zoroastrians, and a delegation of American Indians led by one Mr John Pretty-On-Top from Montana, who thoughtfully brought along his pipe of peace to smoke during the lengthy ceremonies.

Mr Pretty-On-Top offered his pipe 'to the four winds and to Mother Earth'. The Africans prayed to 'the great Thumb we cannot evade to tie any knot, and to the Roaring Thunder that splits mighty trees'. One of Assisi's many churches was carpeted and converted into a temporary mosque for the day to accommodate Muslims. Each group prayed in their own mode and in their own language. In order to fend off accusations of 'syncretism', there was no act of common worship. In his homily the Pope said prayer was an extra dimension of the universal search for peace that had possibly been neglected in favour of negotiations, political compromise and economic bargaining. He had no intention, he said, of reducing all religion to a common denominator, but he felt forced to draw upon what he called 'the deepest moral sources' in the search for peace. At the end of the day olive branches were raised in the air and exchanged and doves of peace were released to flutter over the hallowed stones of Saint Francis's town. The proceedings were relayed by radio and television to a worldwide audience and the Pope was content that he had made his point.

CHAPTER 6

Salvation Politics

Some Christians depict Jesus as a political activist, as a fighter against Roman domination and the authorities, even as someone involved in class struggle. The concept of Jesus as a political figure, a revolutionary, the subversive from Nazareth, does not tally with the Church's teaching
Pope John Paul II, Puebla, Mexico 1979

In January 1979, only three months after his election as Pope, Karol Wojtyla set out from Rome on a chartered Alitalia jet on the first of his worldwide journeys. His destination, Mexico, was not a random choice. By going immediately to Latin America, the Pope stressed the importance to the Church of what happens in this continent. Both in terms of numbers and basic human rights issues, a lot was at stake in this huge area of the world. In ten subsequent journeys criss-crossing the sub-continent during his first gruelling thirteen years as Pope, John Paul managed to visit twenty-two countries in South and Central America, that is to say every State in the region with the exception of Cuba, Surinam and French Guyana. He made the five-hundredth anniversary of the discovery of the New World by Christopher Columbus, to be celebrated in 1992, the excuse for a crusading effort to re-establish the presence of the Universal Church in politically and socially turbulent Latin America.

Pope John Paul decided early on to challenge the 'liberation theologians' of Latin America. They believe that the Universal Church cannot stand idly by in the face of massive social injustice and degrading poverty, but must literally take up arms to achieve the economic and political liberation which is the birthright of every human being.

Ten years before Wojtyla became Pope, Medellin, in Colombia, had seen one of the most significant gatherings of bishops in the history of his church. Medellin was the city which in the 1980s became known as the centre for one of the world's biggest drug cartels, a place with one of the worst records for violence on earth – one murder on average every three hours. The bishops of the whole of Catholic Latin America gathered in Medellin in 1968 to make a solemn declaration that the social and international structures of this vast area were inherently sinful. Taking their cue from the teaching of Dom Helder Camara, Archbishop of Recife in north-east Brazil, the bishops decided that their Church must in future be a 'Church of the poor', one born 'from within the people' and not the meek recipient of structures imposed from above. This represented a radical change of attitude, truly revolutionary in its implications. This was an area where, for four hundred years, the Roman Catholic church had contrived to be closely identified with local political and economic power structures rather than with ordinary poor people.

Many military-led governments in Latin America had tried to involve local Catholic Churches in their battles against what they considered the major political threat – Communism. 'National security' became the God before which were sacrificed such elementary rights as that of the *campesinos* to organize themselves into co-operatives and farmers' unions. Torture and State terrorism often became the normal response of leaders who felt themselves under threat.

Two key encyclicals written by Pope John XXIII in the early 1960s, *Pacem in Terris* (Peace on Earth) and *Mater et Magistra* (Mother and Teacher), viewed Marxism in a more benevolent light than the excommunication decrees against Communists issued from Rome by his predecessor Pius XII. Pope John distinguished between a potentially evil creed and the goodness which could none the less be manifested by those professing ideologies theoretically hostile to Christianity. He urged Catholics to work more seriously than in the past for peace and justice.

Priests in various Latin American countries became seriously involved in left-wing political activities. Some joined guerrilla groups in Nicaragua and El Salvador. In Colombia, a young priest called Camillo Torres was killed in a battle against government forces in 1966. He became a popular hero for left-wingers throughout Latin America.

However it was a Peruvian priest and theologian, Gustavo Gutierrez, who coined the term 'liberation theology'. This was the title of his book published in 1971, a seminal work whose teaching, the author claimed, grew 'out of the oppressed and exploited land of Latin America'.

Gutierrez said that Marxism had encouraged theologians to ask questions about the transformation of Third World societies. To deny the fact of class struggle was to put oneself on the side of those who dominate the poor. The Church must take sides with the poor for whom

Jesus Christ had shown special love. To eliminate poverty was 'to bring closer the moment of seeing God face to face, in union with other men'.

The instrument by which the social and political change necessary to combat poverty and oppression could be helped along was the base community, *comunidade de base* – a concept of Church fellowship that was traced back by its promoters to what they saw as the very first base community – that of Jesus Christ and his Apostles. 'Base', says Gutierrez, 'means the poor, oppressed, believing people: marginalized races, exploited classes, despised cultures.' The communities are small groups organizing themselves prayerfully and pragmatically outside the command structure of the organized Church hierarchy. Hundreds of thousands of these grassroots communities have sprung up. Bible study is punctuated with discussions on severely practical matters like dealing with sanitation and drinking water, replacing the mud and the open sewers that surround most homes in Latin America with paved streets, and fighting eviction by wealthy landlords.

The presence of a priest is not essential to the functioning of the base community, but meeting as a real community, not sitting in pews avoiding each others' eyes, is. There is a fundamental change of direction in the concept of a Church structured on base community lines. Power flows as in a tree from the roots upwards, rather than descending from the Pope at the apex down towards the submissive sheep at the base.

Not all Latin American bishops were supportive of the base communities, which often put greater emphasis on faith in creating a better society than faith in Christ. They were also fearful of losing control over huge numbers of people whose social conscience was being awakened for the first time, and who were being stimulated to take action on their own behalf instead of resigning themselves to lives of degradation and poverty.

Some priests in Nicaragua put the new theory into practice. Leaders of the revolution, which overthrew the dictatorship of Anastasio Somoza less than a year after Karol Wojtyla became Pope, included priests who felt they had succeeded in welding together the basic concepts of Christianity and Marxism. Five of them joined the Sandinista government, including the American-born Maryknoll missionary Miguel Escoto, who became Foreign Minister. John Paul suspended them all from their priestly functions.

And so when Pope John Paul arrived in Mexico City in 1979, ten years after the Medellin declarations had given a new twist to Catholic teaching, he was faced with the crucial question: where does the Church go from here? Are the People of God in Latin America marching towards social justice in this world, or are they seeking only salvation and liberation in the next?

The Pope's answer was clear. Politics and religion are separate. Liberation from sin, by all means. Liberation from oppressive governments by force of arms, no. Later he was to be able to point to the success of the non-violent protest movement Solidarity in Poland as the correct way forward for oppressed peoples. But there always remained a basic ambivalence about his attitudes towards political change in his native country and political change elsewhere in the world.

Wojtyla first set foot as Pope in the New World on the Caribbean island of Santo Domingo, the burial place of its white discoverer, Christopher Columbus. There were delirious scenes of welcome from the crowds during a brief stopover on his way to Mexico City. But this was only a foretaste of the papal triumph in Mexico. For the following six days Pope John Paul was mobbed wherever he went. Over 20 million people, about one-third of the entire Mexican population (then 67 million, today 84 million) saw him in the flesh.

The Latin American Bishops' Conference, summoned to discuss developments since their last plenary meeting at Medellin a decade before, began their meeting with a mass at the sanctuary of the Madonna of Guadalupe, the holiest Catholic shrine in Central America. Here the Pope was on familiar ground. Here his much-loved Madonna from Czestochowa was transposed into an exotic New World setting. Just in case he failed to get the message, written into a colourful carpet of flower petals in front of the basilica was the motto 'Mexico and Poland, United in Love of Mary'.

Just as Poles venerate the Black Madonna as the enduring symbol of their religious loyalty and integrity through centuries of war, division and national disasters, so Mexicans have their own dark-skinned Indian Madonna. She appeared to an Indian, one Juan Diego, in 1531, ten years after the ancient Aztec Empire had been brutally overthrown by the Spanish. The fact that the Virgin appeared on a mountain which had been sacred to the Aztecs and spoke in Nuahatl, a local Indian dialect, not the language of the conquerors, was regarded as being distinctly subversive by the local Spanish Bishop at the time. Inexplicable happenings occurred; they were linked with the Virgin's apparition, and Guadalupe soon became a shrine for the new people of Mexico, the Mestizos, those of mixed Indian and Spanish blood.

When the Mexicans fought the Spanish for their independence three centuries later, they did so under the leadership of a Mexican priest, Father Miguel Hidalgo y Costilla. His followers flew the banner of the Virgin of Guadalupe decorated with her portrait, believed to have been miraculously imprinted upon Juan Diego's cloak.

What many Mexicans secretly hoped in 1979 was that Pope John Paul had come to announce a new interpretation of the Christian message taking into account their own suppressed culture and religion. They should have known better.

The Pope made no reference to the violence and oppression which had accompanied the spreading of the Gospel message from 1492 onwards. He did not even refer directly to the 800 Latin American priests and nuns who had been persecuted during the previous decade in Central and South America – some of them dying as martyrs to their faith. He paid lip service to some of the ideas of the liberation theologians, speaking of the need to 'humanize political and economic systems', but his basic message was that activist priests were mutilating the Church's faith by setting up a so-called 'people's Church' in competition with the institutional church in Rome. Marxism was fundamentally atheistic and therefore incompatible with Christian teaching. The concept of class struggle was foreign to Christian ethics.

Just before the Pope's second visit to Latin America one of the Catholic Church's champions of human rights in the sub-continent, Archbishop Oscar Romero of San Salvador, was assassinated by his political enemies while celebrating mass in a hospital chapel. The crime was blamed upon right-wing death squads, and no one was ever brought to trial. Archbishop Romero had started out as a traditionalist bishop, refusing to engage in politics, but as his country gradually slid into a full-scale civil war (which is still continuing in the 1990s) he stood up in public to oppose the ruling military dictatorship. He asked the Americans to suspend arms shipments to El Salvador and pointedly stayed away from the inaugural ceremonies for the new Head of State, refusing to open his cathedral for him, although the official Vatican diplomatic representative continued to show a high profile. On a visit to Rome just before his death, Archbishop Romero was warned by Pope John Paul that Marxist ideology could weaken people's Christian faith. Romero replied defiantly, 'There is a form of anti-Communism that is not directed to the defence of religious views, but to the defence of capitalism, that is of the right.'

The Archbishop recorded his diary on tape for two years before his death, including that visit to Rome. (It was transcribed and published

in Italy by La Meridiana in 1991.) The Pope kept Archbishop Romero
waiting for a week for his audience, and the Archbishop worried a lot
about the expense of taking taxis to and from the Vatican as he tried
to get in touch with the head of the pontifical household to make the
arrangements. When he finally managed to speak to the Pope and was
able to tell him about the murder of Father Octavio, one his priests, by
right-wing death squads, the Pope advised 'great prudence in making
concrete denunciations'.

I explained to the Pope that there are situations like that of Father Octavio in
which it is necessary to be very concrete because injustice and violence have
been very concrete.

The Pope recalled his own situation in Poland, where he had had to deal with
a non-Catholic government, and stressed the importance of unity among the
country's bishops.

I replied that I also desired this but unity could not be simulated, it had to
be based upon the Gospel and the truth. I was worried that negative information
about my pastoral mission in El Salvador had preceded me at the Vatican; the
Pope recommended 'boldness and courage, tempered by prudence and necessary
balance'.

In a homily in San Salvador's cathedral on Sunday 23 March 1980,
Archbishop Romero told soldiers and police among his congregation
that they had a right to refuse to carry out orders to kill their fellow
countrymen. 'We want the government to understand that reforms are
no use at the cost of so much bloodshed. I implore you, I pray you, I
order you in the name of God to stop the repression!' The reply came
the next day – three bullets delivered in the chapel of the Hospital of
Divine Providence.

Reacting to the assassination, the Pope deplored the violence which
broke out at the martyred Archbishop's funeral, but called Romero
merely 'zealous', a term of faint praise in Vatican terminology. However,
most Latin Americans already recognized Romero as a saint, their own
twentieth-century Thomas Becket. The Archbishop's simple whitewashed tomb inside the cathedral in San Salvador receives a daily mantle
of fresh flowers from pilgrims. But when John Paul arrived on a whistle-
stop ten-hour visit to San Salvador three years after the murder, his act
of homage to what had already become an important shrine for many
Latin American Catholics was almost surreptitious. A truce had been
declared between government and rebels for the day. Protected by a
heavy guard of jumpy-looking government soldiers armed with auto-

matics, the Pope stopped for ten minutes to pray in private before Romero's tomb during an unscheduled stop on his way from the airport to his main open-air mass at the Metro Centre, a supermarket complex. He expressed compassion for the suffering of the people of El Salvador, and called for national reconciliation, but he made no reference to Archbishop Romero's martyrdom.

After Mexico, it was natural that Pope John Paul should turn his attention to the other Latin American Catholic giant, Brazil. The largest country in South America must figure in any book of religious or secular superlatives; it has the largest Roman Catholic population in the world (over 120 million) as well as being the world's leading coffee and sugar producer, containing the world's longest river, the Amazon, and being surrounded by the biggest rain forest, where lurks the world's longest snake, the anaconda. The Pope devoted almost two full weeks to his first Brazilian visit, longer than he spent in any other single country during his world tours – a measure of the country's immensity and importance. São Paolo is already the southern hemisphere's biggest city and by the year 2000 is expected to reach the size of what is currently the world's most populous megalopolis, Mexico City.

Brazil also comes near the top in the league of the world's most unjust societies. The wealthiest one per cent of Brazilians enjoy the same income as that shared among 50 per cent of those at the lower end of the social scale. Famine is endemic in the impoverished north-east. Land reform has been much talked about, but little implemented. Since the Pope's visit more than 1,000 landless people have been killed in rural property disputes. Brazilian Catholic bishops reported in the year that Wojtyla became Pope, 'Brazilian society today in real terms is not so far removed from the slave society out of which it was born.'

In July 1980, when he first toured this vast country, the Solidarity movement was gaining ground back in Poland. The atmosphere among the 70,000 workers who packed the soccer stadium in São Paolo to hear him speak was electric. The Archbishop of São Paolo, Cardinal Paolo Evaristo Arns, had been opening his churches to enable strikers to take refuge from the soldiers sent to disperse them by the military junta currently ruling Brazil. Among the crowd was the popular trade-union leader 'Lula', Luis Inacio da Silva, later to stand (unsuccessfully) for President – Brazil's potential Lech Walesa.

Pope John Paul trimmed parts of his 'Brazilian Solidarity' speech at the suggestion of his advisers – they felt he might be going too far in championing workers' rights. But his rapturous audience understood his message: there were cascades of applause as he was driven around the stadium in his Popemobile.

In his later social encyclicals the Pope was to try to rationalize his ambivalent attitudes. He explained that societies in which workers' rights are systematically denied and economic policies do not allow satisfactory employment levels cannot be justified from an ethical point of view, nor can they attain social peace and harmony. But at the same time the Catholic Church remained reticent about proposing its own ideal economic and social models to the world. 'Models that are real and truly effective can only arise within the framework of different historical situations,' he wrote in *Centesimus Annus*. The Pope raised one cheer for capitalism. 'The Church . . . recognizes the positive value of the market and of enterprise, but . . . points out that these need to be oriented towards the common good.'

Ambiguity continued to surround the Pope's real commitment to the steps advocated by many of his bishops in order to create a more just society in Brazil. Did he travel to Brazil to learn or to teach, I remember asking the Pope as we flew across the south Atlantic from Rome to Brasilia? His reply cleverly complicated the question. 'My job is to teach, but I teach learning and I learn teaching,' he said.

During his visit to Recife in the north-east, the Pope seemed to react strongly to the dramatic plight of his flock there, and condemned 'particularly painful situations of marginalization, poverty, malnutrition, illiteracy, insecurity . . .'. In front of the television cameras he embraced his local Church leader, Dom Helder Camara, branded 'the Red Bishop' and treated as a non-person by the military regime. 'This man is the friend of the poor and my friend,' the Pope said comfortingly.

However, when Dom Helder retired at the new mandatory age of seventy-five, the Pope appointed an extreme conservative as his successor. The new Archbishop of Recife, Dom José Cardoso Sobrinho, appeared intent on restoring the influence of the landowners whom Dom Helder had fought for two decades. In 1989 Archbishop Sobrinho sacked and disciplined some radical priests and dismissed the entire local Catholic Justice and Peace Commission.

Two of Brazil's most outspoken churchmen have been disciplined by the Vatican for failing to follow the Pope's line. Leonardo Boff, the Franciscan theologian, and Pedro Casaldáliga, the Spanish-born Bishop of São Félix do Araguaia, on the edge of the Amazon rain forest, have both given rare and frank accounts of what it is like to be at the receiving end of Vatican disapproval.

Father Boff arrived in Rome a few days before the publication of the second Vatican document on liberation theology in 1985. He was told he had been summoned for a 'conversation' with Cardinal Ratzinger, but it turned out to be a more formal hearing than he had anticipated, with a stenographer taking down a transcript of everything that was said. Boff was refused permission for some of his fellow Franciscans to accompany him to the Vatican in the limousine that was sent to pick him up from his quarters. 'Too bad I'm not just under plain arrest,' he quipped to the grim-looking prelates who came to accompany him. However, he noticed that his minders did unbend slightly and allow themselves the trace of a smile when their vehicle drew up outside the iron grille of the portico of the Holy Office and Boff commented, 'Ah! the torture chamber!'

After two hours of close theological interrogation, Boff was allowed to bring in his advocates and supporters, Cardinals Aloísio Lorscheider and Evaristo Arns. The text of a joint communiqué euphemistically described the atmosphere as one of 'brotherhood', but it was rather like politicians describing a stormy encounter as 'frank and cordial'. Boff was subsequently sentenced to a year of silence for 'adequate reflection', during which he was forbidden to carry out any public speaking engagements or to publish any books.

Before withdrawing from public dialogue in obedience to the Vatican decision, Boff issued a short statement re-affirming that he was not a Marxist and that as a follower of Christ and Saint Francis he favoured liberty, and 'the noble struggle for justice and towards a new society'. He found it ironic that as Brazil was finally about to emerge from a military dictatorship which had curtailed the right to free speech and practised severe censorship, Rome was using the same techniques to silence one of its own missionaries.

Bishop Casaldáliga paid less lip service to Rome than Father Boff. He had helped to found two of the Brazilian Church's most effective human rights agencies, one protecting small farmers and landless peasants, the other Indian minorities. The Catholic Church had stood almost alone in defending the Yanomani Indians against the Brazilian armed forces, local government authorities, mining companies and gold prospectors. The Brazilian Bishops' Conference accused the government of allowing 100,000 gold diggers into the homelands of the Yanomani tribe (now estimated to number only about 9,000) who continue to face extinction. The Yanomani established contact with the outside world for the first time in the 1950s; their lands have been invaded and polluted in spite of theoretical protection provided by Brazil's new constitution. They are defenceless in the scramble for gold and uranium.

Bishop Casaldáliga refused for seventeen years to travel to Rome to report on the state of his diocese. He said he felt it was useless in the current climate of distrust manifested by the Vatican towards non-conforming Brazilian Church leaders. When the Bishop finally obeyed a summons to Rome in 1988, he was received at a chilly private audience by the Pope.

I explained to him how the different reality of our latitudes and the situations we have to live out oblige us to adopt positions which are possibly not understood by other people in the Church. The Pope recognized this and asserted several times that, 'the Church must take on the social issues. They are human problems.'

He repeated several times that he was aware of the great injustice that is taking place in Brazil, above all in the north of the country.

Afterwards he sat down, opened his arms and – half warning and half jesting – said to me, 'So you see, I am no wild beast!'

'I didn't think that for one moment,' I smiled. But in truth being so much nearer to it during those days, I felt just how this Vatican resembles a cage, albeit a golden one.

Cardinal Arns of São Paolo had the rug pulled from under him by the Pope's decision to divide up his diocese into five parts. The Cardinal was left in command of the central metropolitan area, while the rest of the sprawling city, where most of the low-income workers live, was handed over to four new conservative appointees. According to José Queiros, a theologian at São Paolo's Catholic University, the Vatican is now 'deliberately trying to nullify the Church's active participation in the social, economic and political problems of the country. In this sense they are trying to restrict and police the actions of the progressive clergy.'

Cardinal Arns's plans for continuing a powerful social training programme for priests in his diocese were compromised. He had incurred papal displeasure by travelling to Rome to defend Leonardo Boff in person before Cardinal Ratzinger.

The small but strategically important Central American state of Nicaragua was the crucible in which liberation theologians believed the practical results of their social creed would be tested. During the 1970s the local Roman Catholic hierarchy, under the leadership of the Nicaraguan Cardinal Miguel Obando y Bravo, in the true spirit of Medellin, denounced the cruel and oppressive regime of General Anastasio Somoza.

The overthrow of Somoza by Marxist Sandinistas in 1979 was at first applauded by the local Roman Catholic bishops. Many Nicaraguan priests and foreign missionaries supported the new government's efforts to spread literacy and land reform. But a split soon developed between the hierarchy and many ordinary Catholics who applauded the presence of priests in the new government. The base communities became highly politicized. John Paul entered the debate with a letter supporting his bishops and denouncing the idea of a 'popular Church' as 'absurd and perilous'.

On arrival in the airport at Managua, the capital of Nicaragua, during his whistle-stop tour through Central America in 1983, the Pope was subjected by the Sandinista leader Daniel Ortega Saavedra to an anti-American diatribe. 'The footsteps of interventionist boots echo threateningly in the White House and the Pentagon,' Ortega told him. Later the Pope was angry to find that there was no cross to be seen at the outdoor mass site prepared for the congregation of half a million Nicaraguans bussed in to see him. He quickly understood how his visit was being exploited for maximum political effect by the Sandinistas. Portraits of Karl Marx, Lenin and Sandinista heroes formed the backdrop to the papal mass. A monster banner raised among the crowd read, 'Thank God and the Revolution!' The day before the Pope's visit, a funeral had been held in the same park for seventeen young Sandinista soldiers killed by US financed anti-government forces operating from neighbouring Honduras.

In his homily the Pope called upon Nicaraguan Catholics to support their bishops, and repeated in person his condemnation of the 'popular church'. Christian unity, he said, was threatened when the traditional teaching of Rome was challenged by 'earthly considerations, unacceptable ideological compromises and temporal options including a conception of the Church that replaces the true one'.

That precipitated the heckling. Well-organized claques of Sandinista youths, led by communist cadres from Cuba, began shouting 'We want peace!' and 'Power to the People!' The Pope reacted angrily. 'Silence,' he shouted, and then raised his voice again, 'The Church is the first to promote peace!' He brandished his papal crozier challengingly in the air to emphasize his point, as if to make up for the lack of an altar cross.

The Pope's first document on liberation theology was issued under the signature of Cardinal Ratzinger in September 1984. It warned of the 'terrible contradictions' involved in trying to integrate Marxism with Christianity, since 'atheism and the denial of the human person and his rights are at the core of Marxist theory'. Drawing on the Pope's own experience under a Communist regime in Poland, the document pointed out that revolutionary movements fought in the name of the oppressed often betray the very people whom they claim to be liberating.

The second document published a year later showed the Pope attempting, unsuccessfully in the view of the liberation theologians, to claim that Rome had already admitted the Catholic Church's primary obligations to the poor, and even raised the possibility of using 'armed struggle' to overthrow unjust regimes. But this attempt to combine the non-Marxist elements of liberation theology with traditional Church teaching did not convince Latin Americans.

An awkward test for the Church's attitude towards the overthrow of an oppressive regime arose on the opposite shores of the Pacific Ocean in the Philippines. The outspoken Cardinal Archbishop of Manila, Jaime Sin, openly supported the movement which successfully overthrew President Ferdinando Marcos. At first the Pope was sympathetic to this political intervention by a local hierarchy, but then he made it clear that he thought the Cardinal had gone too far in his support for this Corazon Aquino, although he never publicly criticized Cardinal Sin. The Pope decided that what was deemed acceptable in Catholic Warsaw was not necessarily acceptable in Catholic Manila. Poland was a special case, politically speaking.

The Pope's visit to General Augusto Pinochet's Chile and to Raul Alfonsín's Argentina in 1987 pinpointed some of the inconsistencies he had to deal with in forging new political policies for his Churches of Latin America. He called upon President Pinochet at the President's official residence, the Moneda Palace. This was the building where Latin America's first democratically elected Marxist President, Salvatore Allende, had made his last stand during Pinochet's military coup of 1973. Afterwards the Pope stood with Pinochet to be photographed together on the balcony of the palace, whose bomb scars had long since been repaired. It was a symbolic gesture that was to be strongly criticized by left-wing Catholics, yet was perhaps impossible for the Pope to avoid.

Later, in order to demonstrate even-handedness, John Paul greeted the current head of the Chilean Communist Party among a delegation of opposition leaders. Then serious violence broke out at the main event during his visit to Santiago, the mass in O'Higgins Park for the canonization of Saint Theresa of the Andes, Chile's first native saint.

Armoured vehicles and water cannon moved in on the crowd. White-robed priests, their arms raised in a gesture of peace, moved down from the altar platform to try to calm the half-million-strong congregation as tear gas was used against part of the crowd.

The regime, and some Catholic bishops, said it was all the fault of the left. Other bishops – and the opposition – claimed the disturbances were the work of right-wing provocateurs. During the flight back to Rome, the Pope refused to cast blame and said it had been 'an extremely base, primitive and violent provocation' and that the crowd had reacted with great dignity. But he refused to be drawn into political controversy. 'It is neither my intention nor my duty to enter into technical and political solutions,' he told a questioner archly.

In the two neighbouring Latin American countries the Pope's bishops showed a remarkable lack of political consistency.

In Chile the local Church hierarchy had learned to keep its distance from the Pinochet regime. It spoke out loudly and clearly against state-organized violence and social injustice. When Pinochet was defeated in a plebiscite the year after the Pope's visit and had the bad taste to compare his defeat to Christ's crucifixion, the local bishops strongly criticized him for his blasphemy.

By contrast, during the Pope's visit to Argentina, his bishops there manifestly failed to speak out against the torture and killings of the previous military regime. One bishop had actually justified the use of torture. Two bishops, Enrique Angelelli of La Rioja and Carlos Ponce de León of San Nicolas de Los Arroyas, who had dared to speak out against the regime, had been murdered. No one pronounced their names before the Pope. The mothers of the *desaparecidos* – those who had paid with their lives for opposing the regime – were not invited to meet the Pope, nor was he taken to see the shanty towns of the capital.

'Better to show the Pope beautiful things than sad things,' remarked one of the Argentine bishops to the 1980 Nobel Peace Prize winner Adolfo Perez Esquivel.

The Pope was well aware that all was not well with his Church in Argentina. He added a solemn word of warning to a speech he made to the assembled bishops before he left Buenos Aires, 'Conscious of your role as pastors, pay attention to what your society, even if it is secularized, even if it seems to be indifferent, expects of you as witnesses of Christ.'

The fall from power in 1990 of General Alfredo Stroessner of Paraguay, one of the twentieth century's longest-serving dictators, may have been helped along by the visit paid to his country in the previous year by Pope John Paul. Stroessner, who had come to power in a military coup during the pontificate of Pius XII in 1954, incurred the growing wrath of the bishops of Paraguay – an overwhelmingly Catholic country – for human rights abuses against landless peasants and constantly rigged elections. In Paraguay less than one per cent of the population controls 77 per cent of the territory; at least a quarter of its 3 million population is composed of landless *campesinos*.

The Pope did not repeat the error he had made in Chile by appearing in public alongside the dictator Pinochet. When the official welcome ceremony at Asunción airport had to be cancelled due to a tropical rainstorm, his private meeting with the dictator took place inside the presidential palace well away from the prying eyes of the cameras. While gun-toting police surrounded a near-by church occupied by hunger-striking peasants, the Pope was forced to listen to one of the most hypocritical addresses that a Head of State had ever dared to make in front of him.

'Paraguay today is a country without social or political problems,' President Stroessner said, 'without riots, without political prisoners, without mothers in mourning as a result of political fanaticism; a nation on the road to harmony and solidarity, and to an intensive development of social justice. Look at the serene faces of our people . . . here there are no terrorism, no hunger, no drugs . . .' Stroessner concluded by declaring he was 'the most Christian ruler on earth'.

Pope John Paul lectured the President sternly on his view of political liberty, quoting freely from Pope John XXIII and Vatican II.

'Politics', the Pope said, 'has a fundamental ethical dimension because it is first and foremost a service to man. The Church can and must remind men – and in particular those who govern – of their ethical duties for the good of the whole of society. The Church cannot be isolated inside its temples just as men's consciences cannot be isolated from God.'

There followed what must have been the shortest applause ever to follow a papal speech. President Stroessner clapped his hands four or five times and then, stony faced, stood up. Government officials and diplomats present in the ornate reception room took this as their cue to remain silent and allow the Pope to leave.

Later, in public, the Pope took up the moral cudgels again on behalf of the impoverished *campesinos* of Paraguay. 'How many *campesinos*, workers and unemployed people lack their daily bread? The authorities must feel themselves obliged to ensure that more and more people have access to the ownership of land,' he said.

Stroessner tried – and failed – to prevent the Pope from meeting opposition leaders in his one-party State. He was also unable to prevent the Pope's final engagement in his country – a youth rally – from turning into a vast political protest meeting. Hundreds of thousands of people of all ages took part. They chanted, 'Freedom! Freedom!' The Pope avoided political rhetoric in his message to Paraguayan youth, but his parting words at Asunción airport – 'By building a Christian nation and being faithful to your roots you can build a Paraguay for tomorrow' – were heeded within a matter of months when the 75-year-old Stroessner was deposed and a (slightly) more liberal regime was installed.

The Pope's second visit to Mexico in 1990, eleven years after his first pace-setting tour at the beginning of the pontificate, provided an interesting benchmark in assessing to what extent politics outweigh the purely pastoral aspects to his visits. Mexico is an almost unique case in the Catholic world. Although a country as Catholic as Poland, with the Vatican claiming 90 per cent church membership and with Catholic schools playing a vital role in the nation's educational system, it is still an offence for a priest to appear in public in clerical garb, or for the Church to own property or to take any official part in the nation's life.

The reasons for this are connected with Mexico's turbulent anti-clerical history in the nineteenth and twentieth centuries. Formal ties were broken with the Vatican as far back as 1859. Then in the 1910 Revolution the Church had backed the losing side; when the liberals triumphed over the conservatives, the victors took their revenge by enacting discriminatory legislation against all Church activities. Under the 1917 constitution the Roman Catholic Church has no official exist-ence in Mexico, public religious services are forbidden and priests are neither allowed to vote nor to take any part in politics.

The Pope set about correcting this. 'A theme that certainly concerns us, as pastors of the church in Mexico, is the present civil legislation,' he announced.

'The Church in Mexico wants to be considered and treated not as something strange, nor as an enemy that must be confronted and fought, but as an ally of all that is good, noble and beautiful.' John Paul expressed this hope while opening a new headquarters for his Mexican bishops. A few months before he had persuaded President Carlos Salinas de Gortari to nominate a 'personal representative' to the Vatican, and there was never a hint during the eight-day papal visit that the proceed-ings were, technically, illegal. No one dared to suggest that the Pope ought to doff his white robes in order to comply with Article 130 of the Mexican constitution.

The Pope kept returning to his anti-abortion, anti-contraceptive message as he criss-crossed the largest Spanish-speaking Catholic country. But significantly he failed to persuade the Mexican government to reverse one of the Third World's most successful family-planning programmes. According to government figures, Mexico's rate of population growth has almost halved (down from 3.7 per cent to 1.9 per cent) during John Paul's pontificate. Even so, the population of Mexico had increased by a massive 30 per cent in the eleven years that had passed since his first tour.

Perhaps surprisingly, Rome's most serious threat in Latin America comes not from liberation theologians, but from Protestant fundamentalist sects. The Vatican believes these have been gaining new converts at the rate of 3 million people a year – 400 an hour – during the 1980s. The sects attack the Vatican as a manifestation of the devil. The Roman Catholic Primate of Brazil, Cardinal Lucas Moreira Neves, has warned that 'the springtime of the sects could be the winter of the Catholic Church'. Ten per cent of Brazilians now belong to one of that country's more than 4,000 fundamentalist churches, and the Vatican estimates that by the year 2000 there will be 34 million evangelical Christians in Brazil alone.

Many of these are former African spirit worshippers. Millions of Brazilians, who may for statistical purposes call themselves Catholics, actually follow cults which originated in the Yoruba and Bantu religions and were brought to Latin America by African slaves. At mass in the poor sections of Rio de Janeiro you can see the congregation swaying to the throbbing beat of the *atabaques*, the wooden drums used in Candomble spirit rituals.

The Universal Church of the Kingdom of God, a Brazilian fundamentalist sect which was founded in 1977 with only thirty members, now had more than 600 churches in Brazil, two in New York and one in New Jersey, with a daily total attendance of half a million people. This Church directs its message directly to spirit worshippers and conducts exorcism ceremonies.

United States' financed Pentecostalists, who emphasize the emotional side of religion and the believer's direct relationship with Jesus Christ without priestly intervention, find Central and South America fertile ground for conversions. The Catholic Church finds the long theological training necessary for priests a handicap in competing with Evangelicals who can persuade people to 'surrender their lives to Jesus' instantly, and who can persuade these new recruits to go on and convert hundreds more.

During his second Mexican tour the Pope responded to the steady flow of Indian converts to fundamentalist religion by travelling to Indian country near Mexico's border with Guatemala and addressing Indians haltingly in their native tongues. Protestant sects, which have translated the Bible into many native languages, find fertile ground for conversions among an Indian population inexorably driven by poverty and hunger towards the shanty suburbs of the mushrooming cities. Six million people in the Tuxtla Gutiérrez area speak only Indian dialects, and ancient Mayan is a growing language. The Pope greeted the Indians in their indigenous Tzotzil and Zoque tongues, drawing roars of laughter and cheers as he joked about his own pronunciation. 'Now I have a difficult task,' John Paul remarked as he was about to twist his tongue around a few lines of Tzotzil translating the phrase, 'Jesus loves you, as he loves all the disciples who are "the salt of the earth and the light of the world".'

A rhyming Spanish chant of 'Indios, amigos, el papa es con tigos' (Indians, friends, the Pope is with you) went up; and the Pope joined in the chanting.

In Guatemala, the Head of State during the Pope's 1983 visit was a born-again Christian, General José Efrain Rios Montt, a member of a California-based organization called Gospel Outreach; along with other fundamentalist sects operating in Guatemala they received *carte blanche* from the President to evangelize the Indian population with the army's help, at the expense of the Catholics. Before Rios Montt was ousted for abusing the theoretical separation between Church and State, nearly one-quarter of Guatemalans had been converted by the evangelicals: the fundamentalists confidently predict that by the year 2000 half the population of Guatemala will have abandoned their allegiance to Rome.

The 1990 presidential election in Guatemala was won by another fundamentalist, Jorge Serrano. His election was marked by intense trading of religious insults between evangelicals and Catholics, who accused the Protestant sects of 'wanting to snatch 500 years of Catholicism from the people of Guatemala to impose a religion originating in the United States'.

The Catholic Church's best antidote to the fundamentalist threat seems to be the base communities. They now number over 300,000, are spread all over the South American continent and are still growing.

And Catholic bishops report that where a community flourishes, the fundamentalists are unlikely to gain ground. Although the final document of the Puebla conference praised the base communities as 'motives for hope and joy in the Church' and 'the focal point of evangelization, the motor of liberation', the Pope has remained ultra-cautious about them. The base community represents a democratic challenge to a Church which finds it impossible to abandon its hierarchical structures; yet there is a strong argument that the base communities are Solidarity's equivalent for Latin America: organizations where the poor can find equality, understanding and true Christian solidarity, instead of being encouraged merely to suffer in silence.

The base communities also offer a remedy for the growing shortage of priests, but not one which the Pope wishes to accept. As far as he is concerned, a church without priests is not a church at all and therefore pragmatic considerations do not apply. At a Vatican Synod convened in Rome in 1990 which dealt directly with the problem of how to provide celibate pastors for the Catholic Church's growing Third World flock, Bishop Valfredo Tepe of Ilheus, Brazil, proposed that the ordination of married men could help to alleviate the shortage of priests in many areas of his country.

'One should study more seriously, without fear of taboo, the need and possibility of ordaining the *viri probati* who are present and working in the numerous communities,' Tepe said. (*Viri probati* is a Latin term referring to those, including married men, who have proven themselves spiritually 'mature'.)

He went on, 'This study is required for pastoral motives, given that there are no signs that in coming generations a sufficient number of truly celibate vocations will emerge.' He noted that in Brazil many priests work alone in vast, densely populated communities 'whose needs and expectations exceed all human possibility. In some Brazilian parishes, five or six masses are celebrated each Sunday. These parishes are under stress and feel frustrated because they don't succeed in giving an adequate pastoral assistance to their own community.'

An American cardinal, Joseph Bernardin of Chicago, told his fellow bishops that the rule requiring Roman Catholic priests to be celibate 'often appears unattractive and unattainable'.

The Synod chairman appointed by the Pope, Cardinal Neves, a conservative whom John Paul put in command of his Brazilian church, imperiously ruled the whole discussion out of order. He said the celibacy issue had already been resolved 'in a definitive way'.

During one of his visits to Latin America the Pope tried to explain in a simple parable his aversion to conventional political and economic labelling. This was addressed to a crowd gathered in the cathedral at Santa Cruz in Bolivia – the town where Ché Guevara started his Marxist rebel movement in the 1960s. The Pope suggested that the poor Third World might have lessons to impart to the wealthier First and Second Worlds.

The Pope was impressed by the bubbling spontaneity shown by impoverished Bolivians – Bolivia is the poorest country in the poor subcontinent. He acknowledged their 'inhuman' living conditions, but praised their festive capacity for life. 'You know how to pray, how to weep, how to sing and how to dance,' he said.

'The Pope has arrived here in this cathedral walking on the right, and now he goes away walking on the left. As soon as he turns around, his left becomes the right.

'What does this mean?' he asked. 'Does it mean that it is the Pope's destiny always to walk on the right?

'Here, I believe I have found the answer to that question. The Pope and the whole Church, all of us, have to create a meeting point between the so-called world of the left and the so-called world of the right. A point of reconciliation because the world cannot live in continuing division, it cannot live in conflict.

'In part this is a comment on my last encyclical which speaks not only of left and right, East and West, but above all of the Third World, of the majority of the world of today and of tomorrow. I want to tell you who belong to this Third World that the solution for overcoming the divisions of left and right must be found right here in your human, Christian and social reality. That is my hope.'

In another speech in Bolivia he blamed the unjust local structures of society upon the process of capitalistic, free-market expansion. In other countries, he said, people had suffered as a result of Marxist collectivism. 'In both cases these sufferings have their origin in the ideologies of the dominant cultures, and they are both incompatible with your faith and culture.'

The Pope's meeting with the unemployed miners of Oruro was perhaps one of the most dramatic in all his worldwide travels. The local Bishop, Julio Terrazas, said, 'The faces that you see in front of you, Holy Father, are marked by grief and suffering. They demand a liberation that has never arrived. Here in the mines the workers have destroyed their lungs to create wealth for their country.'

Lopez Arias, a trade-union leader, said, 'You have not been able to hear the wail of the mine sirens because the mines are deserted; the only sound you can hear is the crying of hungry children. Thirty thousand unemployed miners are pleading for justice. Their wages are an insult to human dignity. We feel ourselves protected by the Church here. That is why we ask you to denounce the injustice in which we are forced to live.'

A *campesino* wearing the colourful Bolivian poncho and woollen headgear grabbed the microphone. 'My name is Primo Arce Contreras. I belong to the Aymaras Indian tribe. We are suffering. We cannot sell our produce. The authorities treat us like animals. When we say these things they say we are Communists.' An Indian woman with a baby strapped to her back presented the Pope with an empty saucepan.

A miner ran up to the pontiff and cried into the microphone, 'We are hungry, we have no bread. Thank you for having welcomed liberation theology, thank you for your encyclical on workers' rights.'

The 1987 encyclical letter, which few among Pope John Paul's Bolivian peasant audience were likely to have read in person, is called *Sollicitudo Rei Socialis* (The Social Concern of the Church). It is a distillation of the Pope's thoughts on the overall economic and social background to the crisis affecting contemporary relations between rich and poor nations twenty years after his predecessor, Paul VI, first pronounced on the subject in his 1967 encyclical *Populorum Progressio* (The Development of Peoples). Pope John Paul gave a new twist to Paul VI's attempt to bring up to date the social teaching of the Catholic Church in *Populorum Progressio*. John Paul made a revised ethical assessment of the huge and growing gap between the world's 'haves' and 'have nots'. He suggested prophetically that the North-South economic conflict might soon supersede the tensions of East-West political divisions. He also pointed out that the world had not benefited from the development plans of the hopeful 1960s; this he put down to the fact that the mere accumulation of wealth and goods and services, even when it is to the benefit of the majority, is not enough for the realization of human happiness. Science and technology cannot bring freedom from every form of slavery. He wrote in *Sollicitudo Rei Socialis*:

Unless all the considerable body of resources and potential at man's disposal is guided by a *moral understanding* and by an orientation towards the true good of the human race, it easily turns against man to oppress him. Man finds himself up against a form of mega-development consisting in an excessive availability of every kind of material goods for the benefit of certain social groups. People become slaves of possession and seek immediate gratification, with no other horizon than the multiplication or continual replacement of things already owned with others still better.

This is the so-called civilization of 'consumption', of 'consumerism' which involves so much throwing away and waste. An object already owned, but now superseded by something better, is discarded with no thought of its possible lasting value in itself, nor of some other human being who is poorer.

In other words Western man worships at the altar of consumerism and experiences 'radical dissatisfaction because one quickly learns – unless one is shielded from the flood of publicity and the ceaseless and tempting offers of products – that the more one possesses the more one wants, while deeper aspirations remain unsatisfied and perhaps even stifled.'

However the Pope added an important *caveat*. There exists a basic human right of 'economic initiative', that is to say the right and even the duty of each citizen to exercise his or her own creative potential to help build society in a responsible way.

Experience shows that the denial of this right, or its limitation in the name of so-called equality of everyone in society, diminishes or in practice absolutely destroys the spirit of initiative, that is to say the creative subjectivity of the citizen. As a consequence there arises not so much a true equality as a 'levelling down'. In the place of creative initiative there appears passivity, dependence and submission to the bureaucratic apparatus which as the only 'ordering' and 'decision-making' body – if not also the owner of the entire totality of goods and the means of production – puts everyone in a position of almost absolute dependence, which is similar to the traditional dependance of the worker-proletarian in capitalism. This provokes a sense of frustration or desperation and predisposes people to opt out of national life, impelling many to emigrate and also favouring a form of 'psychological' emigration.

The Pope went on to discuss the political implications of his social and economic guidelines.

No social group, for example a political party, has the right to usurp the role of sole leader since this brings about the destruction of the true subjectivity of society and of the individual citizens, as happens in every form of totalitarianism. In this situation the individual and the people become 'objects' in spite of all declarations to the contrary and verbal assurances.

He asked Catholics to consider whether the denial or limitation of basic human rights – such as the right to religious freedom, the right to share in the building of society, the freedom to organize and form trade unions and to take economic initiatives – did not impoverish the human person as much as, if not more than, the deprivation of material goods.

The Pope's fear that the diluted Marxist theories proposed by some liberation theologians might help spread Communist rule seems unfounded if one examines the Communists' political record in Latin America during his pontificate. Marxist parties put up a poor showing in elections during the 1980s in many Latin American countries as new democracies replaced military regimes. From Mexico in the north to Argentina in the south, voters preferred to entrust the solution of runaway foreign debt and the growing gap between rich and poor to other political formations than the radical left.

The sort of parliamentary representation achieved by Communist Parties in the course of free elections in Italy or France appeared to be beyond the reach of Latin leftists. In Mexico, the first Latin American country to run out of cash to pay its foreign debt, the far left won only 6.2 per cent in the presidential poll of 1982. After Mexico suffered its worst economic crisis in fifty years, the local Communists increased their vote by just one per cent.

Argentina's Trotskyist Movement to Socialism (MAAS) won less than 3 per cent of the vote in the presidential election that brought Raul Alfonsín to power in 1983, ending eight years of brutal military rule during which thousands of left-wing supporters had been abducted and murdered. After four years of freedom to organize for parliamentary elections the MAAS increased its share of the poll by just one per cent, not enough to gain a single parliamentary seat. Brazil in 1986 saw the extreme left-wing Workers' Party double its support – but only from 3 to 6 per cent.

In Ecuador a Maoist-Moscow alliance presidential candidate did less well in 1988 than in 1984, gaining less than 5 per cent of the votes. Only in Chile and Paraguay, where the Communist Party was banned under the rule of right-wing military dictators, did the Communists seem likely to make a better showing in free elections.

While Czechoslovakia was in the process of throwing off the shackles of Communism in November 1989, on the other side of the globe in El Salvador six Jesuit priests – leaders in the local struggle for human rights – were murdered one night in cold blood by government soldiers in the capital San Salvador. It was chilling proof that ten years after the assassination of Archbishop Romero, the Latin American Church's preferential option for the poor could still arouse the deep hostility of those who wield power. The Pope made yet another public appeal for an end to violence in the 'martyred' Central American country, which of course went unheeded. In September 1991 Guillermo Alfredo Benavides, the army colonel who had ordered the shooting of the priests, was found guilty of the Jesuits' murder at a trial forced upon El Salvador by the United States as a condition for continuing military aid. But the soldiers who actually carried out the shooting were acquitted, and the colonel was likely to be quickly amnestied. In 1989 the Salvadorean Supreme Court decided not to ask the United States to extradite Captain Alvaro Saravia, the driver of the car allegedly used in Romero's murder, who is living in exile in Miami, although he said he was now ready to testify.

The latest unexpected political setback that the Pope suffered in Latin America was the election of a young (37–year-old) black Roman Catholic Salesian missionary priest as President of the Caribbean island republic of Haiti. Father Jean-Bertrand Aristide, ordained priest in 1982, was dismissed from his order in 1988 for advocating violent struggle to create social and political justice in this desperately poor country, which is situated in one of the most impoverished parts of the hemisphere. He won a landslide victory in his country's first-ever democratic presidential elections in December 1990.

Haiti's population of 5 million blacks and creoles are the descendants of the black slaves led by Toussaint L'Ouverture who rose up against the colonial power, France, to proclaim their independence at the beginning of the nineteenth century. For decades Haiti was ruled by the corrupt Duvalier family and their notorious Tonton Macoutes police who had brutally suppressed all political opposition. When I accompanied the Pope on a six-hour stopover in Port-au-Prince in 1983 at the end of a South American tour, I was struck by his bold message to the people of Haiti that the time had come for change. This seemed political dynamite in the local context; and I remember speculating what effect his speech might have had if it had been pronounced at that moment in Poland instead of in the lush tropical island setting.

The Pope criticized the lack of food and medical care, the poor schools and housing, the fear and misery, the degradation of life which had gone on during the rule of President-for-life Jean-Claude 'Baby Doc' Duvalier and his late father 'Papa Doc'. The elder Duvalier had been excommunicated by the Catholic Church for expelling the last white Archbishop of Port-au-Prince. His successor, local-born Archbishop François-Wolff Ligondé, soon became identified with the policies of the ruling family. Opposition to the Duvaliers had become focused within grass-roots religious movements such as Aristide's so-called 'Little Church' or 'Parish of the Poor', for want of a legal political alternative. Among the crowds who heard the Pope's message on that day was the recently ordained Father Aristide, known as 'Titide' by his devoted followers.

Aristide, a slight, soft-spoken priest in private conversation, can arouse powerful emotions with his political oratory. He used a local Catholic radio station – Radio Soleil, the only news source in Haiti to report human rights violations and corruption – as his pulpit. He had studied theology and psychology in England, Canada, Egypt and Greece and became fluent in six languages. As Father Aristide's congregations grew, the local Vatican Nuncio sent alarmed reports to Rome. Eventually the priest was sacked by his religious superiors and told to move to Canada. He refused and redoubled his political efforts to create a more just society in his country.

Shortly after the fall of the younger Duvalier in 1986 and his flight to France, the future President of Haiti survived the first of several assassination attempts. Father Aristide's church of Saint John Bosco was burned down in 1986 by the Tonton Macoutes, who killed and wounded scores of his parishioners at morning mass.

His successful campaign for the presidency – he obtained 70 per cent of the vote even though he had been disowned by the local Catholic hierarchy – played on messianic symbolism and patriotic fervour. The campaign was called *Lavales* – a local Creole word meaning a torrent or a landslide. 'Like Jesus I preach in the spirit of justice, love and peace,' he said in an interview before his election. 'God is not a man with a beard up in the sky. God is you and me and everybody.'

Aristide's simple, vivid language was immediately understood by his fellow countrymen. For too long, he told them, most Haitians had been living 'under the table', while a few privileged people sat 'on the table'. The time had come for people to 'live as brothers and sisters around the table'.

Rome's embarrassment at the political success of Father Aristide was compounded by a physical attack on the Papal Nuncio, Monsignor Giuseppe Leanza, and his assistant, Leon Kalenga, a young African priest in the papal diplomatic service on his first foreign posting. They were stripped to their underpants and beaten during riots triggered off by Aristide's supporters in Port-au-Prince, which culminated in the burning down of the colonial-style wood-built cathedral. Monsignor Leanza escaped humiliation by fleeing to the neighbouring Dominican republic disguised as a woman. The Pope declined to send a Vatican representative to the inauguration ceremony of President Father Aristide of Haiti.

The next major meeting of all the bishops of Latin America with the Pope is in 1992 as part of the Columbus anniversary celebrations in Santo Domingo. Twenty-three years after the historic Medellin gathering Latin America's political and social structures seem hardly less sinful than they were a generation ago. The Pope will trumpet the failure of Communism in Eastern Europe as implying the failure of liberation theology in Latin America. But he will find that even with the support of the conservative bishops whom he has appointed during the past decade there remains a powerful and committed body of Catholic opinion in Latin America which continues to regard the Vatican as a distant ivory tower, cut off from the real and painful world that they know.

CHAPTER 7

Africa: Dealing with Witch Doctors

I don't expect any ecclesiastical coup d'état *in Africa against Rome. I simply say, 'I have got some different kind of flowers.' Instead of saying, 'How beautiful those flowers are!' the Vatican says, 'Oh no! Those flowers are poisonous!'*
Archbishop Emmanuel Milingo, former head of the Roman Catholic
Church in Zambia.

During the reign of Pope John Paul, Roman Catholic churches in various black African nations celebrated the first centenary of their founding by European missionaries. The return of the Christian faith to Africa had coincided with European colonalism at the end of the nineteenth century. Rome's presence in Africa, so strong in the early Christian era in Egypt and North Africa, had been destroyed by the Arabs. It was felt again in the fifteenth and sixteenth centuries south of the Sahara, when Portuguese missionaries accompanied the first wave of European colonizers. But by the beginning of the nineteenth century it had once more totally disappeared. What had gone wrong?

It was a question the Pope would ponder during his seven visits to Africa, which took him to practically every country and major city in the continent, from Casablanca to Nairobi, from Johannesburg (involuntarily, when his chartered jet was diverted by bad weather) to Kinshasa.

Numerically, his African Church now seems to be flourishing. Membership is increasing faster in the 'Black Continent' than anywhere else in the world. During John Paul's pontificate alone, the number of African Catholics had almost doubled from about 50 million to over 90 million souls. One African in six is now a member of the Roman Catholic Church. But Islam, which wiped out Christianity in northern Africa within three centuries of the birth of Mohammed, is again becoming militant, and the Vatican admits that the two religions are on a 'collision course' in some African countries. One African in three is now a Muslim.

During the 1990s Islam will replace Catholicism as the religion with the largest worldwide membership.

There are internal threats as well. The transition from a white-led missionary Church to indigenous-led African hierarchies has raised problems as well as hopes for the future. Although the first indigenous African bishop of modern times, Joseph Kiwanuka of Masaka, Uganda, was not ordained until 1939, about three-quarters of Africa's 481 bishops are now African-born and this proportion will increase. Yet there is still an acute shortage of African priests because of the celibacy rule, which not surprisingly is unpopular in a polygamous society. Priestly vocations are not keeping pace with population and church membership growth. In 1960 there was one priest for every 1,800 African Catholics; now the number has fallen to one for over 4,200 Church members. Many African dioceses still depend for staffing and, even more importantly, for their funding upon the foreign missionaries who re-established the Church's bridgeheads in Africa in the nineteenth century. Yet foreign missionaries are no longer politically acceptable in many independent African regimes.

From its very origins, Christianity has been closely linked to Africa. Jesus Christ himself lived temporarily in Egypt, for all practical purposes as a refugee. Egypt later became the first African country to welcome his teaching. Many prominent figures in the early Church were Egyptians, among them Saints Clement and Cyril of Alexandria, and the biblical scholar Origen. The monastic life first took root here. Christian missionaries set out from Egypt to convert Nubia, the southern part of modern Sudan which is still a Christian stronghold, and Ethiopia. By the middle of the fifth century the whole of Egypt had been converted to Christianity. The Egyptian Coptic Church which survives today is a relic of those times. But Christian Egypt was relatively short-lived. In the year 640 Alexandria, the gateway to the Nile, fell to Arab Muslim invaders and Islamic religion and culture took over.

The Church spread into North Africa as early as the second century AD. The vitality of the early Church there can be judged from the large number of bishops appointed. Several early popes came from Africa. By the beginning of the fifth century almost six hundred Catholic bishoprics had been set up in the former Roman provinces of North Africa – more than in the whole of the African continent today. One of the towering figures of the early Church, Saint Augustine, Bishop of Hippo (now Annaba in Algeria), was an African, a Berber. He played a prominent role in developing the monastic spirit which was later to infuse mediaeval Western European culture.

However, in Africa the Church not only went into decline, it almost vanished. By the end of the first millennium, there were only three bishoprics left in the Continent, and even these had disappeared by the end of the thirteenth century.

One reason for the African Church's weakness in the face of the Muslim challenge was internal dissent and division caused by heretical movements such as the Donatists. These were a group of extremist Christians, led by a certain Donatus, who split away from other North African Catholics, actively seeking martyrdom in actions of fanatical violence. Another reason was physical attack by the Vandals. Many persecuted Christians fled for their lives to Italy and Gaul. Most serious of all perhaps was the failure of the first carriers of Christianity into North Africa to translate the Bible and the church liturgy into the local languages, Berber and Phoenician. When the Latin language and culture disappeared from North Africa, the Church went with it, whereas in Egypt and Ethiopia where the Church has used local languages, it survived.

The evangelization of Africa south of the Sahara by the Portuguese, begun in the fifteenth century, did not endure much more effectively. By the early nineteenth century there was little to show for the efforts of generations of Portuguese missionaries in West and southern African. The mistake the popes made was to grant Portugal the right of 'patronage', an official monopoly to send missionary monks and priests to convert the Africans. The Portuguese were unable to provide the huge numbers of dedicated missionary priests necessary to carry out effective evangelization in this vast region of the world. Besides, the overriding interest of the Catholic kings of Portugal was political and commercial, not religious. No effort was made to penetrate into the interior of the 'Black Continent'. The names of the Portuguese trading posts established in West Africa betray the commercial motives for their creation – Slave Coast, Ivory Coast, Pepper Coast, Gold Coast. The tropical climate was another implacable enemy of the Church – in the malarial swamps of West Africa Portuguese missionaries frequently fell victim to tropical diseases shortly after their arrival.

The Vatican, therefore, is now engaged in its third major attempt to evangelize Africa. Cultural and political problems may have changed with the centuries, but reconciling local needs and Roman doctrine can still cause conflict.

One modern African Catholic Church leader, Archbishop Emmanuel Milingo, former head of the Church in Zambia, was considered by the Vatican to be exercising his ministry in an unacceptable way. He was duly punished by being brought back to Rome for re-indoctrination and enforced exile.

The case of Emmanuel Milingo illustrates both the dilemma that Pope John Paul faces in Africa and his strong-arm methods for dealing with dissent. Zambia is a textbook example of the overall success of the nineteenth century's resurgence of Christian missionary activity in Africa. Three out of every four Zambians now profess allegiance to one or another of the proliferating Christian Churches or sects, even if only about one in four pledges allegiance to Rome. This was the country where the great Scottish evangelical missionary and explorer David Livingstone lived, worked and now lies buried.

Archbishop Milingo's predicament was first brought to my attention in April 1982, when an African student carried a scribbled handwritten note from him to my Rome office. The Archbishop pleaded for help, explaining that he was being held incommunicado at the monastery of the Passionist fathers, just behind the Colosseum. He said he was permitted neither visitors nor telephone calls.

I became concerned when I checked and found that Milingo's accusations were absolutely true. The nun on the monastery switchboard refused to put my call through to the Archbishop. When I finally succeeded in getting permission to see him, he told me the appalling tale of what it is like to face John Paul's displeasure.

Archbishop Milingo, consecrated Bishop in Uganda by Pope Paul VI in 1964, during the first-ever papal visit to Africa, had fallen into disfavour because of his healing ministry, which drew crowds of many thousands to his masses in Lusaka. Dozens of people claimed they had been restored to health after a laying on of hands by the Archbishop. Many claimed miraculous cures even at a distance, after a letter or a telephone call to Milingo.

Milingo has described vividly what he felt was the turning point in his life in 1973, the moment when he discovered in a blinding moment of illumination that dealing with the spirit world of Africa could be combined with his work as a Christian pastor.

There was a woman who had suffered from Mashawe, a common type of spirit possession in Zambia, for five months. She ate nothing, could only drink water or soft drinks. She feared her child because she did not consider him a human being. She constantly heard voices. She was treated at a mental hospital, but to no avail. At that time I did not know how Satan behaves once he is in possession of someone. Suddenly an idea glowed in my mind.

Look three times intently into her eyes, and ask her to look three times intently into yours. Tell her to close her eyes the third time, and order her to sleep. Then speak to her soul, after signing her with the sign of the Cross. The woman was overshadowed by the power of the Lord. She relaxed calmly and so I was able to reach her soul. I prayed as much as I could, then I woke her up. Neither of us knew what had happened to us. The Lord was leading me to the healing of Mashawe. This disease cannot be treated in a hospital.

Archbishop Milingo announced to his flock in Lusaka in July 1973, 'We have suffered for a very long time from Mashawe, and we have had to find doctors to treat the disease from outside our own Church. But we can heal this disease within our own Catholic Church. So, if any of you suffer from this disease let them come forward and we shall try to help them.' The result was the beginning of what soon became an overwhelming demand for Milingo's healing powers, first of all locally then quickly spreading beyond Zambia's borders. It was not only the unschooled masses of Zambians who flocked to Archbishop Milingo's house and cathedral, but also people from higher social levels, including government ministers, teachers, bank executives and businessmen who were attracted by the Archbishop's growing reputation.

But some white Catholic missionaries in Lusaka and the majority of Milingo's seven fellow Zambian-born, Rome-trained bishops, did not like what they saw. They felt the Archbishop's activities smacked of 'mumbo-jumbo', witchcraft and sorcery, and they complained to the Vatican. A commission of enquiry was sent to Lusaka, headed by a high-ranking Kenyan prelate, Cardinal Maurice Otunga from Nairobi. Milingo was summoned to Rome at twenty-four-hour's notice. He found himself treated by his Vatican superiors almost like a prisoner. He was forced to remain in the Passionist fathers' monastery for months on end and was ordered to undergo a series of psychiatric examinations and medical tests. To him, a senior figure in the African Church at the still relatively young age of fifty-two, it certainly seemed as if the days of the Inquisition had returned.

After being kept waiting for more than a year, Milingo's request to see the Pope was finally granted. To his surprise, the Archbishop learned that the Pope himself had been an admirer of a well-known Italian healer, the late Padre Pio, a Franciscan monk credited with many cures for which there was no obvious medical explanation. The Pope announced that Milingo was to be given a regular job at the Vatican, in the pontifical department dealing with migration and tourism.

This meant he was sentenced to what amounts to permanent exile in Rome. He had to resign his post as the Catholic Church's leader in Lusaka, and was only allowed to carry on his healing ministry in Rome under strict Vatican surveillance. He was provided with an apartment in a Vatican-owned block of flats just outside one of the main gates of Vatican City, where a uniformed doorman watches everyone entering and leaving.

Milingo fervently believes that the casting out of evil spirits – an important part of the African religious tradition – can be of help in dealing with disorders that are considered to belong to the realm of psychiatry in Europe. He also believes that he remains firmly in the mainstream of Christian tradition in his practice of exorcism. According to Milingo, the world is in greater need of spiritual than of physical healing. Oppression by evil spirits is not a phenomenon limited to Africa.

Accusations of witchcraft came directly from the office of George Zur, a priest from what was then East Germany, the Vatican's Pro-Nuncio, or Ambassador, in Lusaka. 'I am not a witch doctor,' Milingo protested. 'It is offensive to say that. Under Zambian law it is an offence to call someone a witch.'

In the Catholic Church all priests are by nature of their function, also exorcists. But they have to ask their bishop for permission to carry out a solemn exorcism (meaning of a person who has all the symptoms of being possessed and is totally under the control of evil spirits).

'I as a priest have this power of exorcism and, as a Bishop, have the authority to delegate. Since 1973 I have carried out exorcism not only in Africa but in Europe and the United States. I think the Church needs to bring the situation back to normal. Christ gave bread to the hungry, healed the sick and cast out demons. The Church therefore should accept once more the total value of the Gospel, including exorcism,' Milingo told me.

What seems to have worried the Vatican most is that Archbishop Milingo, a supporter of the charismatic renewal movement, whose adherents believe they enter into direct contact with the Holy Spirit, might encourage the unbridled growth of quasi-Christian cults in Africa. Many of the 2,000 separatist churches which now exist in southern Africa alone offer their adherents an easy way out of their everyday troubles and in Rome's view are little more than traditional African religions dressed up as Christianity.

But Milingo offers a strong defence of his healing activities which have now, he says, obtained the approval of Pope John Paul.

'Africa feels so small before Europe, because Europe is an elder brother whose superiority, it is claimed, is based upon the order of nature. The inferiority complex which haunts Africa is a perpetual humiliation . . .'

In Africa as elsewhere it is often difficult to draw a clear distinction between politics and religion. In many of the independent states set up, like Zambia, in former colonial territories during the last fifty years, political legitimacy has still not been fully established over the various peoples who cohabit within frontiers imposed by nineteenth-century European powers. Political authority in Africa may be founded on local traditional religions and is often exercised through rites or symbols charged with religious meaning. One reason why colonial regimes failed to gain acceptance was because they had no supernatural authority.

Africa is still too much viewed through the eyes of non-Africans, Milingo says. 'My own mother grew up in her African tradition and never had the ambition to be a European. Neither did she feel she was missing something. To convince me that I shall only be a full Christian when I shall be well brought up in European civilization and culture is to force me to change my nature. If God made a mistake in creating me an African, it is not yet evident to me.

'One must realize that in many parts of Africa we are still speaking as to Christians of the first century, in a language they can comprehend and in terms with which they are familiar.

'I personally have no ambition to form a separate African church. I love the Church as an African and I express my love for her through what I am and what I have as an African. Historically an African is a German, a Belgian, an Englishman, or a Frenchman; the Church should not continue the same trend of mental and spiritual colonialism.

'I want the Gospel to be understood according to the mentality and culture of my people. We Africans do not want to say that cultures cannot marry; they are interrelated.

'We have learned many things from the saints. Most of them come from Europe. We have very few African saints. The attitude of Africa is not so much to do away with all that is Western, but rather to tell Europe that we have some values, an inheritance that the law has given us. Anyone who interprets the search for identity and authenticity of Africans as racism, as discriminatory, is just being prejudiced.'

After a period of agonizing, it seems that the Vatican has finally decided to come to terms with Archbishop Milingo, if for no better reason than it has become apparent that there are many worse poisons affecting the Church than the Archbishop's healing powers.

Ironically, the African prelate now has a devoted following of Italians. The Vatican telephone switchboard has received instructions to put through calls to him from anywhere in the world from people seeking his healing powers, and he receives a huge international mailbag each week. After his last meeting with Pope John Paul, *L'Osservatore Romano* published a photograph of the Pope and the Archbishop together, and restrictions on Milingo's exorcist sessions in Rome were withdrawn. Milingo was told that, provided he lets the Vatican know his travel plans and informs the local bishop in advance when he holds healing services, he may continue his work as a healer wherever he wishes – except his native Zambia.

The removal of Archbishop Milingo from Lusaka has not solved the Vatican's dilemma of how to deal with evil spirits, or rather with independent churches and evangelical movements which centre upon healing. Milingo failed to observe the accepted demarcation lines between Christian and traditional African beliefs, between the natural and the supernatural, between a priest and a healer, between a pastor and an administrator. He upset the sytem and changed the balance of forces, and for that had to pay the price of exile. He was only thirty-nine when he was first appointed to the see of Lusaka in 1969. 'They shortened my youth,' he says of his treatment by his superiors.

On the feast of the Epiphany in January 1989 Pope John Paul announced that the first Synod of African bishops in the history of the Roman Catholic Church would be called during the early 1990s. With new converts joining the church and the Catholic population increasing in Africa at the rate of more than 8,000 a day, the continent is one of Rome's key target areas. Some 500 African bishops are expected to be called to Rome to take part in what many African Church leaders have been requesting for years, the holding of an 'African Council'. Most would have preferred the meeting to take place in Africa, not in Rome. The Special Synod for Africa falls short of a full Church Council. It will be yet another regional Church meeting on the lines of those already held at Medellin and Puebla for Latin America, and will discuss what the Pope rather vaguely terms 'organic solidarity'.

Cardinal Josef Tomko, the Slovak head of the Vatican's Congregation for the Evangelization of Peoples (the former Propaganda Fide department) and a close friend of the Pope, was appointed head of the organizing committee of the Special Synod for Africa. Other members are

Cardinal Francis Arinze from Nigeria, president of the Vatican department now called the Council for Inter-Religious Dialogue, Cardinal Christian Tumi from Cameroon, and the Coptic Patriarch of Alexandria, Stephanos II Ghattas.

A detailed questionnaire was circulated by the Synod's organizers at the Vatican to all Catholic Bishops' Conferences in Africa. This asked for information about three critical areas – the battle for converts with Islam, the role of animism or African traditional religion, and the proliferation of sects and new religious movements likely to syphon off future converts.

In a preliminary Synod report on the Church in Africa circulated in 1990 the Vatican admitted the seriousness of the problem of competing with Islam in Africa.

There is a renewed drive for the propagation of Islam worldwide. In Africa the objective appears to be to convert as many Africans as possible to Islam and to work towards a refashioning of African society according to Islamic principles: in government, legal system, culture, financial institutions, etc. These two objectives complement and depend upon each other.

Acknowledgement is readily made of the rights of Muslims to live their faith and witness to it. But it must be firmly stated that the Church also has the same rights . . .

Islam is an important and often a difficult partner in dialogue. It is important because of its genuine religious values, its large following and the deep roots it has struck among many African peoples. It is a difficult partner because of lack of a common concept of and language for dialogue. As both Christians and Muslims seek to make many converts, great prudence will be required to avoid a dangerous collision course between Islam's Da'wah (the Call) and Christian evangelization . . .

Two important growing tendencies in world Islam are affecting dialogue in Africa. There is an increasing consciousness concerning Islamic Ummah (Community) and the individual Muslim as a member of an Islamic community, with structures and institutions to express its identity and pursue its objectives at local, national and world levels.

There is also a corresponding universal consciousness of Islam as a religion with worldwide goals, through international organizations for collaboration, solidarity and sharing ideas and ideals.

Both tendencies in themselves could facilitate dialogue with Islam as a religion by making available qualified Islamic counterparts. However these tendencies generally work in the direction of radicalism and integralism, thus making dialogue difficult both at individual and group levels.

Much depends on the official status of Islam within each African nation.

In July 1980, the Pope spent two weeks touring Brazil, the world's largest Catholic country, both in terms of population and of territory. He addressed Brazilian workers in the soccer stadium in Sao Paolo, where expectations ran so high and feelings were so tense that he had to tone down some references to workers' rights.

John Paul's immediate predecessor was Cardinal Albino Luciani, former Patriarch of Venice, who reigned as Pope John Paul I for a brief thirty-three days in 1978.

One of Pope John Paul's first visitors after his election was the head of the Catholic Church in Poland, Cardinal Stefan Wyszynski, who had been responsible for propelling the young Cardinal from Krakow onto the world stage.

In 1981, doctors at the Gemelli Catholic Hospital in Rome saved the Pope's life after he was seriously injured in an assassination attempt by a Turkish gunman during a General Audience in Saint Peter's Square. Here the Pope leaves the hospital again after a relapse caused him to return for a second period of treatment.

In each of the countries that he visited for the first time as Pope, John Paul knelt on the airport tarmac upon his arrival to kiss the ground. It was his way of showing his respect for the universality of the Church.

During a visit to Australia in 1986, the Pope posed with a Koala bear for photographers in Alice Springs. There were few pauses for rest or recreation during the Pope's whirlwind travels.

During his travels, the Pope has collected some exotic headgear given to him by enthusiastic members of his flock. He posed for this shot during a visit to Colombia in 1986. At the Vatican, John Paul's travel souvenirs fill a large storeroom.

In 1984, bad weather prevented the Pope's charter plane from landing at Fort Simpson to visit a community of Inuit Indians during a tour of Canada. He promised to return on another occasion, and in 1987 he kept his promise by making a lightning stopover on his way back to Rome after a visit to the United States.

Each Good Friday the Pope fulfills his duties as an ordinary parish priest and hears confessions by Catholic pilgrims visiting Saint Peter's Basilica. The ceremonies of Holy Week mark the culmination of the Church's Year at Easter, the feast of the Resurrection of Christ.

President George Bush was received in Private Audience by the Pope at the Vatican in 1980. Much of the Pope's working day consists of meetings with foreign dignitaries and visiting Church officials from around the world. Most Wednesdays during the year he receives pilgrims at a General Audience at the Vatican. Only VIPs get a Private Audience.

In 1988, Pope John Paul toured five countries in Southern Africa, an area where Catholicism is expanding rapidly, but where other Christian sects compete strongly with Rome for converts and where animist cults still attract millions of adherents.

Mother Teresa of Calcutta, the Catholic nun who founded a new missionary order, the Sisters of Charity, which now has 50,000 workers in almost 100 countries, is one of the Pope's close advisors as well as a trusted friend. In 1979, she was awarded the Nobel peace prize for her work among the starving, the destitute, and the dying.

During President Mikhail Gorbachev's first visit to the Vatican in December 1989, he and the Pope agreed to reestablish diplomatic relations between the Vatican and Moscow, which had been suspended for over seventy years. This meeting marked the beginning of a new era for the Catholic Church in Eastern Europe.

John Paul has always shown particular pleasure in his extensive visits to the young Catholic Churches of Africa. He has visited practically every country in the continent except those ruled by Islamic regimes. Here he hugs an African child during a ceremony in Saint Peter's Square in Rome in 1990.

On April 13, 1986, Pope John Paul paid a historic visit to the Jewish community in Rome at their synagogue on the banks of the river Tiber. It was the first time in history that a Pope had entered a Jewish synagogue to take part in a joint prayer meeting. He was greeted by Rabbi Toaff, the chief Rabbi in Italy, and referred affectionately to the Jews as "our respected elder brothers."

Saint Peter's Basilica, where the tomb of the first Pope, the Apostle Saint Peter, is venerated, remains the hub of the Catholic Church. At Christmas, the square is illuminated at night to enable visitors to admire the life-size nativity scene which recreates the scene of Christ's birth in a manger.

If it is the State religion, as in Sudan for example, the Vatican's problems in helping to protect the rights of local Catholics are very different from that in say Tanzania, a pluralist society where there is more religious freedom. In fact for the Pope's visit in 1990 to Dar es Salaam, President Ali Hassan Mwinyi, a Muslim, hosted fund-raising dinners and made a personal cash contribution towards the estimated 2 million dollars that the papal visit cost.

By contrast, in 1985 the Pope had to cancel a planned stopover in Senegal, where over 85 per cent of the 6 million inhabitants belong to the Islamic faith. The leader of one leading Muslim sect, El Hadj Abdulaziz threatened to lie down with his followers on the airport runway to prevent the Pope landing in his country. The Vatican rearranged the Pope's schedule omitting Senegal. However, he is now scheduled to visit it in 1992.

Nigeria, the most populous nation in Africa, with a population estimated to be in the region of 100 million, is perhaps the most significant example of the 'collision course' between Islam and Christianity so feared by the Vatican. The banning of political parties during the 1980s meant that religion tended to fill the political void. Over 150 Christian churches were destroyed when rioting broke out in Kaduna state in the Muslim-dominated north of the country in 1987. Attempts to bridge the divide through a national advisory council on religious affairs have done little to slow down the religious polarization of Nigeria. Abubakar Gumi, former Grand Khadi of the Northern Region, has openly stated he wishes to see the country become an Islamic republic. 'If we want Nigeria to be a great country, to join hands,' he said, 'we have to follow one faith. I don't think we can accept a Christian as our leader unless we are forced to. Nigerian unity, if I am to do my best, is to try to convert Christians and non-Muslims as much as possible – until the other religions become a minority and will not affect our society.' A meeting planned between the Pope and local Muslim leaders when he visited Kaduna in 1982 had to be abandoned when none of the Muslims turned up.

In Sudan the Pope caused a political row and was accused of interfering in the country's internal affairs. He had told Roman Catholic bishops from the Christian south on a visit to the Vatican in 1988, 'No individual, or group, or the State can claim authority in the sphere of religious convictions. Where that State grants a special status to one particular religion as representing the belief of a majority of its citizens, it cannot claim to impose that religion upon all its people or restrict the religious freedom of other citizens.'

Since 1983 a bitter civil war has been going on against government forces in southern Sudan by Christian-led rebels who are demanding a greater role for ethnic and religious minorities and the repeal of Sharia laws. These laws, which include flogging for drinking and the amputation of hands for repeated theft, were introduced into the whole of Sudan in 1983 and applied to Muslims and non-Muslims alike.

The relationship between Catholicism and the animist cults of Africa is hedged about with mistrust and ignorance. The theory laid down by the Second Vatican Council is that 'inculturation', as it is awkwardly termed by the Catholic Church, is intrinsically a good thing, that the Christian gospel can borrow from local non-Christian religious traditions.

However, when it comes to embracing animist cults the church recoils. It is one matter to acknowledge that 'African traditional religion is the religious and cultural context from which most Christians in Africa come', but another for Rome to accept the mixture of tribalist culture and Christian tradition seen, for example, in the experimental Zairean Catholic mass. How is one to assess the impact of the celebration of a mass such as I witnessed in Kinshasa: the celebrant, a Belgian clergyman clad in a cap of monkey skins, the headgear of a tribal chief, leads twenty or thirty acolytes in a dance around the altar carrying spears along with the Christian cross? The swaying, chanting congregation plays a vital part in a colourful liturgy which often goes on for two hours or more.

Do Africans taking part in this rhythmic ethnic mass distinguish successfully between the Christian saints and their ancestral spirits, between the priest and the tribal chief? I remember a banner at Kinshasa airport as we took off on the papal charter flight which read, 'May the God of our ancestors bless our chief and the Pope.'

The Zairean mass, celebrated in Lingala and other local languages, may be by far the most successful example of 'inculturation' – the grounding of the Christian message in African tribal culture. But it strikes the observer that this token gesture towards the Africanization of the African Church may have attracted undue attention among foreigners, while the Zairean Church has studiously avoided taking any public stand against the serious social injustices being perpetrated in their country. There is little talk of 'liberation theology' in Zaire, a country of institutionalized corruption, the profits from whose mineral riches have gone mainly into the private coffers and Swiss bank accounts of the dictator, Mobutu Sese Seki Kuku Ngbendu Wa Za Banga.

The Catholic Church in Zaire represents a safety net for Africa's most numerous Catholic community (over half the population of 35 million), who are almost totally deprived of State welfare services and depend on Church missions for many basic essentials. When the Church stood up to Mobutu in the 1970s it had to retire badly mauled. President Mobutu threw Cardinal Malula, Archbishop of Kinshasa and former head of the Church in Zaire, out of the country. Now the Church concentrates on providing the essential services in a collapsing State and doesn't get too involved in politics. The West, which needs Zaire's materials, has always considered Mobutu a reliable friend. Whatever the leader gets up to at home is not the concern of outsiders. In Kisangani cathedral there is an example of 'inculturation' which may not exactly be what the Curia has in mind when it sits down to debate policies to follow in Africa. A mural shows God as black, dressed in a loin-cloth and wearing the symbol of power, the leopard-skin cap, which is habitually worn by Mobutu. God also holds a spear and a fly whisk – the symbols of Zairean temporal authority.

When he visited Togo in 1985, the Pope made a studied if token gesture towards African traditional religion. In the capital Lomé, tribal chiefs dressed in colourful robes gathered to greet the Pope and hear him preach. They sat in a phalanx in the hot sun, many of them wearing elaborate crowns of gold encrusted with precious stones. Drumbeats reverberated during the Pope's mass. At another ceremony where he ordained new African priests, the Pope drank water mixed with millet from a ceremonial calabash, and then poured the remaining contents on the ground, a passing tribute to local religious customs. The Pope travelled by boat to a grove near Lomé on the swampy shores of Lake Togo which is sacred to local animists. The shrine there, now dedicated to the Virgin Mary, owes its popularity to a pre-existing animist cult dating back at least five hundred years. The cult's devotees still worship the trees of the tropical rain forest. The sighting of a python, which slithered over the mission-station wall early on the morning of the Pope's visit, was interpreted as a favourable omen. The Pope met with the High Priest of the tree-spirit worshippers and his college of dignitaries including the Purifier, the Tender of the Sacred Flame, the Guardian of the Talking Drums and the Priestess in charge of the Goddess of the Waters, and said these friendly words of comprehension in French: 'Nature exuberant and splendid in this place of forests and lakes, fills spirits and hearts full

of its mystery, and orients them towards Him who is the Author of life.'
In a metaphor he thought the animist priests might easily grasp, he
compared the Catholic Church to the rainbow linking heaven and earth.

During his visit to Togo the Pope received gifts of antelope horns,
headdresses decorated with cowrie shells, and exotic gear for initiation
rites decorated with the hair of a ram and the horn of a gazelle. All the
ethnic bric-à-brac that the Pope's aides gather up during on his African
tours usually ends up in a Vatican store room. A special Vatican committee of ethnic art experts has to meet periodically to decide how discreetly
to dispose of this growing mountain of souvenirs.

Once back at the Vatican the Pope strongly condemned Voodoo rites
originating in Africa and now widely practised in Brazil, such as the
Macumba, the Umbanda and the Candomble, a rhythmic dance
accompanied by percussion and drumbeats imitating the human heart-
beat, which often sends participants into a trancelike state.

'These are grave deviations of popular piety and misunderstood ecumenism,' the Pope said. And he condemned the international tourist
industry for encouraging the symbols, rites and festivals of Voodoo
magic in the name of folklore. Yet the preparatory document for the
African Synod admits that African traditional religion can be seen as
'part of the religious patrimony and cultural heritage common to all
members of a particular ethnic group, irrespective of their [Western]
religious affiliations'.

The proliferating new sects and revivalist religious movements of
Africa are a painful thorn in the side of the Vatican. A variant of the
traditional Gospel message known as the Gospel of Prosperity, which
originated among gospellers in the United States, has found a ready
audience in many parts of the continent. The basic idea is that by
choosing God you choose wealth and prosperity. If you are not prosper-
ing then you are clearly not a true Christian. Four thousand Protestant
evangelists from all over Africa who attended a 'Fire Conference' in
Zimbabwe in 1986 were treated to enthusiastic expositions (with extensive quotations of biblical authority) of the theory of prosperity as a
sign of divine grace. Speakers like the Evangelist couple Kenneth and
Gloria Copeland from Texas told the cheering audience how they had
given away – and mysteriously received back in greater quantities and
more expensive versions from even more generous donors – a series of
dazzling motor cars and glittering gold watches. They had never looked
back since espousing the Gospel of Prosperity.

'I'm not a poor man any more,' Copeland said. 'My days of not

having enough are over . . . God just gave us the key to heaven's bank . . .
Our Father is Chairman of the Board! Alleluia!'

Such sentiments go down as well among the whites of South Africa as
among the poor blacks of West Africa, where for example one prosperity
preacher, Benson Idahosa of Nigeria, has founded more than 1,000
churches. It is comforting for the whites of Johannesburg to hear that
the wealth they enjoy is no more than their due and has nothing to do
with the unjust political and social structures denounced by mainstream
Christian churches.

In most parts of black Africa – which lack any tradition of religious
asceticism – the Prosperity message is equally well received. Wealth
and success (and many wives, although the Prosperity gospel does not
explicitly extend as far as this) are traditionally the sign of the man
blessed by God and his ancestors.

On his second visit to the teeming Zairean capital, Kinshasa, (the first
in 1980 was marred by the crushing to death of nine people during the
rush to get into a papal mass at the football stadium) the Pope beatified
Africa's first modern saint – a black nun, Anuarite Nengapeta. She was
clubbed and then stabbed to death by Simba rebels in 1964 when her
mission station in the bush was overrun during the Congo civil war.
What made the ceremony unique in the annals of the Roman Catholic
Church was the fact that 25–year-old Anuarite's murderer and would-
be rapist was present at his victim's beatification ceremony. The murderer's name was Pierre Olombe. Local newspapers, which published
his photograph, said he had undergone a religious conversion since
trying to force Sister Anuarite to become his 'wife' at bayonet point. He
had escaped from prison after receiving a life sentence for his crime and
had subsequently been pardoned by President Mobutu. The Pope
declined a request for a private meeting with the former 'Colonel'
Olombe on the grounds that he had failed to make an official application
in time; but the Pope did add a sentence to his homily stating that he
forgave the murderer 'with all my heart'.

On this African tour the Pope concentrated on countries with leaders
who were, nominally at least, Christians, and some of whom were
members of his Roman Church. President Mobutu of Zaire, a Catholic,
thoughtfully decided to celebrate the sacrament of marriage with his
latest wife a few days in advance of the Pope's second visit to his country.

The political message that the Pope delivered to these usually single-
party States was typically as follows: if the dictator will respect the view
that to have a political opinion different from his own is not a crime,

will make at least an attempt to stamp out the more flagrant forms of corruption, and will keep the Catholic schools going, then the Pope for his part will use his good offices to keep the aid from rich donor countries flowing and will personally see that the Roman Catholic Church's often essential work in education, health and emergency relief is maintained.

A typical example was the Pope's six-hour stop in Bāngui, capital of the Central African Republic. The military ruler paid tribute in front of the Pope to the work of some 600 foreign Roman Catholic missionaries and lay workers. Their continued presence was as important to General Kolingba as that of the 50 or so native-born Catholic priests, or the 2,000 French soldiers protecting his country, a former French colony. It remains one of the poorest countries in the world. Life expectation is only about forty years and two-thirds of the population are still illiterate. There are virtually no roads in the landlocked Central African Republic, and the river is only navigable for seven months in the year. Fresh monkey flesh and live yellow caterpillars were among the gastronomic delicacies on sale in the capital's central market.

Brightly coloured exotic butterflies, some as large as European song-birds, fluttered around the papal podium as the Pope spoke to the crowds held back at bayonet point by General Kolingba's soldiers. The Pope lectured the Central African Republic's quarter of a million Catholics on the importance of leading the future development of their country after the disastrous Bokassa reign. The Pope tactfully made no mention of the previous dictator, the self-styled 'Emperor' Bokassa, a leader with cannibal instincts who believed he was a modern African Napoleon and who sometimes fed his political enemies to the lions he kept in his private zoo within the palace grounds. Bokassa's triumphal arch still remains in Bangui – a monument to his follies and cruelties.

In most African countries a papal visit is often a welcome political gift to the ruler and his local Party machine. The arrival of the Pope presents a heaven-sent opportunity for an African Head of State to re-inforce his political authority in a society which may be lacerated by tribal, religious and liguistic differences.

The Pope is well aware that he is being used politically when he sees his portrait twinned with that of a local President-for-life on miles of cotton costume and headdress fabrics, all printed and distributed for people to wear in celebration of his visit. But he is usually willing to pay this price for the opportunity to get close to his followers and to encourage his dwindling number of missionary priests and his new but inexperienced African clergy in their difficult task of adapting the Christian message to local African conditions and susceptibilities.

He has paid three visits altogether to the Ivory Coast, the West African territory grabbed by France during Europe's scramble for Africa in the second half of the nineteenth century. The country gained independence in 1960 under Félix Houphouet-Boigny, who had been the first black ever to serve in Paris as a French government minister. Houphouet-Boigny, one of the founding fathers of the Pan-African movement, developed his native village Yamoussoukro as his nation's capital, despite the fact that it was situated in the remote bush over 200 miles from the coastal port city of Abidjan, the country's economic hub.

The centrepiece, the ruler decided, was to be the biggest Roman Catholic cathedral in Africa, rivalling Saint Peter's in Rome. Our Lady of Peace, five years in the building, which today rises like a mirage out of the red earth and the tropical vegetation of this still incompleted capital city, has a steel and aluminium cupola closely modelled on Michelangelo's marble dome which crowns the head church of Christendom in Rome. The cross surmounting Our Lady of Peace soars 525 feet above ground – higher than the apex of Saint Peter's cupola.

Architect Pierre Fakhoury from Lebanon, who designed the huge Yamoussoukro cathedral complex, dismissed criticism of this slavish imitation of Renaissance architecture as entirely unsuitable for the African bush. He argued that the architects of Saint Peter's had copied the classical buildings of Greece and ancient Rome, which in turn were inspired by Africans – the designers of the temples of the ancient Egyptians in Thebes.

Houphouet-Boigny spent more than 150 million dollars on his cathedral, which was also expected to serve as his mausoleum when he died. Construction work coincided with a period of dramatic decline in the Ivory Coast's economic fortunes. The President deflected the charge that he was squandering the resources of a deeply indebted African State by explaining that the money came out of his own pocket, and that his family had donated the site – a former coconut plantation.

Our Lady of Peace has four times the area of stained glass that there is in Chartres Cathedral, is clad in expensive Italian marble, and its African mahogany pews can seat a congregation of over 10,000 worshippers in air-conditioned comfort.

The Pope, well aware of international criticism about the lavish new cathedral in the African Bush, was at first unsupportive when asked by Houphouet-Boigny to bless his new creation. The Vatican was also chary about accepting a gift which would entail heavy maintenance costs. But in September 1990 the Pope agreed to make an overnight stop in Yamoussoukro to inaugurate the basilica at the end of his seventh African tour. The Ivory Coast President agreed in exchange to build a hospital and social centre inside the cathedral complex, and to set up a maintenance fund.

Only about 15 per cent of the Ivory Coast's 10 million population are Catholics. Animists, Muslims and Protestants (in that order) far outnumber them. At the inauguration ceremony, Cardinal Francis Arinze from Nigeria defended the Pope's decision: 'We Africans know that man does not live by bread alone. An African may not have a good house, but he rejoices to see a beautiful house of God. We Africans have our poor, our sick, our hungry, our homeless and our refugees. But these suffering Africans appreciate the value of giving God our best. They realize that nothing is too expensive to offer to God,' he concluded. When he got back to Rome the Pope made a vigorous defence of his decision to accept the gift of the new African basilica in the bush.

A starred editorial in the Vatican newspaper, indicating that the article had been approved at the top, said the Pope had made an 'historic gesture on behalf of Africa's poor' in consecrating the new Church. The poor would be 'the privileged guests of the new basilica. They are the ones asking for it, and they will fill it up.'

The editorial attacked criticism of the basilica in the European press as the work of 'a moral lynch mob' and said that the building of Our Lady of Peace at Yamoussoukro marked 'an important stage for Africa as a whole'.

For political reasons, the Pope has refrained from carrying out any pastoral visit to his 2-million-strong flock – 80 per cent black – in South Africa. But he has visited all the black-ruled frontline States bordering South Africa, and even spent a few hours by accident in the republic when his plane was diverted there through bad weather on a flight from Botswana to Lesotho during his 1988 southern Africa tour. Foreign Minister Pik Botha was hurriedly despatched to meet the Pope and exchange courtesy greetings, but there was no substantive discussion of the problems of apartheid. The Pope strongly denounced the apartheid system on each of his African travels, but always sought to place the problem in the context of his overall worldwide evangelizing mission.

Talking with the flying Vatican press corps as we flew over the Sahara desert from Nairobi to Casablanca on another African tour in 1985, the

Pope was unusually frank about how he views apartheid – a hateful system but a problem to be seen in its global context.

'The world speaks a lot about apartheid, but it is not the only human rights problem,' he said. 'My style of activity is not political. I am not discussing with leaders such and such a political problem. I am teaching what the Church teaches and human rights are only one of the problems of evangelization.

'Certain African situations cannot be judged by our criteria, neither from the standpoint of democratic systems, nor from that of human rights. This does not mean tolerating abuses. It means only that Africans find themselves at a different moment of history. You have to visualize what European countries were like five, six or seven centuries ago. The Africans are just beginning their indpendence.'

He believes that Christians in South Africa must reject violence in combatting apartheid. The system of racial segregation had exacted a 'terrible toll' on the lives of individuals and families and the whole of society, he told a visiting nine-man delegation of South African churchmen, including Anglican Archbishop Desmond Tutu in Rome in May 1988.

The Pope restated his Church's opposition to all forms of racial discrimination, but he went on to prescribe 'a change of heart', rather than economic sanctions imposed from abroad, as the best way to change the situation in South Africa. 'Christians in South Africa are called to work together to promote among all peoples in your society a sense of effective solidarity,' John Paul said.

The delegation from the South African Roman Catholic Bishops' Conference and the South African Council of Churches, representing 7 million of South Africa's Protestants (but excluding those belonging to the racially separate Dutch Reformed Church) held a prayer vigil against apartheid in a Rome church the night before they met the Pope at the Vatican.

Tutu, a Nobel Peace Prize winner, told reporters he was happy the Pope would not visit South Africa during his African tour later that year. Church sources said the Pope had decided to exclude South Africa from the 1988 tour at the suggestion of the country's Roman Catholic bishops.

In a cable sent to Addis Ababa marking the twenty-fifth anniversary of the Organization of African Unity (OAU), which coincided with the South African churchmen's visit to Rome, Pope John Paul insisted that the nations of Africa must be permitted to guide their own development, 'free from unwarranted external pressures'. He told leaders of OAU member nations he shared their concern over racism, ideological conflicts, drought, famine, disease and debt afflicting the continent.

At the same time he underlined Africa's enormous capacity for advancement 'on the basis of the human potential and the resources at its disposal'. With appropriate and effective international help, Africa could look forward to a development 'truly capable of meeting the needs and aspirations of its peoples', he said.

When he arrived in Zimbabwe four months later, the Pope heard an impassioned defence by President Robert Mugabe of the use of violence in the struggle against apartheid. The African leader recalled that his own young country's independence struggle had cost tens of thousands of lives. 'We did not do so for the sake of violence, but because we felt we could not achieve justice through a peaceful solution,' he said, adding that after declaring independence he had practised a reconciliation policy. But the Pope, while again condemning the evils of apartheid, stubbornly refused to sanction violence as a means of achieving political change in South Africa.

However intractable the problems that he finds in Africa, it is evident that the Pope appreciates the enthusiastic welcome he has received practically all over the continent. He enjoys the singing and the drumming and the chanting and the dancing that bursts out spontaneously on his travels. In return he tries to treat the Africans gently. It was to a group of brightly turbaned and colourfully dressed African matrons that he told what is, as far as I know, his only papal on-the-record joke.

He arrived ten minutes early for a speech scheduled at Saint Joseph's cathedral, in Kaduna, northern Nigeria, on Saint Valentine's Day, 1982. It was his last public engagement of the day after a long and tiring series of masses and meetings. His normally gleaming white papal vestments were soiled and limp. His sleeve had been touched by thousands of admirers. Black make-up powder used by African women had left many telltale smudges, and he tried in vain to brush it off.

The bus carrying his suite of Vatican officials had been caught up in a traffic jam. In order to while away the time before they arrived, the Pope began, speaking in his inimitable English:

'Dear Catholic women, I have a long speech, eight pages . . . but before reading it I shall tell you a short story. It is a story of my imagination.

'In my imagination I return to Rome and meet Saint Peter and I greet him of course.

'I say to him, "You know, I was in Nigeria!"'

'Saint Peter looks not quite confident and says, "I don't believe!" '
Laughter and applause.

' "Yes, I was in Nigeria and I visited Nigeria. Last Sunday I was in
Kaduna."

'Saint Peter is still hesitant.

'And so I say to him, "Yes, I was in Kaduna. I ordained about a
hundred priests!"

' "Impossible!" ' Loud laughter and applause.

'So I don't know what to do. I say to him, "In the afternoon I met
the laywomen of Nigeria."

'Saint Peter is still unconvinced. So I show him my white soutane
(covered in black powder) and Saint Peter says, "Yes, now I believe!" '
More laughter and applause.

Africans usually seem to be colour blind when they see the Pope. At
an airport mass at Bamende in West Cameroon, where the Pope preached
in English, not French, for this part of the country used to be under
British colonial rule, I met a twenty-two-year-old African university
student called Javran. He had come to perform a welcome dance with
some friends from his village 100 miles away in the bush. Music was
provided by drums and xylophone made out of the trunk of a banana
tree.

Javran was covered in a fake leopard skin, his face was hidden under
a sort of fishing net and on top of his head he wore a baboon face mask.
As he removed his baboon's head to reveal his less alarming natural
features, I asked him if he was conscious of the Pope's colour when he
saw this white man dressed entirely in white.

'No,' he replied disarmingly, 'we regard the Pope not as a white man,
just as an ordinary person sent to us black men.'

John Paul seems to be as enchanted with Africa as Africans are with
him. Relaxing for the occasional moment on tour he can frequently be
observed tapping his feet to African rhythms. When lecturing Africans
on their moral failings he treats them gently, much more gently, I noticed,
than when castigating, for example, the 'hedonists' of some Western
European countries.

The Pope's biggest African challenges lie ahead – the holding of the
first-ever Synod of the young Churches of Africa, and a planned visit to
the Republic of South Africa. Meanwhile he is well aware of two glaring
facts: first, that events in Eastern Europe, since the political changes of
1989, have tended to obscure Africa's continuing need for injections of

available international economic, financial and technical aid – aid which now has also to be shared out also among the needy economies of his own Slav world; and, second, that the African continent provides perhaps the most serious challenge that the Roman Catholic Church faces to its presence in the developing world as the new millennium opens with the prospect of endemic famine, an AIDS epidemic threatening to lay low whole populations, and signs of an increasingly bitter battle for converts with Islam.

In northern Nigeria Christians and Muslims sporadically take up arms against each other. In Egypt systematic discrimination is taking place against the Christian minority, squeezed between Muslim fundamentalists and the Egyptian State. A human rights organization based in Britain, Christian Solidarity International, reported after a fact-finding visit to Egypt on the eve of the Gulf War that Christian converts there were frequently being detained for questioning by the secret police. Christian Solidarity found that most Christian converts from Islam in Egypt join the Protestant not the Catholic Church, as 'Protestant leaders appear the most willing to accept the risks involved in teaching Muslims the Christian faith'. This report should give Pope John Paul food for thought as he prepares for his African Synod.

CHAPTER 8

The Population Explosion

One cannot deny the existence, especially in the southern hemisphere, of a demographic problem.
Pope John Paul II, *Sollicitudo Rei Socialis*, 1988

Cocooned behind the bulletproof windows of the papal limousine, or in that curious vehicle, half Land-Rover, half glass box, called the Pope-mobile, invented to show off the Pope to his followers at minimum personal security risk, Pope John Paul has passed by some of the most wretched and overcrowded slums in the world. Even connoisseurs of Third World poverty would find it difficult to pinpoint the worst example of human degradation that the Pope saw, or almost saw. Was it during his 1980 visit to the dank, waterlogged shanty towns of Salvador de Bahia in Brazil, where small children often disappear between the rotting plankways separating the shacks built out of driftwood and old oil-drums to drown in the sewage-infested water over which they live? Or was it in Chile in 1987, when he passed through the slums of Santiago, accurately described as a filthy bandage wrapped around the capital city? Or was it on the terraced mountainsides of human misery near Rio de Janeiro, where he visited the sanitized slum or *favela* of Vidigal, which had running water, a miracle specially laid on for the day of his apparition? Or was the most squalid scene in São Paolo, or Caracas, or Lima, or Manila, or Calcutta, or Kinshasa?

By the end of this century, according to a study by the International Labour Organization, most major Third World cities will be swamped by rural migrants and expanding slums. The world's squatter settlements are expected to increase from just under one billion when Pope John Paul took office, to over 2 billion by the end of the century.

Usually a big whitewash operation by State, city and Church authorities would be organized to tidy up the scene for the Pope's whirlwind arrival. In Guayaquil, Ecuador's biggest city, situated among banana and sugar-cane plantations on the Pacific coast, I was present at his

1985 visit to the *guasmo* or city of the poor. Foreign visitors are normally discouraged from forays into this extended shanty town because the local police have given up trying to maintain law and order in an area where tens of thousands of hungry and homeless families squat in shanties built out of a cardboard, driftwood and petrol cans.

The Vatican press was taken under heavy police escort at dawn into what was, with unusual honesty, described to us as a 'no go area'. Families here lived in such promiscuity and poverty that it seemed difficult to believe that we observers should have been quartered for the night in a comfortable hotel only four miles away in the 'real' Guayaquil. I tried to imagine what it was like during the rainy season when the dusty unpaved 'streets' turned into rivers of mud and sewage. One squatter, standing on the floor of his family's flimsy home, built on stilts to avoid the rats and the flooding, explained to me how he went off to work each day as an ice-cream vendor in the 'real' Guyaquil, sometimes wading waist-deep through water, before he reached the tarmac road to the city.

The Pope arrived with his retinue by helicopter in a swirling cloud of dust, said mass in front of a group of buildings freshly whitewashed to screen off the near-by horrors and told families in his homily to avoid the dangers of contraception and abortion, as well as of pornography, drugs and prostitution. The people of the *guasmo* appeared to show little interest in what he had to say. The crowds which had gathered out of curiosity began to melt away even while he was speaking.

In a place where parents and children lived and slept together fifteen or more to a room, it seemed highly incongruous to be telling the population to avoid sensuality, to give a Christian education to their children, and to remember that responsible parenthood is the foundation of an orderly society.

Ecuador, like many of the debt-ridden countries of Latin America, has a steep 2.9 per cent annual rate of increase in its population. The idea that life might be more tolerable for Ecuadorians if there were fewer of them simply does not occur to the Pope. He rejects outright the implications for his Church's teaching of the demographic explosion in the Third World that has grown ever more dramatic during his pontificate.

Briefly, the facts, as gathered by the Population Reference Bureau in Washington, are as follows. It took the human race from the time of its first appearance on the planet until about AD 1830 to reach its first billion. It took just under another century, until about 1920, to double its numbers to 2 billion. Since then, better hygiene, the eradication of diseases such as malaria, smallpox and cholera, and declining infant mortality resulted in a lengthening expectation of life in the more populous parts of the world. The multiplication of the human family speeded up beyond the most far-fetched expectations of those who lived before 1950. The British scientist Sir Julian Huxley confidently predicted that world population would reach 3 billion by the end of the century. He underestimated badly. The third billion was reached in 1958, the fourth in 1975, and the fifth billion during the ninth year of the pontificate of Pope John Paul II, in 1987.

Demographers forecast that the sixth billionth member of the human family will be born before the end of the twentieth century. World population, they say, could stabilize sometime during the twenty-first century at a figure of about 10 billion. The worst-case scenario is a 15 billion population by mid-century.

Lester Brown, Director of the Worldwatch Institute in Washington, says the world can now be more meaningfully divided not into developed and developing countries, according to income, but into areas of rapid or slow population growth. The demographic middle ground has almost disappeared. Either countries multiply at an alarming rate − 2.2 per cent each year or more − or they stagnate.

Africa is the continent where change has been most dramatic. In 1950 Africa's population was half the size of Europe's. By the next century, it will be three times bigger. Nigeria, Africa's most populous nation, now just over 100 million strong, is projected to reach a population of over 530 million before it stops growing towards 2050. Nigeria will by then be the world's third most populous nation after India and China. India is projected to overtake China around the year 2010, when it reaches 1.7 billion.

The latest world growth rate is estimated at 3 babies born every second, 300,000 a day, or 90 million new mouths to feed each year. Even if scientific and technological progress means the planet can support a world population of 10 billion by the early decades of the twenty-first century, there are serious doubts about whether the ecosystem could tolerate the damage that such multitudes would inflict upon the world's non-renewable resources.

These facts and figures are well known to the Pope. But he steadfastly refuses to use his influence over the world's Roman Catholic population, shortly expected also to reach its first billion, to use any artificial birth-control methods to limit the size of their families. Wherever possible the

Church actively opposed all government family planning programmes, even though the Pope knows full well that abortion, which he also denounces as a sin, will continue to be the most commonly practised form of birth control in the poor countries.

In what may eventually come to be seen as one of the most realistic pronouncements of his pontificate, the encyclical *Sollicitudo Rei Socialis* of 1987, the Pope observed that 'unfortunately instead of becoming fewer, the poor are becoming more numerous' and recommended that the world's leaders should pay more attention to the phenomenon, without of course suggesting any real plan of action.

On his first trip to Africa in 1980, after observing the teeming humanity of Kinshasa, where nine people were crushed to death in the crowd which flocked to one of his masses, the Pope was overheard to remark to a member of the Vatican group accompanying him, 'So many people, so many . . .'

Catholic teaching on birth control remains anchored to Pope Paul VI's encyclical *Humanae Vitae*, published in 1968 when the world's population had reached only 4.5 billion. The encyclical, which confirmed the Roman Catholic Church's previous teaching on the immorality of contraception, was never defined as an infallible papal document. Pope John Paul holds that *Humanae Vitae* is a matter of fundamental Catholic belief. He cannot pretend, however, that it forms part of the infallible teaching of his Church. If this had been Paul VI's intention, he would have said so at the time. Infallibility cannot be declared retrospectively. Theologians find it hard to sustain that papal teaching on birth control can be placed in the category of dogma defined as essential to the very basis of the Christian faith. Paul VI's encyclical was written in the light of the findings by a commission of theologians, doctors and other lay experts appointed by the Pope to report on Catholic birth-control teaching with regard to current medical and scientific knowledge. They found after three years' research in the early 1960s that the ban on contraception could not be proved to be Church doctrine from Scripture, tradition, theology, natural law or philosophy, and accordingly advised Pope Paul in favour of change.

The gist of the commission's report was that traditional Church teaching that the purpose of sex within marriage is the transmission of life rather than the mutual pleasure of the spouses should not be interpreted in a narrow and restrictive sense. It is nonsensical to examine each individual sexual act to see if it allows procreation. The experts agreed that what matters is the pattern of a couple's sexual behaviour. The old guard at the Vatican panicked. They saw the threatened change in the Church's attitude to sex as a challenge to the very basis of papal authority rather than a fresh look at birth control. It was to no avail that the experts had stated:

There is no sound basis for fearing that a change would cause a loss of trust in the Church's teaching authority or would make it possible to raise doubts on every other doctrine. Such a change is to be seen rather as a step towards a more mature comprehension of the whole doctrine of the Church.

Cardinal Ottaviani, the then head of the Holy Office, wrote a fifteen-page position paper to Paul VI, putting forward three powerful arguments why official Catholic teaching on birth control should not be changed. First, it would undermine confidence of the faithful in the Church's teaching authority; second, it would open wide the door to promiscuity and hedonism; and third, if individuals were allowed to use contraceptives, governments would be able to claim the right to organize State family planning. Father Henri de Riedmatten, the Swiss Dominican who was secretary of the Papal Commission on Birth Control, set up outside the normal Vatican bureacracy, gradually found an invisible barrier growing up around him as the Curia pressed home its organiational advantage. One day the Swiss priest discovered he no longer had private access to the Pope.

Against the desires of a large proportion of the world's Catholics, the encyclical was drafted and signed. Few papal documents in the long history of the Universal Church have caused such immediate consternation and opposition.

Bishops tried as far as possible to ease matters for their congregations. The Belgians, for example, were among the first to make it clear that Catholics who after serious consideration came to the conclusion that the encyclical was not binding upon them should follow their consciences. Gradually, Catholics began to feel that *Humanae Vitae* did not bind them and stopped even mentioning in the confessional that they had been using contraceptives. By the time Pope Paul died in 1978 the encyclical had been so decisively rejected, in the spirit if not in the letter, that it was largely ignored.

In Britain in the 1980s, according to the noted Catholic psychologist Dr Jack Dominian, 88 per cent of the adult population use contraceptives of some sort, while one per cent use the safe period or 'natural' birth-control methods. Of all users of contraceptives, 43 per cent resort to the pill, and Roman Catholics are no exception to this pattern.

Cardinal Wojtyla, as he then was, made an ambiguous speech at a Milan conference marking the tenth anniversary of the document a few months before he became Pope. 'The pivot of the matter is the conscience . . . everything transmitting the teaching of the church is finally aimed at forming an upright and mature conscience in husband and wife.' What did he mean?

It soon became clear. Everywhere during his subsequent worldwide travels, Wojtyla thundered on about the evils of abortion, contraception and divorce, lumping them together as if they were all somehow equally reprehensible aspects of an 'anti-life' mentality.

Divorce seemed to be a lost cause as practically every country now permits it. The Church has also had its own 'divorce' court for centuries. It is called the Roman Rota and has the power to annul the marriages of those wealthy and well-connected enough to turn to the Vatican's own Supreme Court for a ruling. This function has now been handed over to local diocesan tribunals and only the most difficult or socially important cases come to Rome, such as that of Princess Caroline of Monaco, whose case was reportedly handled by Pope John Paul himself. Between 1977 and 1986 the tribunal heard 1,617 requests from couples married in church who wished to contract new marriages, and allowed 822 of them. But this was far too many for the Pope's liking. He has repeatedly told off his ecclesiastical judges for being too lenient. Among the reasons given for recent successful marriage annulment cases have been the Marxist faith of one of the contracting parties, as well as psychiatric troubles.

The Pope believes couples turn too easily towards the psychiatrist's couch rather than to the confessional. Psychiatrists tend to discover inhibitions and traumas and then argue that this is 'proof' of abnormality, he told his Supreme Court in 1988. Normality easily becomes a myth. 'The normal human condition in this world includes moderate psychological difficulties. Catholics must not give up too easily and, in the words of Saint Paul, must learn to crucify the flesh.'

On one visit to South America the Pope used the word 'contraception' no less than sixty times in ten days of public speeches. But his followers did not agree. The gap between theory and practice grew steadily wider. His teaching that contraception is intrinsically evil and that those who practise it are not recognizing God was rejected. The idea that a tiny group of celibate Church officials are better equipped to formulate teaching on married life than those with living experience of the married state helped destroy the credibility of both the teaching and the teacher.

Theologians were scolded and told to remain silent. In June 1987 the Pope instructed, 'What is taught by the Church on contraception is not a matter that can be discussed freely by theologians. To teach otherwise is tantamount to inducing into error the moral conscience of the married.'

When the twentieth anniversary of *Humanae Vitae* came round in 1988, the Pope organized celebrations at the Vatican, inviting more than fifty bishops and theologians from across the world willing to back his stance on contraception. They put out an obedient communiqué accusing Western countries of 'contraceptive imperialism' which, they explained, meant linking Third World aid to 'vast contraception and sterilization programs, thus harming family life, threatening women's health and violating human rights'.

Archbishop Joseph Cordeiro of Karachi claimed that some multinational companies were using poor countries as a dumping ground for contraceptives. The American Auxiliary Bishop of Newark, New Jersey, James McHugh, announced, without giving any reliable source for his figures, that world food output would be sufficient to support up to 40 billion people in the twenty-first century – four times the projected total.

There followed a series of papal broadsides at the waverers, who are most probably the majority of his followers. For John Paul the very word 'contraception' involves blasphemy, and the use of a condom becomes the equivalent of murder.

The Pope admitted at the celebration for *Humanae Vitae* that reaction inside his Church to the encyclical had been at times 'harsh and even scornful', but, he went on, 'in reality, the years following the encyclical, despite the persistence of unjustified criticism and unacceptable silences, have shown with growing clarity how Paul VI's document as not only always of living topicality but even rich in a prophetic significance.'

Addressing moral theologians, the Pope made it clear that as far as he was concerned there were no exceptions to the ban on all forms of artificial birth control, whatever the personal extenuating circumstances and whatever the consciences of tortured Catholics might dictate. (He implied that the ban also extends to the condom when used to prevent the spread of AIDS.) In the two decades since Pope Paul VI had formally banned artificial birth control, many Catholics had accepted the idea that their conscience established moral principles. 'There has been a radical breakdown in the bond of obedience to the holy will of the Creator, which is the basis of human dignity,' the Pope told the conference.

John Paul said that whoever differed with Church teaching because of his or her own conscience rejected Catholic concepts of moral conscience and the magisterium, or the Church's authority. 'You cannot say that a member of the faithful has carried out a diligent investigation of the truth if he doesn't take into account what the magisterium teaches; if, availing himself of any other source of knowledge, he makes himself the judge; or if, in doubt, he follows his own opinion or that of theologians instead of the teaching of the church.

'No personal or social circumstances have ever been able, or will be able, to rectify the moral wrong of the contraceptive act,' he said. Whoever challenges the teaching of the Catholic Church in this field renders Christ's death on the cross vain. John Paul insisted that the *Humanae Vitae* encyclical placed Catholics in general and Catholic theologians in particular under a direct obligation to obey Church teaching on morals.

Dr Nafis Sadik is a Pakistani gynaecologist who used to run her country's family planning programme. Since 1987 she has been head of the United Nations Population fund (UNFPA). She is the first woman ever to run a major voluntary funded United Nations programme, and controls an annual budget of 170 million dollars and an international staff of 500. Her aim is to extend family-planning services to 500 million more women in the next decade. She urges governments to earmark at least 1 per cent of GNP for family planning. Dr Sadik probably has greater expert knowledge about the world population bomb than any other United Nations official.

Her view is that religious taboos are of relatively little consequence in a brutal world where abortion is still the main method of limiting births. UNFPA does not advocate abortion, but recognizes that some 60 million abortions are carried out each year in the world, about half the total number of live births. Although abortion has now been legalized in countries comprising 80 per cent of the world's population, about half of these 60 million abortions are still performed illegally, at huge cost to women living in countries where abortion is still a criminal offence.

In Brazil, for example, the world's most populous Catholic country, the World Health Organization estimates that for every seven women who give birth, another ten have abortions. Under Brazilian law, abortion is punishable upon conviction by prison terms ranging from six to twenty-four years, yet it remains the main cause of death among Brazilian women. Almost half a million Brazilian women die each year as a result of crude methods of pregnancy termination including the use of knitting needles or injections of caustic substances. Although Brazilian doctors are convinced that the legalization of abortion would save thousands of women's lives, the Church insists that the life of the unborn child is paramount and, echoing the heavy anti-abortion campaign of Pope John Paul, refuses to condone what has become a routine event in Brazilian society at all levels. Elsimar Coutinho, President of the Brazilian Family Planning Association, says abortion is practised liberally by the higher social classes in his country with no fear of social stigma. 'Our law only serves to punish the poor, who are caught with blood on their hands when the abortion is badly done,' he said.

Catholic Brazil is changing, however. Although the government opposed family planning at the Bucharest United Nations Population Conference in 1974, two years after the Pope's visit in 1980, they turned to UNFPA for assistance. 'The desire was there to limit births: women were resorting to extreme methods such as Caesarean section as a method of sterilization,' Dr Sadik told me. Now the birth-rate in Brazil has changed direction – it is going down.

It is the nations with the fastest-growing populations which have least to spend upon social programmes. Dr Sadik's latest report shows that many of the poorest countries, strapped for cash, were cutting spending on health and education by up to 50 per cent during the late 1980s. Given the choice, three-quarters of Latin American women not using family planning say they would postpone, limit or delay their childbearing. But, as Dr Sadik points out, about half the world's women live in rural areas and in societies dominated by men and so do not have access to family planning. She says that many educated men do not see any need for equality and education for women, and as for religious fundamentalism, 'It seems to be designed to keep women in bondage'.

Dr Sadik believes that in the absence of State-sponsored family-planning advice, abortion will continue to remain the most widely practised method of birth control.

Abortion was permitted in the ancient Jewish world and also by the Greeks, who allowed it before the *anima* entered into the foetus (which they considered happened forty days after conception). The Romans condemned abortion as a crime which ranked with poisoning. In the Middle Ages it was punishable by death in many countries, including England and Switzerland. Only from the 1960s onward did abortion become generally legalized. In Western Europe, only predominantly Catholic Belgium and Ireland continue to ban abortion.

In the United States, the Supreme Court ruled in 1973 in the landmark case of Roe v. Wade that American women have a constitutional right to an abortion, based on the right of privacy. During the 1980s some 1.5 million legal abortions were performed each year in the USA; but in 1989 the Supreme Court voted 5–4 that individual states were henceforth free to impose new local restrictions. They were also free to take expert medical advice to determine whether foetuses of twenty weeks are capable of surviving outside the womb. The Roe v. Wade ruling had fixed twenty-four weeks as the legal limit for protecting a pregnancy. The Catholic Church teaches that life has to be protected from the moment of conception.

In the Soviet Union, and in the Pope's native Poland, abortion rates are estimated to be among the highest in the world. With contraceptives in acutely short supply, nine out of ten first pregnancies in the Soviet Union end in abortion. According to statistics published in Moscow for the first time in 1988, 8 million out of the world total of 30 million legal abortions are performed annually in the Soviet Union in what women describe as 'assembly line' conditions.

The Pope has extended the automatic excommunication from the Roman Catholic Church – previously incurred by a woman who terminates her pregnancy with a procured abortion – to anyone else remotely involved in the operation, including doctors, nurses and also the man who made her pregnant. A Vatican lawyer, Cardinal Castillo Lara Rosalio José, was told by the Pope in 1988 to go on public record to explain that the relevant section 1398 of Canon Law is all-embracing.

'No human law can morally justify induced abortion . . . nor can the behaviour of local authorities in trying to limit the responsible freedom of parents to decide whether to procreate children be allowed on the moral plane,' the Pope said during his visit to San Juan, Puerto Rico, in October 1984.

Notwithstanding the demographic explosion in the Third World, the Pope regards prevailing attitudes in the West to abortion as a threat to the future of the whole of humanity. 'The future of man is threatened in some nations today by the drop in births, by demographic ageing, by the spreading recourse to abortion and by thousands of forms of selfishness,' he told Italians, who were encouraged to march to Vatican City on a 'pro-life' day in 1989. Only about 2,000 did so.

Abortion was legalized in Italy five months before Wojtyla was elected Pope. The operation is available free on request during the first three months of pregnancy. After that women have to show that the foetus is deformed or that their physical or mental health is in danger.

In 1981 the Pope gave strong support to a campaign by Italian Catholics to get the law reversed. A national referendum confirmed the Italian Parliament's original decision by a big majority – 67 to 33 per cent – but a major concession to Catholic opinion was built in to Italy's abortion law. Doctors, nurses and paramedical staff at State hospitals can be excused from taking part in abortion operations if they object on grounds of conscience. The result was that some 60–70 per cent of doctors opted out of the State abortion scheme, forcing many Italian women back into the former illegal back-street system. Latest estimates are that about 200,000 legal and 130,000 illegal abortions are performed each year. The Pope's favourite Italian Catholic activist group, Communion and Liberation, is campaigning actively to ban mid-term abortions, which are not forbidden by the law, and eventually to organize another referendum to try to overturn the abortion law.

Family planning in Italy has been slow to gain acceptance because of Church opposition, but is now on the rise. Only about 3 per cent of women in Calabria, in the deep south, use 'secure' methods such as the pill or an IUD, while the figure for the industrial north remains about 10 per cent.

In France abortion, which until the reign of Louis XV used to be punishable by death, was legalized in 1975 and the cost of the operation, fixed by the government at 160 US dollars, is now partly reimbursed by the health service. The French pharmaceutical company Roussel UCLAF developed the world's first abortion-inducing pill, RU 486 (Mifepristone), which was authorized by the French government for use with a doctor's prescription in 1988. But Roussel decided to withdraw it from sale after right-to-life organizations campaigned against its use. What clinched the company's decision was a threat by American anti-abortionists to force a boycott of all Roussel's sales in the United States.

An international family-planning conference held in Nairobi in 1987 called on all governments to liberalize their abortion laws and proposed that family planning should be included in all primary health-care programmes. Fred Sai, a Ghanaian health consultant to the World Bank, said it was unethical for health services to shut their eyes to the abortions which are responsible for the deaths of over a million women each year. He pointed out that the lesson to be drawn from the relaxation of anti-abortion laws in the United States, China and Western Europe was that there had always been a drastic fall recorded afterwards in the number of maternal deaths.

Yet two months after this conference, the Pope was again holding forth to a conference of European anti-abortionists, telling them that Europe was gambling away its future destiny and showing signs of moral decadence because it had failed to respect the right to life of the unborn child.

What is still uncertain however is the correlation between the availability of efficient contraception, and the abortion rate in countries where hitherto abortion has been the principal method of contraception. The current situation in Poland, for example, is that although the commercial availability of the pill and condoms has improved since economic reforms began to bite, this has not yet led to a significant fall in the number of abortions carried out.

Dr Sadik of UNFPA believes that the best way to discourage abortion is to make family planning freely available. Yet only half the population of the developing world has access to any form of contraception, and if you exclude China the figure drops to only one-quarter.

Communist China is an excellent example of how doctrinaire theories about population policy can be reversed quickly when the facts are appraised more realistically. Mao Zedong believed that the population explosion was a capitalist myth and that greater social justice would defeat poverty, however many mouths there were to feed.

China's demographic story is worth examining more closely. More than half of the present Chinese population of 1,133 million has been added since the Communist Revolution of 1949. When Jesus Christ was alive, there were about 60 million Chinese. By 1840 there were 412 million. By the time Mao took power just over a century later there were 540 million. The United States, with a similar land area, today has a population of only 246 million, less than a quarter that of China. Even the Soviet Union, with much vaster territories, never underwent such a population explosion in the name of Marxism-Leninism. The world's biggest-ever door-to-door head count, carried out in China in July 1990, revealed that some 20 million people – more than the entire population of Australia – had been overlooked in previous population estimates.

Mao had certainly been warned. As early as 1950, the Beijing University Rector, Ma Yinchu, argued that unlimited population growth would hinder China's economic future. He was dismissed and disgraced. It was not until he had reached the venerable old age of ninety-eight, and his views became official policy, that he was finally rehabilitated. Ma Yinchu died at the age of 101, a symbol of the increased longevity of his race. The Chinese have almost doubled their life expectancy in the past two generations.

Famine, earthquakes, war and disease had traditionally maintained the demographic balance in a country which has over a fifth of the world's population but well under 10 per cent of its arable land. Mao, like the Chinese peasant, regarded his people as China's most important resource. 'Every stomach has a pair of hands,' he used to say. China, which now uses openly coercive policies in an attempt to curb further population growth, is still forced to make exceptions to the single-child families which are now mandatory. In the countryside, where most Chinese live, an extra pair of hands, preferably male, has always been regarded as the best and most reliable form of insurance for your old age.

The election of Karol Wojtyla in Rome coincided with a complete turn-around in official Chinese population policy. As late as 1974 at the Bucharest United Nations Population Conference, the Chinese had expressed remarkably similar views to those of the Vatican. Indeed, ridiculous as it now seems, the Holy See actually felt obliged to deny reports that there had been a secret alliance between Mao and the Pope.

By 1979, one-child families were the legally enforced norm. Newly-weds had to sign a contract with the State to have only one child, who would be entitled to free education and medical care. A second child would forfeit these benefits, while a third would incur fines representing a heavy curtailment of income.

The new law was not respected. There were appalling reports of late-term abortion decrees enforced by officials upon peasant women, some of whom fled from their homes and travelled thousands of miles to deliver their child secretly in the home of relatives. Baby girls were reported to have been suffocated or given away to enable parents to have a male heir, the ultimate aim of every Chinese family. There was enormous suffering. Local enforcement committees would occupy the house of a woman pregnant for a second time and refuse to leave until she agreed to have an abortion.

However, by 1988 the *People's Daily* admitted that the situation was once again getting out of hand. The Communist Party newspaper said there was now little hope of holding the population at the target figure of 1.2 billion by the end of the century. By the spring of 1989 officials were declaring that the population was 'undoubtedly out of control', and for the first time confirmed a 1.1 billion figure. The state science and technology commission was calling for increased birth control among the 86 million people of China's 55 ethnic minorities. Most of them had been exempted from the rules applying to the Han ethnic majority, on the grounds that they did not represent a demographic threat to the nation.

Twenty-two million babies were born in China in 1987, a million more than in 1986. That's a rate of 40 babies a minute, or the equivalent of a town of 50,000 people each day. The authorities announced further rewards and punishments to curb unplanned pregnancies.

The *People's Daily* conceded that one child per couple is 'absolutely not in line with the laws of nature', but added that the rules had to be adhered to for the sake of the nation.

In the countryside, the *People's Daily* reported, more than 90 per cent of the population wants more than one child. More than 30 per cent of births were unplanned and the number of pregnancies among married women was rising. Over 11 million abortions were performed in China in 1986, more than in any other country in the world. A family-planning official appointed in every town and village was to be rewarded if his area kept within its birth quota and punished if too many babies were born; but the abortion rate would not be taken into account in evaluating the birth-control monitor's performance.

Still, the Chinese government takes comfort from the fact that the situation would be much more catastrophic if widescale family planning had not been introduced during the 1970s. They calculate that if nature had taken its course there would today have been an extra 200 million mouths to feed. Bringing up all these children would have cost slightly more than China's current GNP for one year. China has become a major user of the French abortion pill RU 486, which is expected eventually to supplant surgery as the main method of abortion in most of the developing world.

Chang Chongxuan, China's Deputy Minister for Family Planning in Beijing, explained that his government's plans are based upon education and voluntary acceptance of the country's true needs not coercion. In rural areas, he said, exceptions were being made for one-child families where hardship would result, but confirmed that the current baby boom is expected to last at least until 1995 before the population begins to level off.

There are ethically worrying aspects to Chinese government policy on population. One Chinese province went beyond mere limitation of numbers and began compulsory sterilization of the mentally retarded in order to 'increase the quality of the population'. The People's Congress in Gansu passed a law in 1988 forbidding mentally retarded people, estimated at just over one per cent of Chinese society, from marrying without first undergoing sterilization. The authorities are now considering extending this law to the whole country. Only those mentally retarded as a result of hereditary factors rather than through accidents would be affected, and local officials said that only 10 per cent of the estimated 270,000 mentally retarded in Gansu, those now classified as 'severely retarded', would be affected by the new ruling.

The *People's Daily* commented, 'Anyone responsible for allowing mentally retarded people to give birth will be fined and subjected to administrative discipline. The retarded lack productive capability and live on relief funds and grain. They are a great burden to society.'

China's neighbour Vietnam, which is adding one million a year to its present population of 65 million, has also taken strict measures to call a demographic halt. Families with more than two children were punished under a 1988 decree. The aim is to reduce annual population growth from 2.5 per cent to 1.7 per cent. Couples having more than the permitted number of children had to pay towards otherwise free medical care and education and 'increase their contribution of labour for the common benefit of society'. They were also forbidden to move into town centres.

The largest Catholic population in Asia lives in the Philippines. Slightly more than half the estimated 60 million Asian Roman Catholics live in the scattered archipelago of 7,000 islands that was first a Spanish, then an American colony. The Pope saw the pressures of poverty, accompanied by a virtually uncontrolled population explosion, when he toured the notorious Tondo shanty slum of Manila in 1981. Family planning has been encouraged neither by President Ferdinando Marcos, nor by his successor President Corazon Aquino. The World Bank has warned of the threat to the country's national resources posed by the baby boom (latest growth rate: 2.4 per cent).

Fifty million condoms were donated to the Philippines by foreign family-planning organizations in the years before President Marcos was finally ousted from power in early 1986. Only 10 million were ever used. The rest were still being distributed in 1990 free of charge at family-planning centres. Their expiry date – 1985 – was plainly visible on the labels.

The Church's opposition to condoms means that they are hardly ever used by Filipinos, despite the prevalence of sexually transmitted diseases like AIDS. Another reason, according to a popular local newspaper columnist Tita Girom, is that many Filipinos still hold the view that 'Only Casanova types use condoms for protection.'

By contrast Catholic Mexico brought its rate of population increase down by almost one half between the Pope's first visit in 1979 and his second in 1990. The admonitions of the Pope did not prevent the Mexican government from putting into operation a strong State-sponsored family-planning programme during the 1980s. The latest statistics show an annual population increase of only 1.9 per cent in comparison with 3.7 per cent when Karol Wojtyla was elected Pope. About half the women in Mexico now regularly use some form of contraceptive device. According to Dr Sadik, resistance by the Catholic Church to State family-planning programmes in Latin America depends upon the strength of the government. When the government feels secure Church groups lie low, but if the government weakens then the local Church steps up its opposition.

The Pope has had the opportunity to compare at first hand the economic consequences of successful and unsuccessful family-planning programmes in developing countries. But he has refused to draw what his critics see as glaringly obvious conclusions. In 1984 he spent three days in South Korea, a country which has a tiny but fast-growing community of Catholics. South Korea has also had a strong government family-planning programme in operation since the 1960s. Publicity on the theme of smaller families is constant and effective. Population growth is about 1.5 per cent each year, economic growth over 7 per cent.

The following year the Pope visited Kenya, one of the most economically favoured countries in Africa with a growing industrial base and a solid agricultural sector. Yet the contrast with South Korea could not be greater. In Kenya, President Arap Moi has unsuccessfully called for smaller families and has even introduced penalties for civil servants who have more than four children. Kenyan women can on average expect to have eight children – a figure that has remained fairly constant since the country's independence. They usually marry in their teens, less than half are literate, and less than 10 per cent use any form of contraception. The population, 20 million now, is expected to multiply fourfold by the middle of the next century, and may rise to 120 million before it stabilizes. Kenya's real wealth is consequently diminishing as an acute land shortage develops. Poor farmers are forced to use marginal land, which rapidly becomes unsuitable for any purpose and are then forced to migrate to the mushrooming capital city, Nairobi. And Nairobi itself has become an environmental nightmare. Soil erosion, air and water pollution, and inadequate waste disposal are all problems which diminish the quality of urban life.

In East Asia, where most women are literate, they usually wait at least until the age of twenty before marrying and they have a life expectancy ten years greater than that of their sisters in Kenya. In South Korea, for example, deaths during childbirth are extremely rare, and infant mortality is around thirty per thousand, less than half the figure for Kenya.

The unavoidable conclusion is that as long as poor countries cannot control population growth, even a reasonably high economic growth rate will not lead them out of poverty. The International Finance Corporation, an offshoot of the World Bank which deals with private investment in the Third World, noted in its 1987 report that there is no hope of raising living standards in countries where the population continues to grow at a rate of 2 per cent a year and more. The determination of the Vatican to try to influence Latin American countries whenever it can against family-planning strategies may be one reason why Latin America sinks ever further into debt while Asian countries, where Vatican influence is negligible or non-existent, perform economic miracles.

Indonesia, with 175 million people, the fifth most populous nation in the world, was visited by the Pope in 1989 although only one per cent of its citizens are Catholics. A vigorous and well-thought-out family-planning campaign, with strong support from religious leaders in what is a predominantly Muslim country, cut the annual population growth from 2.3 per cent in 1970 to 1.9 per cent by the late 1980s. The aim is to reach a growth of only 1.6 per cent by the mid-1990s. According to the Central Bureau of Statistics in Djakarta, half the married women in Indonesia now use some form of artificial contraception. To overcome reluctance by city dwellers to attend the public contraception clinics which have been set up all over the country, they are being encouraged to buy their own contraceptives. The family planners call it 'social marketing'. But as Dr Haryono Suyono, the chairman of Indonesia's family planning organization, points out, the base from which the population grows has not diminished and therefore between 1980 and 1990 the population was expected to have increased by 35 million in comparison with 28 million between 1970 and 1980.

Indonesia's wealthy and prosperous neighbour Singapore, with a total population of only 2.6 million, was visited by the Pope in 1987. Here he found support for Catholic teaching on birth control from the predominantly ethnic Chinese Singaporeans, who for two decades ran an energetic birth-control campaign under the slogan 'two is enough' but who are now predicting economic calamity as a result of the decline of the birth-rate to one of the world's lowest – 1.44 per cent. The government is spending half a million US dollars a year to try to persuade Singaporeans to have three or more babies, if they can afford them, in order to keep numbers up.

To learn more about the Vatican's attitude to birth control I went to see Father Arthur McCormack, an experienced missionary priest who for twenty-five years was one of the Roman Catholic Church's leading experts on demographic problems. He was a special adviser to the United Nations Population Conference in 1974 and consultant to the United Nations on development and population until Wojtyla's election.

He has scant regard for the 'natural' family-planning methods which are alone permitted by his Church. 'The fact that only some two to four per cent of the people of the world use them, often in conjunction with other methods and with abortion as a safety net against failure, is carefully concealed by the Vatican,' he told me. A World Health Organization report of December 1980 said that natural family-planning methods are 'of very limited usefulness' in developing countries and that more research is needed. Yet this report, whose contents were known when the Pope called his Synod on the family at the Vatican in 1980, was ignored by the bishops meeting in Rome. No recognized population expert was called in to advise the Synod.

Arthur McCormack's views are, needless to say, not welcome today at the Vatican, despite his pastoral experience as a missionary and his academic experience as a demographer. He was chaplain at a maternity hospital in Liverpool, and saw at first hand in Bangladesh and other Third World countries the difficulties involved in proselytizing on behalf of 'natural' family planning.

He was 'frozen out', to use his words, for trying to make the Catholic Church recognize the correlation between world poverty and the population explosion. If, as the Pope nobly says in his 1988 encyclical *Sollicitudo Rei Socialis*, the Church seeks to lead people to respond to their earthly vocation as responsible builders of earthly society, is it really good enough to state that a world demographic problem exists and leave it at that? The Pope admits that the situation of the world's poor has worsened in the twenty years since his predecessor Paul VI wrote his encyclical *Populorum Progressio*, the first major statement to come out of Rome on development problems. Given that, as John Paul argues in his encyclical, the teaching of the Roman Catholic Church is subject both to continuity and to renewal and is subject, as he puts it, 'to necessary adaptions suggested by changes in historical conditions and the flow of events', then is there not a case for a reassessment of *Humanae Vitae*? Worsening poverty and declining food supplies, combined with the fact that the Catholic Church's teaching on contraception is today neither effective nor even obeyed by the majority of its adherents, seem good reasons for reconsideration of the subject.

What are the prospects of feeding the growing human family without the poorest continuing to suffer hunger and even starvation?

James Ingram, the executive director of the World Food Programme was called in by the Vatican in November 1988 to address the Pope's co-ordinating committee for charitable relief, Cor Unum (One Heart). He reported that almost one-fifth of the human race goes hungry each day, in the sense that they live in households too poor to buy the food necessary to provide the energy for work. And of these, one half or nearly 600 million people, equivalent to the combined population of the United States and the Soviet Union, do not even get sufficient nourishment to carry out minimal activity if they are adults or to grow in a healthy manner if they are children.

Expert opinion is that there is no way that this situation is going to change in the foreseeable future – except for the worse. There are limits to what technology can do to fill empty bellies. Only a fairer allocation of the world's food resources can solve hunger on the scale that exists today.

Attempts to estimate how many people the world environment can support depend upon what sort of diet is considered tolerable. If the products of world agriculture were to be distributed equally, and if people were to accept a basically vegetarian diet, then there would be enough to feed a total of some 6 billion people, or slightly more than the present world population. It takes ten times as much land to produce food in the form of meat as it does to produce vegetables which supply the same energy. Yet much of the world's most productive cropland is used to graze beef cattle.

If, on the other hand, meat is considered necessary to human survival, then currently only enough food is produced for the mouths of about 4 billion people, or four-fifths of the present world population. And if the sort of varied diet considered desirable in the developed countries is chosen, there is only room for about 2.5 billion, or half the current world population. As people become richer they also tend to consume foods that are more expensive in terms of the resources used to produce them. For example, in the Sahel people have developed a taste for rice, which cannot be grown locally in sufficient quantities. Demand for white bread is growing in many overcrowded Third World cities, yet wheat cannot be grown in the tropics.

The picture gets more and more sombre the further you delve into the statistics. Intensive Western agriculture uses ten units of energy – mainly oil – to produce one unit of food energy. The world's oil resources will begin to run out during the twenty-first century. After that the developed world may not be able to feed itself, let alone the hungry of the developing world. Even now the ability of the rich countries to feed themselves has only been achieved with heavy subsidies. They spend two and a half times more money subsidizing their own farmers than they give in development aid to the underprivileged 3 billion people of the Third World.

Environmental devastation is reducing crop yields in parts of the world such as sub-Saharan Africa and Central America, which are becoming increasingly dependent upon food imports. The long-term outlook in India, which trebled its wheat production in the years following the development of high-yielding strains during the green revolution, is not promising. Output is now static and there are still more undernourished people in India than in any other country in the world.

When Karol Wojtyla was elected Pope in 1978 AIDS was unknown. The Vatican's reaction to the developing moral and social debate on how to deal with the new disease was at first silence, then, when bishops from the most seriously affected regions, North America and Africa, began asking advice, the suggestion was made that it might be divine retribution for sexual immorality. The aged Cardinal Siri of Genoa, at one time considered a possible candidate for the papacy and one of the Italian Church's right-wing hardliners summed up Rome's view, 'It is right that those who sin should pay.'

However, the view of the man who, during John Paul's pontificate, held the top medical post in the government of the United States, where AIDS now kills more people each year than road accidents, is that the AIDS pandemic has extremely grave international implications. Dr C. Everett Coop, former Surgeon General of the United States, said, 'Even if we find an effective vaccine, I am afraid that the impact of AIDS on the world's cultural, economic and social fabric will last many years after the disease is no longer a public health threat. Before AIDS is checked, many developing nations will lose large numbers of their most productive young adults in fields of important economic endeavour.'

The cost of terminal medical care for the victims is going to be astronomical. The United States is already spending 6 billion dollars a year on treating AIDS victims and the cost is expected to double by 1994. Developing countries simply cannot begin to foot the bill. Cameroon, for example, would have to forfeit its entire export earnings for a year to pay for the medical screening of its population.

In Africa, where up to 20 per cent of people are now thought to be HIV carriers (although the figures do not show up in the World Health Organization totals for lack of reliable statistics), AIDS is spread almost entirely by heterosexual contact and affects men and women in equal numbers. Only three African nations, Algeria, Libya and South Africa, can afford to mobilize resources on the scale of the Americans or Europeans. A regional conference on AIDS held in Kinshasa, Zaire, in 1988 was told that the 'slim' disease, as it is colloquially known in Africa, is gradually changing moral and sexual behaviour. Condom sales in both Congo and Zaire are on the increase. Between 1987 and 1988 they jumped to 300,000 per month from almost negligible sales previously.

The latest major international medical conference on AIDS, held in Florence in 1991, ended with continuing sombre assessments on the spread of the killer disease and caution about the prospects for a cure. Although no less than eleven different vaccines against the HIV virus are under development in the United States and Europe, no satisfactory cure for AIDS is yet in prospect. Doctors made cautious predictions that a successful vaccine, or cocktail of vaccines, might be developed by the year 2000, but most tests have so far been carried out on chimpanzees – there is an understandable shortage of human volunteers to take part in clinical trials.

There is also a cost problem. Different strains of vaccines will be necessary to combat AIDS in Africa, where the disease is most rampant. It is not certain that the international pharmaceutical companies will finance the development of vaccines suitable for use in the poor countries of the Third World – now regarded as the major growth areas of AIDS in the years to come.

The number of AIDS sufferers in Asia has been grossly underestimated the conference was told, and the transmission of the disease in India and Thailand is expected to climb rapidly. By the mid-1990s the number of AIDS sufferers in Asia, where half the world's population lives, will overtake that in the industrialized countries of the West, according to Jonathan Mann, Director of the international AIDS centre at Harvard University. The spread of AIDS in Eastern Europe, hitherto protected against the epidemic by political restrictions on the free movement of HIV carriers, is also expected to gather pace.

The Pope's first public gesture towards the twentieth century's major medical and social malady, did not come until the ninth year of his reign. He met a group of sixty-four AIDS sufferers at the Dolores Mission Church in San Francisco, where the disease was first identified among homosexuals in 1981. The Pope had a message of compassion for the victims, one of them a Catholic priest, assembled in nine pews among the congregation. 'God loves you all without distinction, without limit,' he said. 'He loves those of you who are sick, and those suffering from AIDS.'

Pictures of him cradling Brendan O'Rourke, a four year old condemned to die from the disease, were instantly on the front pages of newspapers around the world. Brendan, infected with AIDS through a blood transfusion after his premature birth, tugged at the Pope's ears when the Pontiff took him from the arms of his father and hugged him.

Outside the mission church a crowd of about 2,000 gays shouted 'POPE GO HOME' and 'SHAME, SHAME, SHAME!' The church is about a mile from the notorious Castro district, centre of homosexual life in San Francisco. There groups of gays clowned an anti-papal happening, dressed in cardboard mitres and disguised as bishops and nuns – including the 'Sisters of Perpetual Indulgence.' Earlier that year the Vatican had denounced homosexual acts as 'an intrinsic moral evil' and recommended a celibate life for gays. Demonstrators at another of the Pope's stops in Phoenix, Arizona, where he called upon Catholics to imitate the Good Samaritan in holding out a helping hand to AIDS victims, carried placards saying: 'GAY, PROUD – AND STILL GOING TO HEAVEN!'

As leaders of the Universal Church in the country most seriously affected by the AIDS epidemic, American bishops decided to take a lead in drawing up Catholic guidelines to help people deal with the difficult medical, social and moral consequences of the disease. Unlike the Vatican which starts from lofty general principles, the Americans' starting point was four real human AIDS tragedies, an infected baby whom no one wanted to adopt, a married woman infected during a previous relationship, a drug addict infected by a dirty needle, and a young homosexual who had just lost his job after revealing he had contracted the disease. The idea was to lift the discussion above the idea of retribution for sexual misconduct.

One paragraph in the American draft document entitled 'The Many

Faces of AIDS: a Gospel Response', which suggested that information about condoms should be part of the Church's educational effort to help Catholics combat AIDS, caused uproar. The Vatican demanded the immediate withdrawal of the document.

It sounded harmless enough: 'We are not promoting the use of prophylactics, merely providing information that is part of the factual picture.' Cardinal Ratzinger wrote back that the document gave the impression that the Church had modified its position on contraception and was therefore unacceptable. He ordered them to draft a new version.

The Pope belatedly realized that it was not good enough for his representative, Cardinal Fiorenzo Angelini, the Vatican City State's Health Minister, to go to a world conference on AIDS in London and criticize the 'unseemly' publicity being given to the condom. 'An outsider', Cardinal Angelini commented, 'might have the impression that the purpose of this meeting is to advertise a product!'

L'Osservatore Romano waited until March 1988 before coming out with its first leader on AIDS: 'To seek a solution to the problem of infection by promoting the use of condoms is to enter a road not only unreliable in a technical sense, but also and above all unacceptable in a moral sense.' The only solution was to 'avoid the cause of infection, which means in about 95 per cent of cases abstaining from sex outside marriage and from drug-taking'. The fundamentals were 'chastity, conjugal fidelity, self control'. It was not enough for doctors and researchers to join battle against AIDS. Spiritual health helps physical health and vice versa.

A split is now developing between the Vatican and Catholic leaders in these prosperous Western societies where AIDS is now a major health problem. The argument is over the morality of using the condom as a protection not against conception but against infection. The French hierarchy has come out squarely in favour of allowing the condom in order to avoid spreading the disease both between married and non-married partners. AIDS victims have a duty not to spread the disease as well as the right to compassion, the French bishops say. America has followed suit. Catholic Ireland has decided to pay for free condoms and syringes for Dublin drug users at risk from AIDS.

The Vatican sponsored its own international AIDS conference in November 1989, hoping to deflect attention from medical and scientific aspects towards the ethical problems that this new world health threat poses. The proceedings did not go entirely according to plan. World experts on AIDS, such the two scientists who first identified the virus,

Professors Robert Gallo of the United States and Luc Montagnier from France, politely but firmly told the Vatican gathering that they did not agree with prominent Church leaders such as Cardinal John O'Connor of New York, who had stated bluntly, 'The truth does not lie in condoms and clean needles.' Lieutenant-Colonel Robert Redfield, head of AIDS research for the United States Army, told the conference that the disease was shortly expected to become the leading cause of death in the American armed forces.

John White, a priest who claimed he was an AIDS sufferer, was hustled out of one conference session after holding up a banner which read 'The Church has AIDS.' The voice of AIDS sufferers was not heard. Cardinal Angelini sophistically explained that the conference was 'for AIDS sufferers, not of them'.

In his summing up, the Pope said the Catholic Church faced a double challenge over AIDS: first, in helping to prevent the further spread of the disease, and, second to provide assistance to the growing number of those already suffering from it; but there was to be no concession to 'palliatives' such as the condom.

New ethical problems have arisen as a result of rapid medical and scientific developments during John Paul's pontificate. Many Catholics find the Pope's 'pro-life' stance provides an overly simplistic answer to the complex field of human genetic research. Is it right to seek to make permanent changes in the genes of victims of inherited diseases? Should French and American cosmetic companies be allowed to use human foetal tissue to test their products? After all, it was not only Catholics that found something grisly about cases like that of the divorced American couple Mary Sue Davis and her husband Lewis from Tennessee, who quarrelled over the custody of seven fertilized embryos deep frozen before their divorce. To give life, or not to give life, can often involve delicate legal as well as ethical issues.

The Pope's major statement on these questions came in a document published by Cardinal Ratzinger in February 1987, entitled *Instruction on Respect for Human Life in its Origin and on the Dignity of Procreation*. This document provides a strongly negative answer to all questions relating to test-tube conception and manipulation of the human embryo for any purpose whatever. *In vitro* fertilization to help childless couples to conceive is forbidden to Catholics, as are surrogate motherhood, the freezing of embryos, sex selection and all forms of genetic engineering. All children must be conceived by natural methods without external artificial aids. If in doubt, Pope John Paul's answer is 'no'.

The document attracted rueful comment from medical researchers like Dr Patrick Steptoe, who in the year of Wojtyla's election, 1978, succeeded in giving life to the world's first test-tube baby from an embryo fertilized outside her mother's womb. 'I cannot see how if God has given us brains to use, and brains to go and do these things, it can be wrong to give a childless couple life through *in vitro* fertilization,' Dr Steptoe said. 'I think it is going to be very hard on Catholics. I cannot agree that women who could have children by this method should be told that they are not allowed to.'

About 1,400 test-tube babies have been born in Britain and another 1,500 in the rest of the world as a result of Steptoe's pioneering work. 'It's nonsense to suggest that there is no love in *in vitro* fertilization. There is a great deal more love and care with those children than with many who are conceived normally,' Dr Steptoe said.

French opinion on the Pope's ruling was equally hostile. The leading French gynaecologist Emile Papiernik said, 'French opinion will not follow these Vatican injunctions, any more than it followed those on contraception and abortion.' The rectors of four major Catholic university teaching hospitals in France, Belgium and the Netherlands travelled to Rome to tell the Pope that they had no intention of giving up their research on artificial conception. When they continued to refuse to toe the papal line, Cardinal Ratzinger in a signed article in *Osservatore Romano* accused them of 'very serious rebellion'.

Difficult legal as well as ethical issues are raised by the use of human tissue to produce commercial biological products. In the United States a congressional advisory body, the Office of Technology Assessment, decided that in the absence of clear legal restrictions, the sale of tissues and cells is generally permissible, unless the circumstances surrounding the sale suggest a significant threat to individual or public health or strong offence to public sensibility. A report by the Office said both the Christian and Jewish religions generally favour the transfer of human biological materials, such as hearts and other organs, as gifts, but that Congress would have to decide on the commercialization of biological products derived from human tissue.

Is it enough to argue, as the Pope does, that some forms of scientific progress do not coincide with the true welfare of mankind? Does it really mean anything to say, 'The study of life should serve life'?

And, above all, is it really 'pro-life' to allow population levels to increase to such an extent that living systems in certain impoverished regions of the planet will never recover?

The latest United Nations report on the state of world population (1991) says that the planet's population could double again within the next sixty years. The natural resources required for human survival are being consumed at an ever-increasing rate. Dr Nafis Sadik explained that fertility must be lowered from the current rate of 3.8 births per woman to 3.3 by the end of the century in order to stabilize the situation. 'Reaching our family planning and fertility targets for the next decade will be crucial for future progress – and even for human survival – in the next century,' she said. I am not suggesting that Pope John Paul is responsible for this worrying state of affairs, or even that his opposition to contraception is going to be decisive for the world's future. Mexico's experience is proof of this. But his narrow interpretation of *Humanae Vitae* has boxed his church into a corner as far as the development of a coherent Catholic response to the population explosion is concerned.

CHAPTER 9

King Karol's Court

The Divine Right of Kings has lapsed in most of the world's sovereign states, and the papal triple tiara, dating from mediaeval times and symbolizing the Pope's rule over his temporal kingdom, his spiritual authority over his subjects' souls and his moral authority over all other monarchs, has been consigned to a museum. None the less Karol Wojtyla, Bishop of Rome, Vicar of Jesus Christ, Successor of the Prince of the Apostles, High Pontiff of the Universal Church, Patriarch of the West, Primate of Italy, Archbishop and Metropolitan of the Province of Rome, and Servant of the Servants of God, continues to count among his many titles that of Sovereign of the Vatican City State.

The Papal States of central Italy once covered thousands of square miles, but the kingdom is now squeezed into an area of a mere 110 acres adjoining Saint Peter's basilica in the centre of Rome. The Vatican is a walled fortress city; the walls were strengthened and buttressed to protect the Pope from further invasions by Christian princes after the sack of Rome and of the Vatican in 1527 by the mutinous armies of the Holy Roman Emperor Charles V.

Much of the territory of the world's smallest sovereign state, apart from its palaces, museums, administrative buildings and churches, consists today of well-manicured parks and gardens. These were spared the frenzy of real-estate speculation and development which, between 1870 and 1990, transformed Rome from a sleepy provincial city of 200,000 into a densely overbuilt and disorderly metropolis of 3 million inhabitants. Vatican City even continues to boast a bosky dell full of sturdy oaks and elms, a tiny remnant of the forest that used to surround Rome during the legendary age of the Etruscan kings and Romulus and Remus.

Inside the territory Karol Wojtyla is a king in every sense, with full executive judicial and legislative powers. His kingdom issues its own car licence plates (the Pope's stretched Mercedes limousine has the Vatican registration SCV001, standing for Vatican City State), is served by a railway station where duty-free goods enter courtesy of Italian railways through a sliding steel portcullis cut into the Vatican walls, contains a helipad for the Pope's frequent travels, a Mint which produces its own coinage (although the Italian lira circulates freely inside the kingdom), a Post Office which issues its own stamps, a police force (the Vatican Gendarmerie, not to be confused with the largely ceremonial corps of the Swiss Guard), a supermarket, a petrol station where Vatican employees can fill their tank for less than half the cost in Italy, a library, a fire brigade, a radio station which transmits programmes worldwide in thirty-two languages and a nascent television service, a newspaper and publishing house, a bank, a prison, a court of law, a press office, a fine arts restoration department, and a pharmacy which does a brisk trade in tranquillizers but is forbidden to sell contraceptives.

The Catholic Church claims twenty centuries of continuity for this site, set over and around the 'rock' of Saint Peter (whose tomb in the Roman cemetery cut in the rock under the high altar of the basilica was positively identified only late in the twentieth century by the eminent Italian archaeologist and scholar Margherita Guarducci). Yet during many of those centuries popes did not reside at the Vatican.

For almost a thousand years they used to live on the other side of the city in the Lateran Palace next to their cathedral church of Saint John Lateran. The popes moved, temporarily during the fourteenth century, from Rome to Avignon, and thence back again to Rome, where they took up residence and transferred their court to the Vatican on the opposite bank of the Tiber. In the seventeenth century Pope Gregory XIII found the Vatican unhealthy because it lies too near to the river. He built a new papal palace (now official residence of the President of Italy) on the Quirinal hill and moved the papal court once again.

Vatican 'traditions' often turn out to be considerably less ancient or significant than you at first assume. The custom by which popes always dress in white, for example, dates back only as far as the reign of Pius V in the latter half of the sixteenth century. Pius was a member of the Dominican order and chose to wear the distinctive white religious habit of his order after his election. His (non-Dominican) successors found his example convenient to follow.

The old Saint Peter's was built upon the Vatican hill, where tradition said Saint Peter had his tomb, by the Roman Emperor Constantine after his conversion to Christianity in the fourth century AD. In mediaeval times, the building became an architectural marvel full of historic tombs and relics. Unfortunately today little trace remains of this Constantinian basilica, with its glittering exterior mosaics and inlaid marble pavement trodden by generations of Christian pilgrims. At the beginning of the sixteenth century on the eve of the Protestant Reformation, Pope Julius II, faced with the prospect of carrying out major structural repairs to the 1100-year-old building, boldly decided to pull down the historic centre of Christian worship in Rome. He commissioned Donato Bramante and others to design and build a new, bigger and more splendid monument to the first of the popes.

The new Saint Peter's completed during the century that followed the Reformation with the help of artists such as Raphael and Michelangelo, became the visible symbol of the Counter-Reformation. This movement attempted to fight back against the success of Martin Luther's reforms, which had so seriously diminished the Catholic Church all over northern Europe. The arts of architecture, painting and sculpture were mobilized to bring life to a dynamic new Catholic vision of the universe. Baroque art aims to stab the heart and shock and delight the eye. A series of art-patron popes then went on to embellish the whole city of Rome with new churches, piazzas and streets; the sculptor and architect Gian Lorenzo Bernini was commissioned in the seventeenth century to build the colonnaded forecourt in front of the basilica which holds up to a quarter of a million people at today's papal outdoor masses or general audiences.

The miniscule Vatican City State as it exists today was delimited by the Lateran Treaties signed by Pope Pius XI (or more correctly his Secretary of State Pietro Gasparri) and the Italian Dictator Benito Mussolini in 1929. This agreement (under which the Italian State also paid compensation to the Pope for the loss of his territories) put an end to a transitional period which had existed for the previous half century since the abolition of the Papal States and the founding of the modern unified Italian State. For over fifty years the reigning Pope had been 'the prisoner of the Vatican', rarely venturing outside its walls except to the papal summer Villa at Castelgandolfo in the Alban hills.

A labyrinth of mediaeval streets and buildings which had previously hidden the impressive distant vista of Bernini's piazza and Carlo Maderna's façade for Saint Peter's was demolished at Mussolini's orders, and a triumphal approach to the See of Peter was hacked through the ruins. The naming of the street, the Via della Conciliazione, marked the official reconciliation between the initially anti-clerical Italian State and the Roman Catholic Church.

When you reach the coblestoned piazza at the end of Via Della Conciliazione you are already, technically, inside the Pope's kingdom. Joint Italian and Vatican territorial jurisdiction extends over the piazza; so, for example, when the assassination attempt on Pope John Paul took place there in 1981, Italian and Vatican security agents together arrested the Turkish terrorist Ali Agca, who was then handed over to the Italian authorities for trial.

For most Catholics visiting Rome, access to the Pope's kingdom is severely limited and over most of its area banned altogether. During daylight hours, you can walk around the piazza and into Saint Peter's freely, provided you are suitably attired. If you apply to your Embassy to the Holy See, you may be lucky enough to get a ticket for the Pope's regular Wednesday morning General Audience, held inside the modern Nervi audience hall in winter and in the open air in the piazza in summer. If you are a scholar, a student of archaeology or a VIP or can show some special justification, you may get a written permit to visit the tomb of the Apostle in the archaeological area under the crypt or consult books and manuscripts in the Vatican Library.

If you wish to see the Vatican gardens, you will have to join a guided tour and keep off the grass. Pope Pius XI, who reigned between the First and Second World Wars, was the keenest papal gardener of modern times. He not only planted the tallest tree now growing inside the Vatican, a giant sequoia from California, which is more than 100 feet tall and has to be secured by ropes to prevent it falling outside territorial limits, but accumulated a fine collection of orchids in the Vatican greenhouses, which he rebuilt. When he died in 1939, the papal orchid collection was sold to a Roman prince by his successor Pius XII, a man of more austere taste who anyway preferred roses.

Pius XI also installed a scientific drainage system for the Vatican gardens and buried miles of underground water pipes with automatic sprinklers for irrigation, enabling the carefully cropped lawns – a rare luxury in Rome – and the well-tended flower gardens to survive the searing Roman summer heat. An abundant water supply comes to the Vatican from Lake Bracciano, a freshwater lake lying in the crater of an extinct volcano thirty miles to the north of Rome. The water arrives in Vatican City through an ancient Roman aqueduct repaired by Pope Paul V at the beginning of the seventeenth century.

Pope John Paul employs only about thirty gardeners in comparison with Pius XI's garden staff of more than a hundred. They grow flowers and hothouse plants for the decoration of the Pope's private apartments and those of senior cardinals, and supply fresh vegetables for the Pope's table. The Vatican even produces its own honey from a dozen beehives hidden behind the hothouses.

These days almost as many visitors travel to Vatican City to see the Pope's art collection as to pray at Saint Peter's tomb. Two million visitors tramp each year through the miles of corridors of the Vatican museums, which house one of the world's richest collections of marble and bronze sculpture, manuscripts, paintings and *objets d'art*.

Museum entrance fees and the sale of Vatican City postage stamps to collectors go a long way towards meeting the running expenses of the City State, which levies no taxes or customs duties, but which manages, unlike the Holy See, to produce an annual surplus of a few million dollars. Just next to the railway station is the Governatorate or the equivalent of the Vatican's town hall, an office complex put up after the 1929 agreement to create the modern Vatican City State. Here ecclesiastics and lay clerical staff deal with such mundane matters as refuse collection, street lighting, fire prevention and traffic regulations (there is a chronic parking problem inside the Vatican and wheel clamps have been introduced by the Vatican gendarmerie in an attempt to discipline priestly parking offenders).

By far the most popular exhibit in Vatican City is the Sistine Chapel, where the conclave meets to elect a new Pope on the death of the incumbent. Michelangelo's monumental fresco paintings – the Creation (1508–12), which covers the entire vault of the ceiling, and the Last Judgement (1535–41), above the main altar – are newly restored, resplendent in their original colours. The Pope may not be the most innovative of the long list of papal patrons of the arts, but he must be given credit for having authorized what is perhaps the most important Italian art-restoration project of the twentieth century – the meticulous cleaning of Michelangelo's frescoes, darkened with the soot of four centuries of candle smoke and the dust and grime raised by millions of visitors.

One change inside Vatican City during Pope John Paul's reign of which the ordinary visitor will remain unaware has been the construction of a huge underground bunker. Here, twenty feet under the courtyard of the Belvedere Palace, is held the overflow of precious codexes, manuscripts, books and historical documents previously housed on the upper floors of the Vatican Library and the Secret Archive. The scale of the excavations – there are over thirty miles of new shelves – prompted rumours during the mid-1980s that the Pope was building a nuclear bunker for himself, his staff and his art treasures, as a precaution against an atomic holocaust. This was denied by Vatican officials.

The engineering works for the bunker were financed by a loan from

German Catholics, and by the sale of limited facsimile editions of some of the most famous volumes in the Vatican archive; they included an edition of Dante's Divine Comedy with illustrations by Sandro Botticelli, and the codex of Saint Benedict with illuminated miniatures painted by monks at the great Benedictine abbey of Montecassino during the eleventh century. A German publishing house presented the Pope with a high-technology printing press to produce the facsimiles, orders for which have been received from collectors and libraries around the world.

The Vatican Library, the oldest public library in the world, was founded by Pope Sixtus IV in 1475. It is consulted by up to 150 scholars every day. The Secret Archive, a separate collection, also open to scholars, had a complicated history. Many papal documents were removed to Avignon for safe keeping by Clement V in 1309 and it took five centuries to retrieve some of them. The whole collection was then taken off to France again by Napoleon's armies, and was shipped back to Rome only after the Congress of Vienna. Vatican archivists are still trying to persuade the Bibiothèque Nationale in Paris to return some of the indexes and catalogues.

Other commercial publishing ventures begun during John Paul's pontificate include the production and marketing of compact discs under a Vatican label, and the joint marketing with a Swiss company of solid gold reproductions of historic seals, including coronation seals of the Bourbons and the Hapsburgs attached to parchments and manuscripts in the Vatican archives.

The Pope's own apartments are situated on the top two floors of the Apostolic Palace. Below, there is an enfilade of high-ceilinged reception rooms facing south and east. They include the large papal study overlooking Saint Peter's Square, from the window of which John Paul addresses the crowds at his regular Sunday midday Angelus prayer; and the private library where he receives Heads of State and official visitors. The Pope's own penthouse apartment lies above. His living quarters are comfortable, but not luxurious. There is a gymnasium for exercise and a roof garden built by Paul VI, where John Paul often relaxes in the open air after lunch. Six Polish nuns take care of the cooking and cleaning and an Italian private valet serves at table. The Pope sometimes drinks a glass of white or red wine with his meals, but is no trencherman. On his travels he eats and drinks very little. He says mass in his private chapel at seven o'clock each morning. His secretaries and a few invited guests are present and normally take communion from his hand. They may be asked to remain behind to share a usually hearty breakfast, his preferred meal of the day. Lunch and dinner are usually also the occasion for continuing Church and diplomatic business at table.

King Karol's courtiers run the Roman Curia, as the central government of the Roman Catholic Church is officially known. The Curia in its present form is of relatively recent origin – the Catholic Church is still governed through structures set up during the Counter-Reformation. The modern Curia was the creation of the energetic late sixteenth-century Pope Sixtus V, who was also responsible for the building of many of Rome's monuments. The top body of the Holy See (not to be confused with the Vatican City Administration) is called the Secretariat of State; it is headed by the Pope's deputy (currently Italian Archbishop Angelo Sodano, a Vatican diplomat with long experience in Latin America) and is divided into two sections, one dealing with the Church's internal affairs, and one with the Vatican's international relations with other states (headed by a Frenchman, Jean-Louis Tauran).

The Holy See maintains one of the world's most extensive and cost-effective diplomatic services. It keeps representatives in 125 countries at the relatively modest cost of about 10 million dollars a year. Vatican diplomats – traditionally regarded as future ecclesiastical high-fliers – are trained at a pontifical academy for diplomats in Rome. Vatican ambassadors are called 'nuncios' when they are working in a country where the Catholic religion is dominant and where they automatically become deans of the local diplomatic corps; in countries where the Dean receives his status by seniority, the Vatican Ambassador is styled 'pro-nuncio'; elsewhere when the papal envoy is merely representing the Pope among the local Catholic Church and has no official accreditation to his host State he is called 'Apostolic Delegate.' From the world's capitals Vatican diplomats report by telegram and diplomatic bag to the eight language desks – Italian, Polish, English, German, French, Spanish, Portuguese and Latin – of the Secretariat of State. Financial economies are achieved by skeleton staffing arrangements and a certain amount of doubling up. In Africa and the Middle East, for example, envoys sometimes cover up to four different countries in a given region.

Very occasionally a Vatican nunciature becomes the scene of international attention. In December 1989 the ousted ruler of Panama, General Noriega, took refuge in the papal nunciature in Panama city when he was being chased by American troops after their invasion of his country. Following some frenetic days of negotiations, the General was finally persuaded to give himself up and was taken off to America for trial on drug-trafficking charges.

The internationalization of the Roman Curia, formerly heavily Italian-ized, began in earnest under the reign of Pope Paul VI and this process has continued under Pope John Paul. The Holy Office is currently under the command of a German cardinal, Propaganda is under a Czechoslo-vak, Bishops under an African, Education is run by an Italian, Justice and Peace by a Frenchman, Christian Unity by an Australian.

However, it would be misleading to suppose that the seemingly cosmo-politan character of the Curia makes it a true cross-section of world Catholic opinion. The Pope's men remain very much the Pope's own appointees, and can be relied upon to carry out his policies discreetly, obediently and to the letter.

Under the umbrella of the Secretariat of State come a series of 'Pontifi-cal Congregations', which can be loosely described as the equivalent of government departments in a secular State. Each is headed by a resident cardinal and has a specific Church responsibility. Lower down the Vati-can hierarchy come various councils and commissions which deal, among other matters, with relations with other Christian Churches, other religions, non-believers and the press.

Most prestigious of the Congregations is that for the Doctrine of the Faith, the former Holy Office and Inquisition, the Pope's watchdog which deals with wayward theologians. The Holy office used to be responsible for drawing up and maintaining the Vatican's Index of Prohibited Books (abolished in 1966). Once it was powerful enough to order the burning not only of offending texts but also of their authors. A monument in the Piazza Campo dei Fiori, one of Rome's busiest fruit and vegetable markets just across the river from the Vatican, commemor-ates one of the best-known victims of the Roman Inquisition, Giordano Bruno, mathematician, astronomer and precursor of modern science, burned alive for his allegedly heretical writings in 1600.

The congregation for Bishops is in charge of administering the world's 3,000 Catholic bishops and putting forward names for their replacement when they die, retire or become incapacitated by age. It is headed by an African cardinal from Benin, Bernardin Gantin.

The Congregation for the Clergy looks after the Catholic Church's 400,000 priests and the fabric of their churches. The Congregation for Institutes of Consecrated Life looks after over a million nuns and monks in the religious orders.

One of the busiest congregations deals with the dead, not the living. Pope John Paul will go down in history as the Pope who made the most saints. In the first thirteen years of his pontificate he raised to the altars more than 250 new saints and over 300 new blesseds. For the sake of comparison Paul VI created only 21 saints, and Pope John XXIII 10. (The technical distinction between venerating a Saint or a blessed is that the latter is considered to have reached only an intermediate stage on the road to full sainthood, and that his or her heroic virtues have been officially recognized for celebration at a local or regional level rather than worldwide by the whole Catholic Church).

Many of the new saints were proclaimed outside Rome during the Pope's worldwide travels. 'Sainthood is possible in all nations, in all civilizations, in all latitudes,' John Paul has said. 'The saints are truly among us!'

The Roman Catholic Church's calendar of saints has hitherto been heavily weighted in favour of the religious heroes of the old Catholic countries of Europe – Spain, Italy and France – and in favour of celibate priests and nuns.

'In Europe, we have been saint-making for a long time. We had a head start, while some Third World countries have not got a single blessed or saint,' said Robert Sarno, an American Jesuit priest who works at the Vatican's saint-making bureaucracy, the Congregation for the Causes of the Saints, located on the third floor of one of the Vatican offices overlooking Saint Peter's colonnade.

Many of the Pope's new saints come from Asia. During visits to South Korea and Japan he created a phalanx of new Catholic role models. In Rome, in June 1988, despite criticism from the Communist government in Hanoi that he was making an undesirable political statement by carrying out the ceremony in Rome, he carried out the biggest mass canonization in history. The Pope declared saints 95 Vietnamese and 26 European missionaries to Indo-China, who died during anti-Christian persecutions by the emperors of Tonkin in the days before the French took over modern Vietnam.

The process of selecting modern saints often involves the Pope in complex political judgements. The killing of Archbishop Romero in San Salvador comes under this category. Was his murder carried out for political or religious reasons? Similar considerations are also holding up decisions on the beatification of some victims of Nazism and of the Spanish Civil War whose names have been put forward as possible new saints.

At the offices of the Congregation for the Causes of Saints, theologians are poring over the case histories of 7 potential new saints from Thailand, a country which until the pontificate of John Paul never had a single official martyr. Two Thai nuns, Agnes Phila and Lucy Khambang, and five Thai Christian lay workers who were shot to death in December 1940 by order of the Siamese government during a period of crackdown against Christians in support of the country's official religion, Buddhism, are now potential candidates for sainthood. Their case or 'cause' as it is called in Vatican jargon, is being given special priority among more than 1,400 dossiers currently under examination by the Vatican's 'saint factory'. Ultimately it is the Pope who decides whether a given candidate or group of candidates for sainthood will have to wait a year, a decade or perhaps several more centuries before his, her or their heroic virtues gain special recognition by the Church.

Under new Vatican rules approved by John Paul in the fifth year of his reign, Catholic bishops all over the world are invited to identify new and timely candidates for official sainthood. One Rome parish priest, Father Piero Pintus, who was born in Monaco, was moved to start collecting signatures for the beatification of the movie actress Grace Kelly in Rome, Hollywood and Philadelphia, her home town, 'because of her moral stature as actress, wife and mother'.

Under the former rules only established religious orders usually had the necessary cash, time and dogged perseverance to lobby for their candidates in Rome. Now the process of becoming a saint can be started off in any diocese. And the Pope also relaxed the requirement that two authenticated miracles are required. In 1983 he reduced this to only one miracle. Most 'miracles' are medical cures inexplicable by science; occasionally other strange happenings are accepted as evidence of the supernatural at work.

One case was the sudden multiplication of food reported from a poor and hungry community in Olivenza, southern Spain, in 1949. Dozens of witnesses claimed under oath that they had seen three cupfuls of rice plunged into a pan of boiling water swell to provide food for 150 people after the invocation of a locally born and revered missionary friar Juan Macías, who had died in the seventeenth century in Peru.

Computers and VDUs have made their entry into the Vatican during the John Paul's reign, although there seems to have been little initial co-ordination between the different Congregations about installing compatible user-friendly software and in training computer operators. The 'saint factory' reported an inexplicable happening two years after their clerks had started to transfer the complete records of the department on to a computer system kindly provided by a donor in the United States. One morning operators found that the Congregation's computer had wiped clean all the patiently accumulated information on current and past saintly causes; they had to start the job again from scratch. An internal enquiry failed to reveal whether this should be put down to natural or supernatural causes and, if the latter, which frustrated saint or blessed might be considered responsible.

One of the most important Vatican departments is situated not inside the Vatican at all, but in a fine Renaissance palace near the Spanish Steps on the other side of the Tiber. This is the Congregation for the Evangelization of Peoples (formerly, and more familiarly, known as Propaganda Fide, the department in charge of the Roman Catholic Church's worldwide missionary operations). The head of this powerful department, which administers a huge and independent budget running into several hundred million dollars a year — several times the total running costs of the central administration at the Vatican – is colloquially known by Romans as the 'red Pope' (in counterpoint to the 'white Pope' John Paul and Father Peter-Hans Kolvenbach, the 'black Pope' who is head of the Jesuits). John Paul put in charge of this key office a fellow Slav, Cardinal Josef Tomko.

Propaganda looks after the affairs of what used to be called 'mission territories' – meaning most of the Third World's Catholic churches not yet deemed strong enough to stand on their own feet. The term 'mission territories' was dropped when it was realized that it has a racist tinge to it: the whole Church is now seen to have a missionary role; it would be demeaning to consider Nigeria, for example, a 'mission territory' when Nigerian priests may already be filling a missionary role in Europe.

Propaganda would also seem to be the most appropriate name for the Vatican's press and public relations department, but in fact this goes by the ponderous title of the Council of Social Communications. A daily bulletin of the Pope's engagements is published, plus a list of visiting bishops and VIPs who have been granted papal audiences and texts of papal speeches – a non-stop flood of words addressed to every conceivable interest group on the planet which fills a thick volume each year. Occasional news conferences are arranged in the Sala Stampa, or Vatican Press Office, but what really goes on behind the padded doors of curial offices is regarded by the priestly guardians of the Vatican as being top secret, as if the security of the Vatican City State was genuinely under threat by investigating hordes.

Wojtyla neither likes nor trusts the media. He finds its values shallow and its behaviour intrusive. He scans a wide range of daily and weekly newspapers from many countries. He is usually disappointed by journalists. He cannot see why they should not be glad to act as evangelizers.

His authoritarian side abhors the lack of control he has over the media, despite the fact that his activities have probably filled more column inches in the secular written press and have certainly received more air time on TV and radio than those of any other pontiff in history. Soon after his election he banned all senior Curial officials from talking on or off the record to the press. On the occasions when bishops and cardinals from around the world travel to Rome for Synods or other Vatican gatherings, members of the written press, including correspondents fully accredited to the Vatican, are kept firmly but politely out of the way. Members of the Vatican Press Corps are never permitted to sit in at Synod or other official Vatican meetings. They are briefed by priests who may be good propagandists or missionaries but who are not necessarily skilled in précis writing, or the assessment of the legitimate interests of readers, viewers or listeners. Full texts of speeches are rarely made available. Only by unofficial lobbying is it possible to work on Vatican stories. Official information at the Vatican is usually obtained at several removes from its original source. The gap between the Pope's professed desire to make the Vatican, as he once said, as 'transparent as a House of Glass' and the reality is glaring. The Vatican's accounts were grudgingly made public for the first time in 1988, but they did not detail much in the way of income and expenditure.

The appointment of a layman, a professional journalist from Spain, Joaquin Navarro Valls, as the Vatican's official press spokesman in 1984 raised hopes that the openness promised by King Karol was going to be realized. But Dr Navarro is also a committed member of the Opus Dei movement, which puts a different complexion upon his appointment.

Opus Dei, a right-wing religious movement founded among university students in Madrid in 1928 by a Spanish priest, Monsignor José Maria Escrivà de Balaguer, has many critics within and outside the Roman Catholic Church. They are concerned at its secretive nature, the hold it exerts upon many intelligent young Catholics and its obscure connections with the worlds of high finance, universities and the media.

In Britain, Cardinal Basil Hume has publicly criticized the recruitment methods of Opus Dei, which instructs its more youthful adherents to conceal their membership even from their parents in some cases.

Although Opus Dei presents itself as the equivalent of a major religious order, it cannot yet claim to be in the same league as the Society of Jesus. The Jesuits, as they are more commonly known, founded in the sixteenth century by a Spanish soldier, Saint Ignatius of Loyola, carried out the Church's first missionary attempts inside China, and are now best known for their worldwide educational activities. The Jesuits take a special oath of loyalty to the Pope and are uneasy about Opus Dei's ambitions. The current head of Opus Dei is Bishop Alvaro del Portillo. His priestly followers have increased in number by 60 per cent during Pope John Paul's years to over 1,600, while during the same period the number of Jesuit priests has diminished from 20,000 to 18,000.

Opus Dei, which is open to both men and women, now claims over 70,000 adherents all over the world. Just under 2 percent of members are priests. Most members are working professionals who agree to dedicate their lives to Christ while continuing at their normal jobs. Some agree to will their possessions to the movement. The founder moved to Rome in 1946, where he established Opus Dei's international headquarters. He died in 1975; six years later he was already an official candidate for sainthood at the Congregation for the Causes of the Saints, at that time under the command of a fervent supporter of Opus Dei, Cardinal Pietro Palazzini.

Pope John Paul demonstrated his personal support for Opus Dei in 1982 by agreeing to grant the movement the equivalent status of a major religious order by permitting it to rank as a 'personal prelature' under the Vatican's Congregation of Bishops. Technically this means that Monsignor del Portillo, a trained civil engineer as well as a bishop, now takes instructions directly from the Vatican; his diocese stretches worldwide and Opus Dei members are removed from the jurisdiction and control of local bishops. Opus Dei's known connections with the world of international banking have led to the suspicion that it was the channel which helped the Pope to provide secret funds for the growth of the Solidarity Catholic free trade union in Poland before and after the declaration of martial law in the early 1980s, as well as contributing to the huge *ex gratia* payment to the creditors of the failed Banco Ambrosiano, part owned by the Vatican. But an Opus Dei spokesman denied this and insisted that the movement has no connection with any financial organization or political party.

Apart from having its own man in the key position of official Vatican spokesman, Opus Dei makes no mystery about its ambition to take over Vatican Radio from the Jesuits, who have run Vatican broadcasting since the days of Guglielmo Marconi. The organization has now acquired a complex of buildings next to the church of San Girolamo in central Rome. After extensive restoration they have established there a centre

of higher ecclesiastical and theological studies where they hope to coun-
teract what they regard as the over-liberal tendencies of the Jesuit-run
Gregorian University, the principal pontifical theological college of Rome.

Opus Dei men are good courtiers. Pressmen are not. A report on the
Pope's visit to Spain in 1982 by Domenico Del Rio, a former Franciscan
who has been Vatican correspondent for the biggest circulation Italian
newspaper *La Repubblica* during most of the pontificate, was published
under the headline 'Spanish Faithful in a Trance for Wojtyla Superstar'.

It was not meant to be a humble visit. And it was not. Wojtyla was lauded by
the castes who hold power: ecclesiastical, military and political. He never arrived
in a city without being surrounded by the obsequious representatives of these
three ruling castes. The popular triumph came later, but it was held back by
bullet-proof glass and the police. In Spain the Vicar of Christ entered the house
of the King and posed for a smiling souvenir photograph with the royal family.
He never entered the house of a poor man. The poor, when hit by floods, are
viewed from a helicopter, or from the top of a mountain. The poor, especially
when they are out of work, are visited from the top of a platform, as happened
in a popular quarter of Madrid. The poor have no gilded salons, and perhaps
they also shoot.

In Madrid, at the Bernabeu Stadium, packed with young people mad with
enthusiasm for Wojtyla, there was a depressing sight. Even young people today
realize sadly that they are also courtiers. After the ovations, the songs, the
dances, which seemed to be a sign of youthful freshness, came the gifts.

Two by two, boys and girls climbed the steps of the dais bearing flowers,
fruit, rich cloth, carpets, a bullfighter's cloak. The stadium fell silent. A loud-
speaker boomed out a message about 'the colossal figure of His Holiness John
Paul II'. The boys and girls queued to kneel in front of the Pontiff to present
their gifts. Like the conquered to the conqueror. Wojtyla was up there, serious,
hunched on a low throne, his hands dangling from the armrests. He was not a
Pope, he was an oriental satrap.

On later travels in Africa the Pope would very occasionally ask his
motorcade to stop to allow him to enter the mud and wattle house of
a poor man for a quick glimpse of how the majority of mankind lives.
But Del Rio was right, humility was never Wojtyla's distinguishing mark;
most people who glimpsed the Pope during his travels saw him seated
or standing on a dais above the crowds.

Other articles in similar critical vein followed, but when Dr Navarro
took over at the press office, Del Rio found his name had been taken
off the list for the next papal charter flight. Like many other journalists

covering papal journeys he now feels freer if he makes his own travel arrangements.

The semi-official Vatican daily newspaper and propaganda organ *L'Osservatore Romano* was founded in the mid-nineteenth century. It has changed its style very little since then, although it now publishes extra weekly editions in Polish, French, English, German, Spanish and Portuguese. The *Osservatore*, which for a brief period during Fascism had the distinction of being the only uncensored newspaper in Italy, is not noted nowadays for the quality of its international reporting or for separating news from comment. Its unsigned editorials make heavy reading and it seems that the Catholic faithful have declined to follow the Pope's exhortation to buy the newspaper 'to follow the ordinary magisterium' of the Church. Total circulation is reputed to be less than 20,000 copies, mostly sold by subscription.

Inspired by the setting up of the first Polish free trade union, Solidarity, the Vatican's 2,000 or so lay employees – those who are not priests, nuns or members of the various religious orders – decided soon after the beginning of the Pope John Paul's reign to found their own trade union to press for higher wages and pensions. Vatican wages had remained indexed to the cost of living in the 1970s and had fallen way below remuneration levels inside Italy. Until Pope John Paul's reign, no one had ever dared to suggest that Vatican employees had enforceable labour rights. Notwithstanding the Pope's commitment to workers' rights expressed in his 1981 encyclical *Laborem Exercens*, it took ten years of negotiations for him finally to agree to set up his own labour office. It is called the Labour Office of the Apostolic See and appropriately, has premises in Via della Conciliazione.

In 1981 the Pope had rather offhandedly written to his Secretary of State about the prospects for organized labour inside his kingdom, 'It is not part of the social doctrine of the Church for this type of organization to indulge in strike action or class struggle, or to serve the interests of any political party . . .'

Mariano Cerullo, elected president of the Vatican trade union, found negotiating with senior officials of the Curia exasperating and extremely long winded. He felt they were getting nowhere; in February 1988 he organized the first recorded strike inside the Vatican when the payroll office suddenly announced that wages and salaries were going to be paid in arrears at the end of each month instead of in advance at the beginning of the month as previously.

It was a very gentlemanly strike. Workers stayed at their posts but announced they would voluntarily dock three hours' wages from their pay and give the money to the Pope to help feed the hungry somwhere in Africa. Archbishop Jan Schotte, in charge of the Labour Office, described the strike as 'completely unacceptable'. He angrily accused the Pope's employees of 'creating useless apprehension about the Church in the public mind' and at first refused to accept the 40,000–dollar cheque handed over by the union.

Conditions of service inside the Vatican – a basic thirty-six hour week – are not particularly onerous. Office hours are from eight in the morning until two in the afternoon six days a week, with a generous sprinkling of religious holidays added to the numerous Italian public holidays. It is practically impossible to get answers to urgent enquiries at the Vatican after lunch, except from a handful of senior members of the Curia who sometimes return to their desks to catch up with their backlog of work for an hour or two after the afternoon siesta.

Karol Wojtyla is not only the first Pope from Poland, he is also the first Pope who skis and enjoys hiking in the mountains. John Paul refused to allow the heavy duties of his office to deprive him totally of the chance to indulge in the sport that he enjoys most. After spending his first four Roman summers limited to the confines of the gardens of the papal villa at Castegandolfo (where he had promptly installed a twenty-five-metre swimming pool at the beginning of his reign) John Paul surprised everyone at the Vatican by taking off in 1984 for a short Alpine holiday in the Italian Dolomites in the company of his close friend, the unconventional octogenarian and President of Italy, Sandro Pertini. There, with a small party of bodyguards and his faithful secretary, he was able to take to the slopes again for the first time since he left Kraków, clad in black anorak, ski trousers and a woollen bonnet to protect him from the cold.

During subsequent winters the Pope often made unannounced day trips from the Vatican to ski resorts in the Abruzzi mountains of central Italy, where a *piste* was closed off by police for his private use. In summer he started to take a regular week or ten-day holiday in the Alps during July. He usually stayed in a church-owned chalet, going for long mountain hikes with a stout walking stick each morning, sometimes sharing a modest picnic of bread, sardines and salami with mountain guides, and surprising more than one lonely woodsman by knocking unannounced on the door of his hut. One day he shared a meal which included the local delicacies – polenta and stewed goat – in the home of a village priest. Sometimes he would take a helicopter trip to a near-by glacier to get in a few hours of summer skiing. Groups of young Catholics occasionally exchanged a few words with the Pope during these Alpine interludes. He usually managed to give a suitable ecological twist to their meetings, telling one group, 'The command up here in the mountains is "Walk!" And the next command is "Breathe!" Looking after the earth's resources is a moral duty.'

Asked whether he did not feel better in the fresh mountain air than in the 'prison of Saint Peter's' he replied diplomatically, 'I must say you have to know that prison to appreciate this freedom!'

The Pope's renowned reluctance to take time off surfaced even during these short breaks in the mountains. Arriving in the Alps for his latest summer break, he announced that besides taking some long hikes he would also be working on a new encyclical and learning a new language – Hungarian – in preparation for a pastoral visit to that country. 'This vacation won't simply be *"dolce far niente"* – lazing time away', he informed reporters who toiled up the mountain valley to his Italian summer hideaway at Introd in the Val d'Aosta. 'There are other things to do!'

During most of the year, every Sunday afternoon, the Pope leaves his Vatican kingdom. He puts aside his care for the Universal Church and becomes for an hour or two the ordinary Bishop of Rome, chief pastor of a city that, as he once remarked, is beginning to resemble a Third World metropolis. The Pope's five hundred parish visits have taken him above all into the sprawling suburbs which mushroomed around Rome after the Second World War, and which are visibly lacking the amenities and the public services worthy of a European capital city. During these visits he has been kept informed by his parish priests about the problems of abandoned old people, the mentally infirm who wander about the streets now that Italy has closed its lunatic asylums, the drug addicts, the homeless, the jobless coloured migrants, the gipsy robber bands, the purse snatchers and the AIDS victims. Ordinary Roman parish priests have been frequent guests at the Pope's dinner table, rubbing shoulders with princes of the Church from far countries.

The contrast between the artistic and cultural treasures of the Vatican and Rome, and the reality of daily life in a city that is now representative of de-Christianized Europe, strikes the Pope every time he leaves the Apostolic Palace in his limousine for one of his city engagements.

'Rome is a city with two faces,' he told Mayor Pietro Giubilo when the first citizen called at the Vatican to present his New Year greetings in 1989. 'Next to immense treasures of religious, cultural and human wealth may be observed sectors of multiple moral ills; corners of the Third World; points of great wealth and pockets of great poverty. There are the few who possess much and the many who possess little.'

The decline in daily mass attendance at Rome's 900 churches may not be directly attributable to John Paul's influence at the Vatican, but the fact remains that most weekday and even Sunday masses attract only a handful of believers. Father Livio Pescaroli, a Roman parish priest with a theoretical flock of 30,000 told the Pope at a diocesan meeting in 1989 that average attendance at Sunday mass in his church is barely 3 per cent. It is rare for the dying to ask for the last sacraments to be administered. At baptisms godparents have no idea of their religious responsibilities, they simply give an expensive present. In fact the word 'padrino' (Godfather) in Italian has now lost all religious significance and is normally taken to refer to the Mafia.

Four out of five Roman couples may still choose to be married in church rather than at the City Hall, and there is a splendid choice of ancient and beautiful Roman edifices for society weddings. At the same time, cohabitation outside marriage has become much more common-place during Wojtyla's pontificate. The number of both civil and religious marriages celebrated in Rome dropped by a quarter during the 1980s and divorces more than doubled. One out of three Roman marriages now ends in separation or divorce.

Meanwhile evangelical Christian sects continue to win converts in the capital of Catholicism. The Cardinal Vicar of Rome during the greater part of John Paul's pontificate, Ugo Poletti, said he was particularly worried about the Jehovah's Witnesses, who with ninety-five communities and 17,000 members in Italy have made Rome their headquarters for Europe, Africa and Asia. This essentially administrative decision became in the eyes of the Curia a symbolic throwing down of the gauntlet to the headquarters of the Roman Catholic Church.

CHAPTER 10

Peter's Pence

Go and sell that thou hast, and give to the poor, and thou shalt have treasure in heaven.

Matthew 19:21

Take nothing for the journey, neither staves, nor scrip, neither bread, neither money . . .

Luke 9:3

When Karol Wojtyla took over his Vatican City kingdom in 1978 he found he had inherited from his predecessor a worrying financial crisis. The fabled wealth of the Vatican existed only in the popular imagination, certainly not in the Vatican's bank deposits and share certificates.

The accounts of the central government of the Roman Catholic Church are one of the world's most closely guarded secrets. The former Cardinal from Kraków, who had administered the financial affairs of Poland's second most important diocese for many years, had no difficulty in reading the balance sheet when his financial advisers put the figures before him for the first time.

Cardinal Egidio Vagnozzi, the Holy See's Comptroller, told his master that expenditure was outstripping income by about 12 million dollars a year, and that he would have to dip into investment capital to make ends meet. Circulars had gone round to all heads of department asking them to trim their expenses and see if they could manage with fewer staff. Contributions to the Papacy from Catholics around the world had been falling off steadily during the last years of Paul VI's pontificate. During the reign of Pope John XXIII at the end of the 1950s contributions had risen to as much as 15 million dollars per annum, but by 1970 the figure had fallen to under 4 million dollars. A new fund-raising campaign was well overdue.

The reason for the steady increase in expenditure was the Vatican's greatly extended administrative activities resulting from the decision of the Second Vatican Council to open up relations between Rome and the outside world. Ten new Vatican departments had been created. Regular meetings of bishops from all over the world entailed expensive airfares and board and lodging, all on a much larger scale than in the more leisurely days of Pius XII. The Vatican payroll was also increasing, to the point where more than half the total costs of running the Church's headquarters were attributable to wages and salaries. In former days not only did much of the Vatican's work devolve upon clerics or nuns who were paid low wages, but a devoted band of Italian lay workers performed the menial tasks of the Vatican City State in feudal style, often continuing from one generation to another in the Pope's employ, content to accept low remuneration in exchange for the honour and lifelong security of a Vatican job.

In 1991 the financial stewardship of Pope John Paul has not apparently led to any radical improvement in the situation. The annual deficit has risen fivefold (see Appendix A) and the formerly financially independent papacy is still spending almost twice its annual income. In 1988, an appeal had to be made to the world's 3,000 Roman Catholic bishops to collect funds and pledges of continuing financial support for the central administration of the Church to stave off bankruptcy.

At the eye of the storm was the Pope's chief banker, Archbishop Paul Casimir Marcinkus. After having become the subject of worldwide publicity and unfavourable comment for involving the Holy See in a major Italian Banking scandal, he was quietly retired by the Pope in 1990 and went back to work as an ordinary priest in his home diocese. The story was splashed in the gossip columns all round the world. Pictures of Marcinkus were even sandwiched between the nudes in the pages of the French edition of *Penthouse* magazine. The Vatican Bank was forced to pay out more than 240 million dollars in part compensation to the creditors of an associate bank, the Banco Ambrosiano, which had gone into forced liquidation after its chairman, Roberto Calvi, fled the country and was subsequently found dead in London.

The reputation of the Holy See suffered from Pope John Paul's decision to maintain almost total secrecy over the disastrous management of the Vatican's own private bank, the Istituto per le Opere di Religione (Institute for the Works of Religion, or IOR in the Italian acronym), during the 1970s and 1980s. His stubborn refusal for many years to remove Archbishop Marcinkus from his post – for fear of confirming at best ineptitude, and at worst, fraud – was equally damaging. The only indication that the banker from Cicero, Illinois, might have disappointed his employer came when he was twice passed over for promotion to Cardinal, and when in 1983 he was suddenly removed from his post as bodyguard and chief organizer of the Pope's foreign travels. Father Roberto Tucci, a Jesuit formerly in charge of Vatican Radio, replaced him as papal travel organizer.

Indeed, for the sake of appearances, Archbishop Marcinkus was appointed acting Governor of Vatican City State and remained for another six years at the head of the IOR, a job he had held since 1971 when Pope Paul VI rewarded him for successfully organizing papal foreign travel. Once the spotlight of publicity had been switched off, he was gradually eased out. Marcinkus's job as bank director was abolished and a troika of experienced professional bankers from Germany, the United States and Switzerland was brought in to oversee the running of the Vatican bank.

Although the sums administered by the Holy See may be paltry in comparison with the budget of even a modest-sized international business corporation, outside observers – and the English-speaking Catholic world in particular – felt considerable unease. It was simply not good enough for Vatican officials to complain that the Archbishop had been duped by scheming Italian financiers, nor for the Pope to deplore the 'brutal' treatment meted out by the world's media to his chief Banker. Ordinary Catholics faced with an urgent appeal by Rome to dig deeper into their pockets for more funds wanted to know, in the words of Professor Michael Dummet, the eminent British Roman Catholic layman and Wykeham Professor of Logic at Oxford University, how John Paul's bank had engaged in practices 'from which the most pungent stink of corruption arises'.

And if suspicions were voiced by lay people in rich Western countries, how much more scandalous did the stories from Rome appear to religious workers operating on shoestring budgets in the developing world. The Holy Cross Sisters of São Paolo in Brazil, for example, used to run an expensive girls' school for the local élite until they decided that their true place should be with the poor. They sold off their school buildings and went to live in the shanty towns of the biggest city in the southern hemisphere. Sister Mary Nolan, an American nun of the Holy Cross order, put it this way, 'For many centuries the Church has been connected with power and money, and has been identified with power and money. What we are trying to say is that we must identify with simple people. Not that we should become completely like them – we have our books, our cars, our education. But we try as much as possible to identify with them and to share in their struggles.'

In order to follow the sometimes unedifying history of how the successors of Saint Peter have run Church finances, two preliminary points must be made.

First, the Vatican has always held to a quite obsessive secrecy over money matters. Behind the bronze doors all facts concerning finance, including budgets and balance sheets, are regarded as State secrets. Not without reason are the office doors of all the senior financial administrators in the Vatican doubled and padded with soundproofing material for security. Twentieth-century writers on the finances of the Vatican all admit that they have based their researches largely upon guesswork and deduction. Although under Pope John Paul II, the Vatican has at last begun to publish a few general heads of income and expenditure, and has promised to call in outside auditors, there is as yet little sign of any sense of true public accountability.

Second, popes have traditionally been big spenders – always of course in the interests of the Church and for the greater glory of God. They have been responsible for embellishing the city of Rome with impressive and expensive churches, palaces, villas, monumental gardens and fountains, and for commissioning great works of sculpture and painting.

The origin of regular papal income known today as 'Peter's Pence', formerly a voluntary tax paid by Church members, dates back to Anglo-Saxon times. The romscot was a tax originally created by the kings of Mercia. Each year money was sent to Rome from British pilgrims to pay, among other papal expenses, for oil for the lamps in the basilicas of Saint Peter and Saint Paul. In the Middle Ages feudal dues were collected in many other parts of Europe and paid to the Pope, sometimes in exchange for his military protection.

With the creation of the papal territories of central Italy, the popes financed themselves with taxes and customs dues just like other temporal rulers. They also created and sold for profit offices of State and sinecures with such intriguing titles as 'Bearer of the Golden Rose'. In times of financial crisis they did what any other monarch did in similar circumstances. Pope Innocent VIII pawned the papal tiara. Pope Gregory XVI went to the Rothschilds' merchant bank in Paris for loans.

The last non-Italian Pope before Karol Wojtyla, Hadrian VI from Utrecht in the Netherlands, who reigned in the mid-sixteenth century, had set out on a radical economy drive which involved abolishing the sale of titles. But his cardinals rebelled against northern parsimony and obstructed his planned reforms.

Sixtus V, at the end of the sixteenth century, was the most successful and ruthless financier of all the Renaissance popes. He administered the finances of the Holy See with consummate skill, amassing a fortune of five million gold crowns as a reserve for his successors, which he placed in treasure chests still to be seen in the fortress of the Castel Sant'Angelo. 'The Pope considers not only the waves which rock the barque of Peter, but also the storms that threaten from a distance . . . He follows the example of the fathers of the Old Testament who used to keep a considerable sum of money in the temple of the Lord,' Sixtus wrote.

In the nineteenth century, Sixtus's treasure having long since been squandered, financial mismanagement of the Papal States led to a popular uprising. In 1848 Pius IX had to flee to Gaeta on the coast south of Rome to escape the anger of the mob and was only able to return home under the protection of French troops.

At the suggestion of a group of French Catholics, the mediaeval custom of Peter's Pence was revived in 1849. This contribution, still collected all over the world in Catholic churches on the last Sunday in June, the feast of Saints Peter and Paul, gradually became the main financial support of the Papacy, when all other income from the Papal States ceased with their incorporation into the new kingdom of Italy in 1870.

Although the new Italian State offered an annual contribution to the Holy See of 3.25 million lira, Pius IX and his successors, fearing this might imply acceptance of the political and economic *status quo*, haughtily refused the money. It was not until the signing of the Lateran Treaties in 1929, that the finances of the Vatican were once again put on a proper financial and legal footing with acceptance by the Pope of financial compensation for the loss of his temporal empire.

The terms were 750 million Italian lira in cash plus consolidated 5 per cent Italian state bonds to a value of one billion lira. A special Commission of Cardinals and Italian financiers decided to divide the investment as follows: one-third in Italian stocks and shares, one-third in real estate and one-third in gold and cash. The Italian stocks bought by the Holy See included banks, public utilities, real estate and insurance companies, and industrials.

In 1942, Pius XII took an important although unpublicized step. He set up the Vatican's own bank, the Istituto per le Opere di Religione. According to its articles of association the bank was to look after the 'capital, in cash or shares, and real estate of persons or organizations, destined for Christian charity'.

Although the Vatican insists that the IOR is not a bank in the ordinary sense of the word, it acts and looks exactly like a bank. I have personally exchanged foreign currency at its premises inside the Apostolic Palace, which are complete with cashiers, counters, exchange facilities and patient customers, mostly priests or nuns, waiting in line.

The IOR runs both current and deposit accounts. As it operates from Vatican territory, it has never been bound by Italy's formerly stringent exchange-control laws. Customers, limited to Vatican City residents, members of religious orders, and diplomats accredited to the Holy See, are expected to contribute a proportion of their stipends and salaries to charity in exchange for the advantages they enjoy in bypassing Italian banking laws and the anonymity granted for all international transactions.

The story of how Archbishop Marcinkus rose to become head of the bank and the key figure in Vatican finance throws an interesting light upon the management methods of the Roman Catholic Church in the second half of the twentieth century.

Paul Marcinkus was born in Cicero, Illinois, in 1922, the fourth son of a family of poor Catholic migrants from Lithuania. His father was a window cleaner. He grew up during the years of the Depression in the heyday of Chicago gangsterdom.

The young Paul, a giant of a man standing six foot four inches in his socks and a keen sportsman, was picked out by his local parish priest as a student of promise. He completed his secondary education at a Chicago seminary, was ordained priest in 1947 and was sent to study in Rome. He obtained adequate but not brilliant degrees in canon law and diplomatic studies, and one summer obtained a temporary clerk's job at the real seat of power inside the Vatican, the Secretariat of State. His face fitted. He met powerful future friends, among them the brilliant financier Cardinal Francis Spellman, Archbishop of New York (the world's richest Catholic diocese), and also a top Italian prelate, Giovanni Battista Montini, later to become Pope Paul VI.

Within a year or two of entering the Vatican administration at the bottom of the ladder, Marcinkus was confirmed in his future career. He was sent first to Bolivia, to work as assistant to the Vatican's diplomatic representative in La Paz, and then to Canada. He returned to the Vatican during the pontificate of John XXIII and began working in the English-language section of the Secretariat of State.

This was the period of the Second Vatican Council. Marcinkus, by now a fluent Italian speaker, became a valuable go-between with the Vatican administration for senior American prelates attending the Council. He set up a travel and information office to help American bishops, and gave a valuable concession to a friend, Stefano Falez, a migrant from Yugoslavia, to found what in effect later became a Vatican-approved travel agency called 'Catintour'. Falez was given a small office inside Vatican territory and he and his wife became directors of this lucrative commercial venture set up, according to the articles of association, to 'develop all activities relative to travel and tourism especially for Catholics'. Later Catintour was to issue air tickets for the travels of Pope John Paul II, and Stefano Falez used to appear as 'baggage master' on papal flights.

Marcinkus's big chance came as a result of another close friendship which developed within the walls of the Vatican – with Don Pasquale Macchi, private secretary to Pope Paul VI. When Pope Paul was planning his first visit abroad to Jerusalem in 1964 he needed a heavyweight fixer who spoke English. Marcinkus seemed perfect. His burly physique and extrovert manner put the Pope's mind at rest both over security and protocol matters.

The Holy Land visit, the first outside Italy by a reigning Pope this century, was deemed a great success by Pope Paul, even if he was mobbed by enthusiastic crowds. Marcinkus had acted as the Pope's bodyguard when the crowds in Jerusalem nearly went out of control. When the Pope decided to visit India and later the United Nations in New York, it was natural that he should turn once again to Marcinkus for assistance, as he was unable to speak English fluently. Marcinkus would coach the Pope in pronunciation each time he had to make a speech in English.

There is an unwritten rule inside the Vatican that once a task has been performed successfully in a certain way a precedent has been created. Marcinkus became part of the Vatican Establishment. He was promoted to the grade of 'Domestic Prelate' and became official body-guard and travel organizer for all Pope Paul's subsequent foreign journeys. Pope Paul's last and longest journey took place just before Christmas in 1970, when he made a gruelling swing through Asia and the South Pacific. Marcinkus saved Pope Paul's life during a stopover in the Philippines, when at Manila airport a deranged Bolivian artist called Benjamin Mendoza lunged at the pontiff with a knife. The ecclesiastical bodyguard, towering over the entourage, easily disarmed the assailant, who shouted at the Pope that his aim was only to rid the world of superstition.

In January 1969, Marcinkus was duly rewarded with promotion to Archbishop. He was also given new responsibility as secretary to the Vatican Bank, the IOR, even though he had no professional training whatsoever in banking or financial administration. According to one of his Vatican colleagues, he could not even read a balance sheet. He entered the world of Vatican finances at a crucial moment. Pope Paul, as part of a major reform of the Vatican's administrative and financial structures, had decided to move the major part of the Vatican's investment capital outside Italy and to abandon the practice of having Vatican nominees on the boards of companies in which the Holy See had a major stake.

A new Prefecture for Economic Affairs was set up to co-ordinate all the Holy See's financial activities. The Administration for the Patrimony of the Holy See (APSA) was created to handle the investment side with a mainly lay staff of professionals.

Yet despite such measures Pope Paul, on a visit to the island of Sardinia, one of the poorest parts of Italy, felt able to plead poverty. 'How easy it would be to demonstrate that the "fabulous riches" which from time to time public opinion attributes to the Church, are often insufficient for the modest and legitimate needs of ordinary life,' he told the people of Cagliari.

The Church's newly enunciated view of private property, as stated in Paul VI's encyclical *Populorum Progressio*, was critical of liberal capitalism; yet at the same time the Vatican's contacts with the world of business were growing. This basic inconsistency was to become even more glaring during the reign of Pope John Paul II.

Michele Sindona, a Sicilian financier who was later sentenced to twenty-five years in gaol in the United States for massive bank fraud, now entered on the scene. Sindona, who had manoeuvred his way to becoming owner of one of the biggest Italian merchant banks, apparently convinced the financially untutored Marcinkus that it was high time that the Vatican began to enjoy the fruits of its huge assets. Pope Paul himself was once reported to have described Sindona, with his plan to multiply the Vatican's capital just as Christ multiplied the loaves and fishes in the Bible story, as a 'man sent from God'. The tripling in value of the American dollar in relation to the Italian lira in the years following the purchase of Gulf and Western, General Motors, and other well-known American blue chip stocks and shares apparently showed that the Pope had made a wise decision. But neither Pope Paul nor Marcinkus were aware that Sindona, while he was advising the Vatican on restructuring its share portfolio, was simultaneously engaged in fraudulent deals which had left his Banca Unione and his Banca Privata Italiana almost without capital.

To make matters worse, at about this time another Italian financier joined the small group of 'consultants' involved in Vatican finances. Sindona took under his wing Roberto Calvi, who during the 1960s had masterminded the rapid expansion of the Banco Ambrosiano, a small provincial Catholic bank set up at the turn of the century in Milan. Calvi had turned the Ambrosiano into an extremely profitable organization with branches all over Italy. As he now wanted to expand abroad, he consulted Sindona, an acknowledged expert on profitable banking havens in such fiscal paradises as the Cayman Islands, the Bahamas, Liechtenstein, Luxembourg and, perhaps, the Vatican.

Calvi became chief executive of the Banco Ambrosiano in 1970 and set up a holding company in Luxembourg as the springboard for his future international operations.

He also rented a luxurious winter residence at Lyford Cay near Nassau in the Bahamas. At the New Year in 1971, Marcinkus, a keen golfer and an admirer of Caribbean beaches – he once went for a holiday to Guatemala with Pope Paul's secretary Don Macchi – was a house guest there together with Sindona. This was a decisive moment in Marcinkus's rise to power. Within a few weeks the priest from Cicero had been promoted to be head of the Vatican Bank, the IOR, and Calvi became director general at Ambrosiano. The scene was set for the Vatican's involvement in the first of two huge international financial swindles.

According to Sindona, who in 1986 was finally extradited from the United States to Italy to face fraud charges but died after drinking a cup of poisoned coffee in Milan prison before he could spill any further embarrassing secrets, Marcinkus and Calvi became close associates. Marcinkus was convinced by Calvi's argument that a good way to combat Marxism and promote economic order in the South American continent, shortly to contain more than 50 per cent of the world's Catholics, would be to channel Vatican investments there. It might even be possible to turn a useful profit as well.

On 23 March 1971 a new bank, the Cisalpine Overseas Bank, was registered in Nassau. The joint owners were Calvi's Luxembourg holding company, the Finabank of Geneva (which belonged to Sindona and in which the IOR was a major shareholder) and the IOR itself.

Sindona's fall was not long in coming. In September 1974 the kingpin of his banking empire, the Banca Privata, went into enforced liquidation with losses to the Vatican estimated at 27 million dollars. Then in October the Franklin National Bank of New York, the twentieth largest bank in the United States, which he had acquired four years earlier, collapsed after the injection of huge amounts of federal funds. In January 1975 the Finabank was closed by the Swiss authorities with losses of at least 50 million dollars.

In 1978, the year that Karol Wojtyla was elected Pope, the Bank of Italy, an institution that is regarded highly for its professionalism and probity among the world's central bankers, but which has no jurisdiction whatsoever over the banking activities of the Vatican, decided to carry out a detailed investigation into the activities of the Banco Ambrosiano. What the Bank of Italy's twelve inspectors found in the books kept at the Ambrosiano headquarters in Milan was not reassuring. They discovered that a foreign network had been set up which allowed the bank to move large sums of money abroad virtually uncontrolled by the Italian currency authorities. In a detailed 500-page report the inspectors also voiced suspicions that Calvi might be using the classic technique of lending money to himself to buy control of new acquisitions, a merry-go-round system that he had learned from the Grand Master of international financial juggling, Michele Sindona. The inspectors found serious breaches in banking law, and reported that the Ambrosiano was under capitalized and so poorly organized that Calvi seemed able to do whatever he liked with the bank's funds.

Apparently these warning notes never reached the ears of the men running the Vatican's finances. Archbishop Marcinkus, who now resumed his frenetic travel organizing activities on behalf of the new Pope (it had been nine years since Pope Paul had carried out his last foreign tour) at the same time as he continued to run the IOR, was about to compromise the Vatican once again.

In between jetting around the world administering the first papal visits to Mexico, the United States, Poland, Africa and Britain, the Archbishop had been taking part in overseas financial operations. These must have aroused his suspicions that Calvi's banking operations were not always above board.

Another obscure episode involving the Bank of Italy must also have provided food for thought to both Pope John Paul and Marcinkus. In March 1979 the Deputy General Manager of the Central Bank, Mario Sarcinelli, was suddenly arrested by police and taken off to prison. He was charged with concealing evidence from magistrates investigating a financial scandal unconnected with Calvi. The Governor of the bank was similarly accused but spared the indignity of gaol because of his age. This amounted to an unprecedented political vendetta against two of Italy's best-respected public servants Sarcinelli and the much-respected Governor, Paolo Baffi, knew they were the victims of a political plot aimed perhaps at 'punishing' them for causing trouble for Calvi and his friends. The charges were never proved, but Baffi resigned, disillusioned after a career of more than forty years at the Central Bank in Rome.

Even after Calvi had been arrested in 1981, and sentenced to four years' imprisonment for fraudulent share dealings and breaches of Italian exchange-control regulations (he was released on appeal having only served just over two months in pre-trial detention), Marcinkus issued 'letters of comfort' to Calvi on the Vatican Bank's headed notepaper. They were addressed to subsidiary banks of the Ambrosiano group, one in Peru and another in Nicaragua, confirming that the Vatican had an interest in dummy companies to which Calvi had made large loans. Although letters of comfort do not provide any legal guarantee that the signatory will repay loans, they are often issued to reassure lenders that a borrowing company has reputable backing. Calvi, by now a desperate man with his financial empire caving in around him, had promised the Vatican Bank in writing when he requested those letters of comfort that by giving its moral guarantee it would suffer no loss. Legally, at least, Marcinkus was in the clear.

Although Marcinkus may have felt he was acting to safeguard the IOR's own interests as well as those of his friend Calvi, it must already have been clear that he was wading deep in murky financial waters. Worse was to come. Calvi suddenly disappeared in June 1982. Although he had surrendered his passport pending the hearing of the appeal against his 1981 sentence, he managed to escape to Britain by a circuitous route, only to be found dead in London on 18 June.

Calvi had apparently committed suicide by hanging himself from scaffolding under Blackfriars bridge in the City. The coroner's verdict of suicide was however overturned a year later, when an appeal was heard and an open verdict was recorded. Calvi's family and most Italians continued to believe that he had been murdered. Calvi's widow Clara told an Italian newspaper that her husband's death was connected with 'ferocious struggles for power in the Vatican' and said her husband had used to tell her, 'The priests are out to get me.' The Vatican, of course, officially denied such a claim as 'groundless fabrication,' but it singularly failed to explain how a high-ranking Vatican prelate later came to be involved with the disposal of the contents of Calvi's briefcase, which had disappeared after his death.

There was a run on deposits, both at home and abroad. Ambrosiano's provisions for bad debts were totally insufficient. The Bank of Italy put a board of commissioners into Milan to try to save the situation, and the Big Six – the leading Italian commercial banks – formed a rescue pool to underwrite the immediate needs of the country's largest private banking group. But news of the débâcle spread quickly and the Banco Ambrosiano was formally declared bankrupt by a Milan court on 26 August. The Ambrosiano went bust owing the not inconsiderable sum of 1,287 million dollars – later jovially described by Marcinkus as 'a heck of a lot of money'.

Pope John Paul had to take immediate action over the international furore which now broke out. The first semi-official Vatican reaction was to blame everything upon the wicked international press. In an editorial headlined 'The Lies of the Media', L'Osservatore Romano commented: 'Calvi's links with the Vatican Bank have caused things to be written which offend the elementary canons of information and are completely lacking in seriousness and competence. The insinuations have not spared the person of the Holy Father himself.'

The Pope had already appointed a committee of three prominent lay Catholic bankers, an Italian, an American and a Swiss to examine the books of the IOR and the embarrassing 'letters of comfort'. Predictably they advised the Pope that there was no legal obligation on the part of the Vatican Bank to reimburse those defrauded by Calvi. The Pope stood by his chief banker, who insisted to his employer, as he insisted to everyone else, that he had been guilty of no wrongdoing. Marcinkus replied to a query from the Italian Treasury that he had no knowledge of the shadowy Panamanian finance companies mentioned in the 'letters of comfort', and claimed he owed nothing to Calvi or his bank. He had simply been duped.

The College of Cardinals, the supreme consultative body of the church, was summoned to meet in Rome in November. Almost one hundred Cardinals gathered from around the world to discuss a confidential report on the involvement of the Vatican in the Banco Ambrosiano scandal. They heard not from the chief protagonist Archbishop Marcinkus, but from the Vatican Secretary of State Cardinal Casaroli, entrusted personally by the Pope with sorting out the mess.

The Pope set the tone for the meeting in a letter to his chief executive

Casaroli, the text of which was released on the eve of the meeting. He defined the rights and duties of his Vatican staff in lofty terms. The Pope wrote:

The singular community that operates in the shadow of Saint Peter is not a typical state. It does not possess the ordinary characteristics of a political community. The Holy See governs the Universal Church and carries out its pastoral work for the benefit of the entire human race.

The persons who take part in its activities are with rare exceptions not citizens of the Vatican City State, and therefore have none of the rights and duties which ordinarily belong to citizenship, including the payment of taxes.

The Pope did not mention of course that Archbishop Marcinkus was one of these 'rare exceptions' and the bearer of a Vatican diplomatic passport.

'The Holy See cannot carry on the economic activities proper to a State. The production of wealth and the growth of income do not form part of its aims.' Now came the key point: 'The main source of support for the Holy See must be spontaneous offerings from Catholics, and other men of good will, all over the world. There must be no resort to other financial means which might not appear to respect the peculiar character of the Vatican.'

The Pope went on to ask his staff, both religious and lay, to show a spirit of parsimony in their work, and to take into account the 'real, limited financial possibilities of the Holy See'. This was the closest he came to rapping the knuckles of his ambitious chief banker.

Cardinal Casaroli's report to the meeting contained few surprises except for a controversial disclaimer. He said the IOR was not really a bank at all 'in the common sense of the term'.

He went on to explain that 'it is natural that the Institute for the Works of Religion has to use the banking services it deems necessary; the profit made will not go, as in the case of banks, to shareholders (which do not exist in the case of the IOR) but will be used in favour of "works of religion", which among other things can also make use of loans on conditions notably more favourable that current ones determined by the money market'.

Casaroli told his fellow cardinals that the Vatican would for the moment continue to keep silent about the 'extremely complex situation' resulting from the relationship between the Vatican Bank and the Ambrosiano. He deplored a smear campaign by the media.

The Pope himself wound up the four days' proceedings. Speaking in

Latin, he made one of his two recorded public statements about the Ambrosiano affair. He promised full co-operation with investigating authorities in establishing the 'whole truth', and attempted to refute the popular image of the headquarters of the Universal Church as a playground for international financial speculators.

'The Holy See lives on charity, which is the distinguishing mark of the Christian presence in the world. It has to carry out its universal mission with extremely limited means. The Vatican's budget, in comparison with the expenses of other organizations of a political, social or international nature, is truly comparable to the biblical "widow's mite". Those who administer the finances of the Holy See must act in a spirit of meticulous responsibility and a spirit of parsimony.'

Pope John Paul then dropped the whole subject of Church finances and went on to announce 'an event of great joy'. This was his decision to call a special Holy Year to celebrate the 1,950th anniversary of Christ's death the following year. Holy Years are normally declared only once every twenty-five years. Roman cynics said the real purpose of the extra jubilee, celebrated only eight years after the previous official Holy Year called by Pope Paul in 1975, was to bring millions of pilgrims to Rome and so bail the Vatican out of its financial troubles with their contributions. In the event, the 1983 Holy Year was a financial flop. Visitors were far fewer than forecast and they spent far less than expected, according to the tour operators who are the best-informed sources on the subject.

Meanwhile a joint commission of enquiry was set up by the Italian government and the Pope to determine the exact financial liabilities of the Vatican in the Ambrosiano affair. A West German banker in his eighties, Hermann J. Abs, was also brought in to join the 'three wise men' appointed internally by the Pope to sort out the problems of the IOR. The appointment was criticized by Jews, who alleged that Abs had been the head of Hitler's Central Bank from 1940 to 1945 and had also been a director of IG Farben, notorious as an employer of Jewish slave labour during the Second World War.

After months of haggling between Italian and Vatican experts it became clear that there was no chance of agreement over the ultimate responsibility of the Vatican Bank in the Ambrosiano affair. A compromise had to be sought as both governments had a moral obligation to international creditors. It took another three years of negotiations to reach the final settlement, signed in Geneva on 25 May 1986, with the 119 foreign banks which claimed to have been defrauded by Calvi.

Without formally admitting liability, the Vatican paid out $240,822,222 as its 'voluntary' share of the settlement, with the Italian government making up the rest of the $406,000,000 compensation.

The Vatican stated, 'While the IOR confirms it bears no responsibility for the bankruptcy, in which it declares it became involved involuntarily because of its special position, it is prepared to make a voluntary contribution . . .'

The Vatican Bank insisted that the settlement was made without recourse to outside borrowing, although there were insistent rumours at the time that Opus Dei played a key role in arranging the payment.

Although the creditors were finally appeased, the judicial consequences of the Ambrosiano collapse continued to make the headlines. In the summer of 1982 Archbishop Marcinkus and his two chief lay bankers, Luigi Mennini and Pellegrino De Strobel, had been formally notified in writing that they might be subject to criminal charges in connection with the suspected fraudulent bankruptcy of the Banco Ambrosiano.

The letters were returned to the authorities in Milan unopened. The Vatican argued that correct diplomatic procedure had not been followed; they should have been sent through diplomatic channels. A long legal battle between the investigating magistrates in Milan and the Vatican ensued, in which the Vatican pleaded immunity, while the Italians became increasingly frustrated at the tactics adopted by the Pope's men.

The judges in Milan, Renato Bricchetti and Antonio Pizzi, received no reply to requests for co-operation from Archbishop Marcinkus. *L'Osservatore Romano* reported that the Pope's bankers had co-operated 'substantially and loyally with the Italian judiciary,' but this was simply not true according to the judges. On 20 February 1987 they lost patience with the Vatican and signed arrest warrants for Archbishop Marcinkus and his two chief assistants. This time they used the correct diplomatic postbox, but the delay enabled the accused to disappear behind the protective walls of the Vatican City State to avoid the ignominy of gaol. As no extradition treaty exists between Italy and the Holy See, they felt safe.

There were protestations of pained amazement from inside the Vatican at the charge of accessory to fraudulent bankruptcy not being levelled against Marcinkus, and his chief managers Mennini and De Strobel. Italian police searched for the Archbishop at a villa he had had built in Rome for visiting American clergymen, the Villa Stritch, where he kept an apartment, but he was not there.

The Italian authorities demanded Marcinkus's extradition under clause 22 of the Lateran Treaty of 1929, which states that the Holy See undertakes to hand over to Italian justice 'persons who take refuge inside Vatican City charged with acts committed in Italian territory which are considered criminal by the laws of both states'. The Vatican lawyers replied that clause 11 of the same Treaty protects 'central departments of the church' from any interference by the Italian State.

Flying over the South Atlantic at the start of a two-week visit to Uruguay, Chile and Argentina, Pope John Paul was asked what he thought about the latest developments in the Marcinkus affair. 'We are taking it seriously,' he said, adding, 'we are convinced that a person cannot be attacked in such an exclusive and brutal way. In all seriousness, we shall take up the case and have it studied by the competent authorities'.

According to Professor Francesco Finocchiaro, who holds the chair in ecclesiastical law at Rome University, the IOR is a financial institution whose function is to manage money and does not hold a central position in the headquarters' organization of the Church.

The Vatican lawyers fought hard to prove the contrary – that the IOR was covered by the immunities granted by the Lateran Treaties – and in the end they won; but not before many churchmen, from Curial cardinals down to humble parish priests, had expressed serious misgivings about the attitude being taken by the Pope towards the management of Vatican finances.

Cardinal Silvio Oddi, for example, told an Italian reporter, 'Archbishop Marcinkus is morally responsible for the involvement of the IOR in the collapse of the Banco Ambrosiano. He knew that Calvi was in deep trouble when he wrote those letters of comfort.'

Monsignor Luigi Pignatello, who edits the diocesan magazine *Nuova Stagione* (New Season) in Naples, criticized the silences of the Italian Catholic press and the legal casuistry of *L'Osservatore Romano*. 'It may be dignified, but it is certainly not illuminating on the part of those whose duty it is to make clear the truth before the whole world. We don't want to hear the truth first from Italian justice, for which we have profound respect. Nor do we wish diplomatic channels to cover the Vatican Bank affair with a veil of silence.'

Father Luigi Mozzo, the editor of a Catholic diocesan weekly in Vicenza, asked, 'How is it that in this day and age there is an archbishop running a bank, even if it is the Vatican Bank? Should not temporal organizations be left to lay people to run?'

Archbishop Marcinkus himself received strict orders from the Pope to say nothing to the press. His only public comment was in an interview printed in April 1987 in the Spanish daily *Ya*. Here he took personal responsibility for helping Roberto Calvi, but said that inside the Vatican this was regarded as an act of ingenuousness, not of wrongdoing. Why did he not resign? Because, he argued, this would give him the appearance of being a fugitive from Italian justice (which in fact technically he was), and because it would mean abandoning his two Italian managers for whom arrest warrants had also been issued.

There was a brief victory for Italian justice when the Tribunal of Liberty, a special court set up during the years of political terrorism to protect the rights of those who considered they had been gaoled without cause, upheld the arrest warrants issued in Milan. The Tribunal found that there had been a 'common will to deceive' on the parts of the Vatican Bank and Calvi. The bank had provided 'cover' for Calvi. There was a case to answer as the alleged offences had occurred on Italian territory.

A Vatican tribunal quickly rejected the Italian extradition demand for Marcinkus and his managers. Then in July 1987, only five months after the arrest warrants had been issued, Italy's highest court, the Court of Cassation, quashed the warrants at the request of the Vatican's lawyers. It was up to the Holy See to decide which departments constituted the 'central departments of the church', the court decided. No further appeal was possible against this finding. Archbishop Marcinkus was once more free to leave Vatican territory without the risk of finding himself under arrest. The Archbishop was relieved. 'My faith in Italian justice has been restored,' he told a reporter from the Associated Press.

The Milan magistrates, furious at the decision, decided to take the case to yet another top tribunal, Italy's Constitutional Court. They claimed that the Court of Cassation had acted unconstitutionally in its interpretation of the Lateran Treaties. Eleven months later this last-ditch attempt failed too, on the grounds that the new objections had been raised too late in the proceedings.

When the Public Prosecutor in Milan, Pier Luigi dell'Osso finally sent forty-one people for trial on fraud charges connected with the bankruptcy of the Ambrosiano, he spelt out quite clearly in the indictment that the IOR had played a major role in the swindle. The number of accused was finally whittled down to thirty-five and the trial started in Milan in May 1990.

Archbishop Marcinkus ended his Vatican career on 31 October 1990 with a brief statement that Pope John Paul had finally agreed to accept his request that he be allowed to return to the United States to continue his pastoral work 'enriched in my priesthood'. He noted ruefully, in an off-the-cuff interview, that he would most likely always be remembered as the villain in the Calvi affair.

Thus ended not only the financial but also the legal responsibilities of the Vatican in the Ambrosiano affair. The moral damage remains to be assessed.

A high-ranking Vatican official once told me that when John Paul was elected Pope in 1978, his first reaction to living amid the wealth and splendour of the Vatican was that this was not seemly for the Church of the poor. He had spoken to colleagues about his belief that the Church should sell off its surplus assets. It took only six months for the Curia to convince the new Pope that this would be a mistake, but there remained lingering doubts.

The story is told by a Polish priest, who now works inside the Vatican, that shortly before the Communist authorities in Poland seized all Church properties in 1948 an aged parish priest stood up at a meeting in Warsaw and suggested that his Church had an unprecedented opportunity to set an example by giving away all its property to the poor.

His colleagues scorned his ideas as naive.

One month later all Church property in Poland was nationalized and yet, the priest remarked, no Polish priest or bishop had ever gone hungry since then.

Visiting a Brazilian shanty town near Rio de Janeiro during his first visit to South America in 1980, the Pope symbolically took off his gold fisherman's ring and gave it to be sold to help the poor. But it was not until the colourful interfaith meeting in Assisi in October 1986, five months after the Vatican had agreed to repay 240 million dollars 'voluntarily' to the creditors of the Ambrosiano, that he spoke out boldly in public. 'We have decided to be poor, poor as Saint Francis, poor as so many great souls who have illuminated the path of humanity. We have decided to have at our disposal only this means, the means of poverty.'

He spelt out his ideas in greater detail in the encyclical *Sollicitudo Rei Socialis* published in 1988.

An innumerable multitude of people are suffering under the intolerable burden of poverty.

Before these tragedies of total indigence and need, in which so many of our brothers and sisters are living, it is the Lord Jesus himself who comes to question us.

The abundance of goods and services available in some parts of the world, particularly in the developed north, is matched in the south by an unacceptable delay, and it is precisely in this geopolitical area that that major part of the human race lives.

Part of the teaching and the most ancient practice of the Church is her conviction that she is obliged to relieve the misery of those who suffer, not only out of her 'abundance' but also out of her 'necessities'. Faced by cases of need, one cannot ignore them in favour of superfluous church ornaments and costly furnishings for divine worship. On the contrary it could be obligatory to sell these goods in order to provide food, drink, clothing and shelter for those who lack these things.

The Pope's words were immediately seized on by the press as a turning point in his crusade against the consumer society. Did it mean that the rich furnishings of Saint Peter's and the baroque churches of Rome were about to go under the auctioneer's hammer?

Certainly not, according to Cardinal Roger Etchegaray, who was deputed to explain the Pope's meaning to the press. 'This passage in the encyclical is an appeal to the imagination more than precise instructions,' the Cardinal said.

Cardinal Giuseppe Caprio, former head of the Holy See's Office for Economic Affairs explained to me the philosophy of poverty as it is officially understood inside the Vatican.

'If you look at the pomp and circumstance in Saint Peter's, or some Vatican ceremony with top-hatted ambassadors in formal attire and cardinals in their red robes, life inside the Vatican looks splendid. But you should see how we live every day. Most Vatican residents get up at six a.m. to be in their offices from nine a.m. to one-thirty p.m. Ninety per cent of our priests do not have a flat of their own, they live in hostels and do their own cooking. I do not have a car, except for official travel and I cannot afford domestic servants but am lucky as I have two religious sisters to cook for me.'

I asked the Cardinal about the extreme reluctance of the Vatican authorities to breach their tradition of financial secrecy.

'It is not convenient to publish everything. The reading of the consolidated balance sheet of the Holy See may create difficulties for those who do not understand its complexities and the relationship of the different organizations which make it up. From this stems the risk that people may not believe us.

'We are in a delicate situation when we are dealing with charitable contributions. Remember the Vatican lives off freewill offerings, not taxation.' And he quoted the biblical aphorism about the left hand not knowing what the right hand is doing, when charity is the aim.

'Our lifestyle is one of dignified poverty. People who work for the Holy See, whatever their grade, do not receive emoluments which permit the accumulation of wealth.'

Cardinal Caprio's valuation of the gross assets and investments of the Holy See during the 1980s was the rather modest figure of 560 million dollars. He explained, however, that after making provision for pensions for Vatican employees, only just over half this figure actually produced income.

A glance at the first-ever balance sheet published by the Vatican in 1988 referring to the financial year ending 31 December 1986 reveals the multifarious activities carried out by the central government of the Church, as well as the fact that the headquarters' annual bill for maintenance, electricity, water and heating alone came to over 3.5 million dollars.

Among the departments of the Holy See reporting their income and expenditure were the College of Cardinals, the Synod of Bishops, the Secretariat of State, the Vatican Library, the Secret Archives, and a host of committees and bodies dealing with science, archaeology and sacred music as well as the Pope's own charitable welfare fund. The monthly payroll of about 5 million dollars ate up 51 per cent of the total budget. On the Pope's payroll were 2,315 employees and 885 pensioners. Vatican Radio, which broadcasts on shortwave all over the world, on medium wave to Italy, and on FM to Rome, cost just over 9 million dollars including capital investment for new equipment. Publishing of books, magazines, papal speeches and religious sheets by the quaintly named Polyglot Press produced a modest profit of 5.5 million dollars, although the Vatican daily newspaper L'Osservatore Romano ran at a loss.

Peter's Pence covered less than half the 56-million-dollar deficit, which was paid off by dipping into reserves from previous years. These reserves were almost exhausted, the balance sheet noted.

Archbishop Marcinkus turned in much better results from his job as acting Governor of the Vatican City State than in his previous job as head of the Vatican Bank. The Vatican City State administration, with its 1,195 employees and 529 pensioners, showed a modest surplus of 6 million dollars on a budget of 64 million dollars in 1987. The Archbishop was responsible for running the Vatican posts, keeping the roads swept, collecting parking fines, (Vatican traffic police decided that wheel clamps were the most effective way of punishing erring Monsignori or ordinary Vatican workers who failed to obey parking regulations) and for the manicure of the numerous lawns and flower-beds which decorate the 110-acre mini-state.

The biggest money earner, of course, is tourism. Some 2 million visitors pay 9 million dollars in entrance fees to the Vatican museums each year, and many buy Vatican stamps and coins as well. A lucrative deal was also fixed up with a West German publisher, Belser Verlag, in a 4 million-dollar contract for the exclusive reproduction rights to illuminated manuscripts and codexes from the Vatican library. The Vatican also moved into the compact disc business.

In order to get the finances of the Vatican into proper perspective, it is essential to distinguish not only between the fixed assets, investments and running expenses of the central government of the Church, and those of the Vatican City State, but also between the finances of the Holy See and those of hundreds of other different independent Church organizations, including religious orders with headquarters in Rome and similar peripheral Church bodies, which may sometimes administer sums far greater than the 140 million-dollar annual budget of the Holy See.

Caritas International, which groups Roman Catholic charities around the world and has its headquarters in Rome, handles well over a billion dollars a year in cash, food, clothing and technical help of various sorts. The major donors are the Germans and the Americans; over a million voluntary and paid workers are involved in Caritas's activities in 120 different countries.

The Holy See's budget is also separate from that of the Vatican department which runs foreign missions, which used to be called Propaganda Fide. It is now officially known by the cumbersome title of Congregation for the Evangelization of Peoples, although it is still generally referred to by its former name. Each year it raises sums considerably larger than the Holy See's total budget. For years the Congregation has employed external auditors and published its accounts, because it found that complete openness is reporting how you spend what you get is the best formula for successful fundraising.

Even the religious orders, at the behest of Pope John Paul, have been encouraged to chip in with their contributions to the Holy See, not just to bail the Vatican out of its current financial crisis, but to help guarantee a regular future income for the Pope. A Canadian monk, Father Leo Paul Norbert, for many years treasurer and bursar of his order, the Oblates of Mary, was elected head of a committee of treasurers of religious orders in Rome, both men and women. They gave the Pope's chief financial officer at that time, Cardinal Caprio, some friendly advice when they handed over their first cheque for 200,000 dollars in 1988. 'Try where possible to encourage a greater simplicity of life,' they wrote. 'Do not burden yourselves with useless, repetitive services.'

The religious orders also asked the Pope to consider putting one of their number on the board of governors of the Vatican Bank, 'considering that monks and nuns are the major contributors and account holders at the Bank'. So far there has been no response to this request.

The cost of the worldwide travels of Pope John Paul II figures in none of the accounts made public by the Holy See. The reason is that the bulk of travel and security costs for the first twelve years of the pontificate, which I calculate cannot be less than 400 million dollars, have been borne entirely by the local churches and states whose guests the Pope and his entourage have been. Many dioceses spend months and even years paying off the debts incurred in honour of a papal visit. Even the cost of chartering planes, which have covered 375,000 miles or fifteen times the circumference of the globe, has been offset by the sixty to seventy international journalists who normally accompany the papal party and whose organizations pay full first-class fare on a single ticket basis, even though they occupy economy class accommodation and all journeys start and end in Rome.

'It is not an unproductive investment if you calculate the benefits in pastoral terms,' Cardinal Caprio said.

Vatican officials never discuss the impact of the Pope's travels upon fundraising in the countries he visits. Annual contributions to Peter's Pence from France (four visits) have increased by 80 per cent, from West Germany (two visits) fourfold, and even poor countries like Argentina (two visits) have stepped up their offerings by a magnificent 600 per cent. The Pope's visit to the United States in 1987 depleted the Vatican coffers by half a million dollars, but this was immediately repaid with 100 per cent interest by the wealthy Knights of Columbus, who presented the Pope with a cheque for a million dollars.

At the end of Pope John Paul's first decade as steward of the assets of Saint Peter, costs and income both soared, but the Vatican's financial problems remained. Cardinal John Krol of Philadelphia, who is of Polish origin and a close friend of the Pope, has been instrumental in setting up the Finance Committee of fifteen cardinals from some of the world's richest and most populous city dioceses. This Committee has been meeting twice a year since its creation in 1981 to oversee Vatican finances.

The Cardinal is blunt about the need for greater 'transparency', the current financial buzzword inside the Vatican. He believed that the Pope's appeal for bigger contributions to Peter's Pence must be followed up by greater public accountability. 'My argument has always been that if you want to keep your financial affairs private, you can do so if you pay your own bills: but if you are appealing for cash, credibility demands that you explain why.'

Cardinal Krol is resigned to the fact that it is extremely difficult to get the Vatican bureaucracy to change its ways rapidly – 'You won't find heavenly perfection in the Church,' he told me with a grain of humour. He is currently looking at untapped resources of American philanthropy to bridge what seems to him to be an easily surmountable gap, given that Harvard University's annual budget is, for example, five times larger than the Pope's.

'In 1986 alone,' he said, 'ninety billion dollars was given by American individuals for philanthropic purposes, almost half of it to religion. This huge sum was given not by corporations but by individuals and mostly during the lives of the donors, not in the form of bequests. We must reach out and get our share.'

For a start, American Catholics have set up a 100 million-dollar trust fund, the principal of which is to be kept in the United States but the annual interest will be sent to Rome.

In 1990 Pope John Paul decided to bring into the Vatican a Polish-American Archbishop to replace Cardinal Caprio, Prefect for Economic Affairs who had reached retirement age. Cardinal Edmund C. Szoka, head of the United States' fifth largest diocese, Detroit, gained a reputation as a fiscal hardliner with his decision in 1988 to close thirty-five of Detroit's inner-city churches for financial reasons. The closures were a dramatic reflection of the exodus of the city's white Catholics to the suburbs. Many priests and parishioners appealed to the Vatican for a reprieve, but they were unsuccessful. Szoka explained that it was uneconomic to keep the churches open with declining membership and with not enough priests to minister to his 1.5 million-member diocese.

Szoka, a former national treasurer of the American Catholic Church, and an expert fundraiser, began his new career in Rome by calling for a 15 per cent cut in expenditure by all Vatican departments. In his first year at the Vatican the Pope's headquarters deficit was cut by 11 million dollars.

For the foreseeable future it will be American Catholics who are going to bear the main financial burdens of the Vatican. Although, in theory, it would only require an annual contribution of one dollar from say 200 million Catholics, one-quarter of the Pope's total flock, to put the Holy See's balance sheet permanently back into the black, such magnaminity on a world scale seems unlikely. A joint study carried out in the United States by Michigan University, the National Opinion Research Centre at Chicago University and the Gallup Poll, found that Roman Catholics in America are less generous than Protestants when it comes to putting their contribution into the collection plate. There has been a big drop in giving by Catholics during the 1970s and 1980s, which has been sharpest among the devout, the better educated and the more liberal. In 1984, the typical American Catholic gave only 320 dollars to churches, while the typical Protestant gave 580 dollars. The report commanded that lay people also be given a larger role in the administration of church funds.

The departure of Archbishop Marcinkus for America marks the end of an embarrassing chapter in the history of Vatican finances. Whether John Paul's reign is also going to mark the start of a new era of openness and public accountability remains questionable. Old Vatican habits of official secrecy die hard, as I found when I tried to obtain the latest Vatican balance sheet. I was told that while this is sent to bishops around the world, it is no longer made available to the general public.

CHAPTER 11

God's Politician

The Church is a spiritual type of society with spiritual aims, without any desire to compete with the civil powers or to deal with material or political affairs which she recognizes with pleasure are not of her competence.
                    Pope John Paul II addressing King Juan Carlos of Spain and assembled
                         Spanish political leaders at the Royal Palace, Madrid, 1982

Take back your Bible and return it to our oppressors. They need its moral precepts more than we, because, since the arrival of Christopher Columbus, America has had imposed on it, by force, a culture, a language, a religion and values which belong to Europe.
                              Peruvian Indian leaders to Pope John Paul, Peru, 1985

The Vatican City State is a garden city, a green oasis in the centre of polluted, chaotic Rome. The guide who shepherds tightly supervized groups of visitors explains that they can see two sorts of gardens inside the Vatican. There are the formal Italian gardens, with strictly delimited low hedges arranged in symmetrical curves and straight lines, a development of the enclosed *hortus* or garden with which the ancient Romans adorned their villas. And then there are the 'English' gardens, a landscape apparently sculpted by nature, with meandering paths and wild cyclamen and bluebells pushing through the undergrowth of the Vatican wood.

Anyone attempting to roam alone through the gardens will be challenged and expelled by zealous, uniformed Vatican security guards. Saint Peter himself would not be welcome if he were to make an unscheduled appearance here. You might catch a glimpse of a trim figure jogging past in a tracksuit. Don't jump to conclusions; it is not the Pope, or a member of his Curia coming up for air, but a member of the Swiss Guard keeping fit. The security-cocooned Pope does not walk or jog here any more. 'His Holiness is too busy,' the guide informs us. John Paul keeps fit exercising on his penthouse terrace, skilfully constructed to enable him to see out over the city while remaining screened from the public gaze.

To get from the formal part of the Vatican gardens to the Vatican wood, with its untended paths and its air of romantic neglect, you have to pass through a narrow passage in the building where Guglielmo Marconi began his pioneer experimental transmissions for Vatican Radio in 1931 with a speech by Pope Pius XI in Latin. Towering over Marconi's studio now is aerial FMC-04, the latest addition to an already impressive array of technological ironmongery jutting aggressively into the Roman skyline. These futuristic excrescences beam the Pope's message through the ether to Rome and the rest of the world: Urbi et Orbi. Satellite dishes now adorn the mediaeval tower of Saint John restored by Pope John XXIII, who had once dreamed of retiring there. The guide agrees that the stark AM, FM and shortwave aerials which now sprout over the Vatican spoil the view, but then, as she so aptly reminds the tourists, 'They are very pragmatic people, here inside the Vatican!'

Those unable to tune in to the wavelengths of Vatican Radio can pick up their telephone anywhere in the world and 'Dial the Pope' to hear a recorded message from the pontiff in their own language. The text is changed every day. Even the Vatican is now into televangelization.

The allegory is obvious. The two gardens are two alternative models of a living Church which are now in fierce competition. One is pyramidal in structure. The Pope stands at the apex of a hierarchical organization run by ecclesiastics who are more interested in the application of rules than in kindling the religious convictions of their faithful. Rome imposes its own interpretation of unity on the base. For the Vatican there is no such thing as the North American Church, the Latin American Church, the African Church; there is only one Universal Apostolic Church whose leader, the Pope, is still technically infallible in his teaching. The clergy, under his direction, decides; the laity obeys orders. This garden is formal, structured, hedges are severely trimmed, avenues are straight and you must keep off the grass.

The other Church sees itself as a decentralized 'grass-roots' Church consisting of a network of Christian communities who, together, make up the whole People of God. This Church grows naturally, like the Vatican wood. It finds ecology, looking after the whole of the Creation, as important as ecclesiology, looking after the interests of the Vatican. The 'grass-roots' Church, only a tiny fraction of whose members are professional religious or priests, prefers to turn the pyramid of command upside down. If the Pope is truly the 'Servant of the Servants of God' as he officially styles himself, then these 'grass-roots' Catholics believe he must listen to and act upon advice from below as well as 'management from above', as he once succinctly described his source of inspiration and guidance. These Catholics believe that their Christian faith can be assimilated by a variety of cultures and can assume different shapes and forms. This garden has space for many species which may be active to Africa, Asia or the Amazon rain forest, and which prefer to be left to grow in freedom without being labelled, ticketed and planted in rows or patterns.

One of Pope John Paul's most characteristic orders to his theological staff was the compilation of a teacher's guide or a universal catechism. As the liberation theologian Leonard Boff remarked, one wonders what exotic Roman Catholic being is going to be capable of creating a text equally applicable to the Eskimos of the Arctic, the destitute of Bangladesh, the German business tycoons of Bavaria, the Yuppies of New York and the Xavante Indians of Brazil.

The new compendium has attracted strong criticism, even before publication, from bishops who question the value of continuing to lay down rules and centralize all decision making in Rome. Can the centre hold? Have things begun to fall apart in the Catholic Church during the reign of Karol Wojtyla? It might seem presumptuous to predict the future of the world's longest-surviving international organization, but inevitably one must ask how the Vatican is going to control the passage of those who choose to abandon the rigid formalism of Wojtyla's garden for the less regimented paths of the Vatican wood.

The renowned Catholic theologian Karl Rahner once described this as the beginning of the third period of the Roman Catholic Church. The first period, in Rahner's scheme, was a very short one, lasting less than a century, during which the Church grew out of its Jewish roots. The next period began when the Christians expanded rapidly into Hellenistic and Judaic culture in the Eastern Mediterranean. During the age of Constantine, Christianity became firmly aligned with Western culture and Western civilization. According to Rahner, this second period lasted through the long period of decline of the Roman Empire, through the Middle Ages, the Renaissance, the Reformation and through all the centuries down to the holding of the Second Vatican Council in the 1960s. The shift into the third period became apparent to him during the Council, which he attended as consultant. A new universality of the Church was revealed to him. The Church could now be seen to belong to many different cultures; it was no longer a monopoly of the West.

The problems posed by this new vision of the Church are self evident. No longer does a single culture or philosophy unite and underpin the interpretation of the Christian faith.

The Synods of Bishops who gather in Rome every three years, in theory to exercise their 'collegial' powers of government over the Church together with their pontiff, have turned into mere talking shops. If the bishops are sometimes allowed to let off a little steam, they do so only under strict papal control.

Rembert Weakland, the former Abbot General of the Benedictine religious order in Rome, was working in American during most of John Paul's pontificate. On his return to the Vatican during a recent Synod he found what he described to me as 'worryingly little interest from bishops in developing countries about First World preoccupations, and vice versa'.

'In 1964 when I attended the Second Vatican Council, it was a humble Church. Now it is a Green Beret Church; a lot of talk about "Communio", but how often is the Kingdom of God mentioned? the new movements all fit into this picture of an aggressive new Church.' (American Special Forces in Vietnam were nicknamed the Green Berets, which became a synonym for ruthlessness.)

'Wojtyla's weakness is in organizational structure. As you become more and more Catholic, in the good sense of the term, then there is need for some new structural thinking. How you bring all those local churches into the mix is going to be the trick. They talk about restructuring at the Curia, but there is absolutely n perspective in terms of the whole Church. If this is going to be a watershed pontificate, the challenge will be to create a forum that creates a new way of being a Church.'

Communion and Liberation (CL) – an Italian Catholic student movement which began in Milan in the late 1950s under Giuseppe Giussani, a priest – has flourished under John Paul's pontificate. Adopting somewhat naïve Socialist-sounding policies, CL is strongly critical of Italy's ruling Christian Democrat Party, which it accuses of having become ethically 'soft' in trying to distance itself from the Vatican in order to demonstrate the Party's independence from the Catholic Church. CL supporters, estimated to number about 70,000 in Italy, see themselves as the new Catholic Church Party.

The Pope told CL students in 1984, 'Your way of approaching human problems is close to mine. I could say that it is the same.' Don Giussani replied in similarly enthusiastic vein, 'We serve Christ in this great man with all our existence. This Pope is the event that God created.'

Cardinal Ballastrero, former Archbishop of Turin, was once reproached by the Pope for not liking the Ciellini, as CL are called colloquially in Italian. 'Holiness,' the Archbishop replied, 'when you get to know them better, you won't like them either!'

Meanwhile, another of John Paul's favorite Catholic bodies, Opus Dei, elevated to the rank of 'personal prelature' by the Pope in 1982, received further marks of papal approval. In 1990, Monsignor Alvaro del Portillo, the Spanish-born head of the secretive Church organization, was promoted to the rank of bishop. And in 1992, the founder of Opus Dei, Monsignor Jos Maria Escriva de Balaguer, was beatified by the Pope in Rome, the first step to declaring him a saint.

John Paul's predecessor, Paul VI, perhaps tiring of the burden of the papal office, considered towards the end of his life the possibility of retirement. There was a precedent in the Middle Ages. Pope Celestine V, who had spent most of his life as a hermit, abdicated in 1294 at the age of eighty-five after occupying the Papacy for only five months. The poet Dante placed Celestine in one of the circles of Hell for what he called the Pope's 'cowardice'. Celestine died a virtual prisoner in the castle of Fumone, south of Rome, where he was sent by his successor. He was later made a saint by Dante's less stern contemporary, Pope Clement V.

For John Paul, however, retirement is something not even remotely to be considered. He will remain Pope for life, and is determined to be laid to rest when he dies in the crypt of Saint Peter's, next to the tomb of the Apostle. Yet while the last chapter in the long reign of the first Slav Pope (the average pontificate is of less than eight years' duration) remains to be written, it is already possible to assess the main political successes and failures of the pontificate, its innovations and its persistent areas of weakness.

Among the successes must certainly be counted Wojtyla's high-profile travels. In his first thirteen years as Pope he made more than fifty trips abroad, which took him away from the Vatican for a whole year, travelling more than 750,000 kilometres, and making 1,670 speeches in over 500 different cities and towns. In a world where political leaders increasingly display a lack of true moral conviction, the Pope's words carry weight even when those receiving his message belong to a different religious tradition or are not in full agreement with his Church's teaching.

It will be difficult for the John Paul's successor not to follow his example and set out from Rome on a new worldwide series of pilgrimages; he has effectively reversed the centuries old pattern of pilgrimages of the Catholic faithful converging upon Rome.

The high point of John Paul' pontificate, politically speaking, can now be seen to have been his first journey home to Poland in 1979. The Russians were perhaps quickest to sense the importance – and the danger – of the election of a Polish pontiff. Not only was the future of Communism in his native country compromised, but so too was Soviet hegemony over the rest of Eastern Europe. Whatever the truth about the origin of the attempt on the Pope's life in Saint Peter's Square in 1981, whether or not the Soviet KGB was in some way behind Ali Agca (Mikhail Gorbachev himself has now denied it), Soviet analysts understood only too well the threat to their system raised by the election of the first Slav Pope.

The Pope's 1979 speech at Gniezno, in which he rejected the artificial divisions of Europe agreed by the victors of the Second World War at Yalta, turned out to be truly prophetic. It marked the start of radical political changes which were to mature over all of Eastern Europe a decade later. He was the catalyst for a new vision of Europe, one which could only emerge once the fallacy of the separation of Europe into two opposing political blocs had been exposed. The Polish Catholic free trade union Solidarity was the vehicle through which the Pope's eclectic vision of post-Communist Europe became a reality.

The resumption of diplomatic relations between the Holy See and the Soviet Union in 1989, for the first time since the Bolshevik revolution, marked another political watershed. The Pope obtained the legalization of the Ukrainian Catholic Church, suppressed since 1946, and seized the chance to rebuild hierarchies to minister to all Catholics – both Latin and Eastern rite – inside the Soviet Union. In 1991 the Pope even felt confident enough to appoint the first Roman Catholic Archbishop of Moscow without asking the Kremlin's permission beforehand. The Vatican's new political strength may indirectly have helped millions of Soviet believers – Muslims as well as Christians – to enjoy a new freedom of worship, and may also have stiffened separatist political movements inside strongly Catholic Lithuania and the Western Ukraine.

The first Orthodox church services to be held inside the Kremlin churches since the Bolshevik revolution were celebrated in 1990. But the Russian Orthodox Church, traditionally nationalist and closely tied to the state, is basically unhappy about growing papal interest in other parts of the Soviet Union, and does not agree with Rome on Church unity. The newly installed Ukrainian Catholic leader, Cardinal Lubachivsky in Lvov, is having a difficult time dealing with the local Orthodox church.

The political successes of John Paul in the Slav world were perhaps predictable given the suppressed frustrations and nationalisms of Eastern Europe. But many of the high expectations raised in 1978 by the election of the first non-Italian Pope in modern times have not been fulfilled.

The moment when a newly elected pontiff announces to the crowds in Saint Peter's Square the name by which he wishes to be known as Pope is always eagerly awaited. Cardinal Wojtyla's choice – 'John Paul' – seemed at the time highly significant. It was interpreted to mean that the Polish Cardinal intended to continue the policies of the Pope of the Second Vatican Council, John XXIII, the first twentieth-century Pope really to come to grips with the problems of making Church teaching more relevant to the times. And by choosing again the name of his immediate predecessor, John Paul I, who died after a brief reign of only 33 days, it was thought that John Paul II pledged himself to implement the promise of innovation at the Vatican given by this humble Italian Pope. But both these expectations were to remain unfulfilled.

Pope John Paul's championship of human rights in many parts of the world – in the strictly limited sense of securing freedom for members of his Church to practise their faith – was an undoubted area of achievement. But his implacable opposition to theological innovation, and the inquisitorial and totalitarian methods he employed to stifle dissent among theologians and bishops, caused considerable disquiet among his followers. Many members of the Catholic Church now regard the Wojtyla pontificate as a bulldozer Papacy, in which all internal opposition has been systematically flattened.

Theologians who dissented from the Church's ban on contraception (like Charles Curran of the United States) or who used Marxist analysis to promote social justice (like Brazil's Leonardo Boff) were summarily silenced. The Pope forced the Jesuit religious order into line when he felt it was veering dangerously toward political involvement; he ordered priests in Nicaragua to leave government posts; and he disciplined U.S. nuns who signed a 'pro-choice' newspaper advertisement on abortion. What human rights do nuns and priests enjoy if they wish to make their voice heard in the governance of the Church? There is no Appeal Court of Human Rights at the Vatican to which, for example, a priest who wishes to be released from his celibacy vow might appeal.

In his most overtly political encyclical, *Centesimus Annus*, the Pope gave only two cheers for democracy. Truth, he stressed, is not something to be decided by a majority vote. At times, democracies seem to have lost the ability to make decisions aimed at the common good; the Church does value the democratic system, but Catholics must beware of totalitarianism disguised as democracy.

Those who are convinced that they know the truth and firmly adhere to it are considered unreliable from a democratic point of view, since they do not accept that truth is determined by the majority, or that it is subject to variation according to different political trends.

If there is no ultimate truth to guide and direct political activity, then ideas and convictions can easily be manipulated for reasons of power. As history demonstrates, a democracy without values easily turns into open or thinly disguised totalitarianism.

Several late twentieth-century dictators in predominantly Catholic countries — Marcos, Duvalier, Pinochet, Jaruzelski, Ortega, and Stroessner among them — fell from power after a visit from Pope John Paul. Yet he resolutely opposed those liberation theologians in developing countries who preached that the Roman Catholic Church had a social and political role to play in helping peoples free themselves from oppressive regimes and social injustice. The Catholic Church's decision to endorse what it calls its 'preferential option for the poor' sounded good, but seemed to mean little in practice. There was no follow up to the suggestion that Pope John Paul made in his encyclical *Sollicitudo Rei Socialis* that his Church should sell off its superfluous ornaments and furnishings.

If the poor response by Catholics worldwide to the Vatican's constant appeals for more money suggested that John Paul was ineffective as a fundraiser, his handling of financial scandal at the Vatican Bank scarcely inspired confidence in his judgement as Chief Executive Officer of the Holy See. The Vatican, which still refuses to admit that it could have made a mistake, allowed Archbishop Marcinkus to remain in office long after he would have been sacked by any other comparable organization.

The Pope's political successes were tempered by his failure to satisfy those Catholics who, preoccupied by the moral and ethical vacuum they sensed around them, looked to him for fresh inspiration. Internally, the Roman Catholic Church has moved more in a spirit of retrenchment than renewal during John Paul's pontificate. Rome, has resisted attempts by the component parts of the Church to develop independent theologies, for local churches to make their own distinctive contributions to the Universal Church. The internationalization of the Roman Curia, which began under Paul VI, has failed to make the Vatican more open. The development of the concept of 'collegial' government of the Church, as proposed by the Second Vatican Council, has come to a halt with the appointment of Vatican 'yes' men in key dioceses all over the world, resulting in an increased concentration of power in the hands of the Pope himself.

The growth in Catholic Church membership during the pontificate, with rare exceptions such as in South Korea, is not due to a higher strike rate in conversions from other faiths or from those who had no religion, but rather to natural demographic increase. According to official Vatican statistics, the increase in the number of baptised Catholics in the world have failed to keep pace with the overall rise in population. While world population increased by 30 per cent during John Paul's reign, the number of Catholics only grew by 25 per cent.

Followers of Islam, in contrast, outnumbered baptised members of the Roman Catholic Church for the first time in history during the pontificate. The completion of Rome's first mosque only three miles from Saint Peter's basilica served as a reminder of another significant failure of the Wojtyla pontificate – the inability of the Vatican to start a meaningful religious dialogue with the Islamic world, at a time when both faiths are seeking to bring religious conversion to the rapidly growing African population.

The major blind spot in John Paul's papacy has been his total disregard for the galloping increase in the numbers of people inhabiting our planet. The evidence has been before his eyes in his many visits to the countries of the Third World. The Roman Catholic Church's ban on artificial contraception continues to be disregarded by Catholics all over the world, yet the social, political and economic implications of the world demographic explosion have not yet even begun to be seriously evaluated at the Vatican. Dr Nafis Sadik's latest population projections for the United Nations Population Fund continue to give cause for alarm. Fertility rates are now dropping in some parts of the developing world, where women are producing an average of only four children instead of six as before. However statisticians gloomily conclude that it is now too late to change the prospect that within the next sixty years world population will again double. The population of Africa, proudly pointed to by the Vatican as a major growth area for the Catholic Church (Church membership up by 46 per cent during Wojtyla's reign), is expected to expand from 650 million to 900 million in the final years of the twentieth century, the highest regional growth rate the planet has ever experienced. Dr Sadik's studies show that only a tiny minority of developing countries suffering from serious population pressures have shown the capacity to maintain stable constitutional governments and guarantee civil and political rights to their citizens.

Abortion is another major issue over which the Pope and many of his critics continue to disagree. In a number of countries with large Catholic populations Pope John Paul has not hesitated to wade into national politics and court unpopularity by supporting pro-life movements and opposing the legalization of abortion. He has denied American Catholic politicians the right to a free opinion on the subject, and is doing his best to influence forthcoming abortion legislation in both Germany and Poland. His sense of the distinction between his Church's spiritual and political aims is all but forgotten when he turns to this subject.

Henceforth Catholics in the predominantly white and wealthy part of the world will have to get used to the fact that the Church's future major potential growth areas are peopled by the non-Caucasian poor: Latin America, where more than half the world's Catholics already live, Africa, and, perhaps in the next century, China, simply because it is the world's most populous country.

Pope John Paul planned to celebrate the Christopher Columbus anniversary in 1992 as the start of a new programme of evangelization in Central and South America and the Caribbean, an area where a natural demographic increase of 100 million is expected by the turn of the century. But what exactly was he celebrating? The imposition of European culture and religion on Latin America in the sixteenth-century coincided with one of the greatest genocides in history, practised upon the very peoples whom the colonialists and missionaries were supposed to be converting. The trend during John Paul's pontificate for civilian governments to succeed military regimes in Latin America has not led to any noticeable improvement in human rights for most of the region's inhabitants.

The rapid growth of Protestant sects inside Catholic Latin America, expected to be the major bastion of the Universal Church in the twenty-first century, is causing concern and even alarm in Rome. Cardinal Ernesto Corripio Ahumada from Mexico reported to a meeting of the College of Cardinals in Rome in April 1991 that there had been a 'Protestant explosion' in Latin America during the past thirty years. Conversions from Catholicism to other Christian sects tripled in the Dominican Republic, quintupled in El Salvador and Costa Rica, and increased sevenfold in Guatemala, which now has a 'born again' President. In the United States, where 12 out of 17 million Hispanics profess the Catholic faith, 60,000 Hispanics are leaving the Church each year to join evangelical Protestant groups or sects. Jehovah's Witnesses, Mormons, Baptists, Pentecostalists and Seventh Day Adventists are also exporting their Church organizations from the America to the Philippines, southern Africa and Europe.

Cardinal Ricardo Vidal, Archbishop of Cebu in the Philippines, which alone accounts for three quarters of Asia's Catholics, reported the arrival in his country during John Paul's pontificate of thousands of Protestant fundamentalist groups who attack Catholic teachings and practices. The scarcity of Catholic priests means that the local Church cannot compete with fundamentalist pastors 'who give personal attention to people and are always ready to answer their questions'. The sects target young people in particular, playing on their basic idealism as well as offering them greater participation in worship than the Catholics. More important, the sects also have plenty of money and a financial strategy. One Philippine sect known as the 'Iglesia Ni Kristo' openly pays its members for every Catholic they convert, and provides them with jobs and a certain economic security.

Less directly, the Pope's refusal to consider alleviating the worldwide shortage of priests by ordaining women, permitting the ordination of married men, or by allowing lay pastoral workers to substitute priests has further helped the spread of these sects.

John Paul has also failed in a series of attempts to bring the schismatic Chinese Patriotic Catholic Church set up by the Communist government after 1950 back into the fold of Rome. He refused to close down the Holy See's diplomatic mission in Taiwan, the first condition placed by the Peking authorities for a dialogue with Rome. During visits to Asia the Pope beamed radio messages into China, but there was no response. For the Chinese, the Pope and his Roman Curia are foreign devils supporting a clandestine Church in their country. Just before the Tienanmen Square massacre in 1989, the Chinese Communist Party issued a directive which stated unambiguously:

The Holy See has never ceased its efforts to take back control over Chinese Catholics, and has continued to send emissaries, to nominate bishops and to support secret congregations. This endangers social stability. Faithful and priests who accept the guiding role of the Communist Party and the principle of religious freedom will be welcomed into the Patriotic Church. Severe punishments will be handed down to those who continue to resist.

At least eight Chinese Catholic bishops belonging to the underground Catholic Church loyal to the Vatican were arrested after the Tienanmen Square uprising. Many of them had already spent years in prison. John Paul's announcement of the promotion to Cardinal of the first Catholic bishop from Mainland China, Archbishop Gong Pin Mei, former Archbishop of Shanghai, who now lives in exile in the United States and who spent thirty years of his life in Chinese jails, merely produced further abuse from Peking.

Pope John Paul has also disappointed many members of his Church who feel that the Vatican discriminates against them for reasons related to their sex or the colour of their skin. Despite paying lip service to the dignity of women, and despite his public devotion to the Virgin Mary, John Paul failed to fulfil expectations – perhaps unreasonable ones, given his Polish Catholic background – that he would allow women to play a larger role within the Catholic Church. Modest proposals for women to become deacons or even to act as altar servers were struck out of the recommendations of the Vatican Synod of Bishops which discussed the role of the Catholic laity, male and female, in 1987. John Paul's view is the traditional Polish one that a woman's place is firmly in the home, raising her children, not going out to work to help augment the family budget. He stated this while Poland was still under Communist rule during a visit to Lodz – a dreary industrial city where wages were so low that more than half the local wives were forced to take factory jobs.

Black Catholics both in America and Europe are also unenthusiastic about Pope John Paul. They feel he continues to see the Church as an essentially white-run European institution which falls far short of the universality it proclaims. Father Edward Braxton, a black priest who directs a Catholic student centre at the University of Chicago, put the matter bluntly: 'The Catholic Church is seen by blacks as the special home of the great ethnic and national groups from Europe. It is in some ways incompatible with the black experience in America. When we reflect upon the scars of the past, we need no longer wonder why there are so few black Catholics. The wonder is there are so many.' There are in fact only 300 black priests and one black bishop in full charge of a diocese in the whole of the United States.

Father Warren Savage, the only black priest among 225 white clergy in the Catholic diocese of Springfield, Massachusetts, appealed to the Pope to 'fight racism' when he visited America in 1987. 'Blacks bring a rich heritage that even predates Catholicism,' he said, echoing the feelings of the former Archbishop of Lusaka, Emmanuel Milingo.

As the second Christian millennium draws to a close, is there a future role for 'global gladiators' (I borrow the phrase from futurologist Alvin Toffler) like Karol Wojtyla? On the eve of the last millennium many Christian believers anxiously awaited the end of the world. This time there is less credulity about apocalyptic happenings. But for Karol Wojtyla, as for many of his fellow Slavs, anniversaries and millenniums take precedence over what some members of his Church consider more important matters.

Early on in his pontificate John Paul celebrated the 950th anniversary of the conversion of his native Poland to Christianity. In Vienna in 1983 he recalled how a Christian army led by a Polish king, Jan Sobieski, had defeated the infidel Turks besieging the Austrian capital 300 years before. On a hillside overlooking the city where the King and his generals had attended mass before riding into battle in 1683, John Paul said their victory had 'decided the political and religious fate of whole nations for centuries to come'. He obviously sees himself as a latter day Sobieski. Later, in Kraków Cathedral where Jan Sobieski is buried, John Paul even quoted his triumphant words: 'We came, we saw, God conquered.'

In 1983 the Pope declared a special Holy Year to celebrate the 1,950th anniversary of Christ's crucifixion. 1988 was the date to remember the 1,000th anniversary of the conversion of Russia, or more correctly, the Land of Rus. In 1992 the 500th anniversary of the evangelization of the Americas, which could be said to have begun with Christopher Columbus's first footfall in the New World, had to be celebrated.

John Paul presides over a less and less tolerant Catholic Church. Western European and North American preoccupations with democracy, women's rights and the free flow of information rather escape the Papal vision of things. As the Pope once scathingly stated: 'The future of the world cannot be Moscow, and it cannot be New York either.' But equally, can the future of the world be teeming, crime-ridden São Paolo with its gangs of hungry street children?

The most positive and enduring legacy of John Paul will be the Vatican's renewed international political role and the Pope's claim to the ethical leadership of an increasingly secularized world society. As Catholics all over the world become less obedient sheep, so the Vatican's role of infallible teacher and interpreter of Roman Catholic religious doctrine will be taken less seriously. Yet Foreign Offices in both the New and the Old Worlds did take serious note when the Pope, speaking at Fatima on the tenth anniversary of the attempt on his life, described the political situation in Eastern Europe in May 1991 as 'precarious and unstable'. Among the VIP's listening to the Pope was a surprising guest: Gennady Gerasimov, former Kremlin spokesman, now Soviet Ambassador to Portugal. It was the first time that Moscow had ever been represented officially at a Roman Catholic religious ceremony. Mr Gerasmimov, asked to comment on his presence at a shrine dedicated to the reconversion of the now rapidly disintegrating Soviet Union to Christianity, said simply: 'The Soviet Union has returned to the world.' By the end of the year, the Soviet Union had ceased to exist.

APPENDIX A

Vatican Balance Sheets

1 Holy See

The first-ever public statement of income and expenditure issued by the Holy See was made in February 1988 and related to the financial year 1986. Subsequently figures were made available each October for the previous financial year. In the 1987 accounts published in October 1988 it was stated that reserves accumulated in previous years from Peter's Pence were exhausted. Since then the Vatican has been spending more than its income. Accounts for 1986 and 1987 were made public by the Vatican press office, but those for 1988 and 1989 have been made available only to bishops and are still considered confidential. Heads of expenditure and income have been changed or bunched together without explanation during the accounting periods, which explains the gaps.

Expenses	1986	1987	1988	1989
	(in millions of US dollars)			
Wages and salaries	}58.0	}71.7	}69.4	50.5
Papal embassies				9.4
Administrative expenses	9.7	12.0	9.4	7.8
Electricity, maintenance and taxes	3.6	3.8	3.1	2.0
Management charges, interest paid	11.0	12.4	17.9	15.5
Vatican Radio	10.3	8.0	}13.7	20.9
Publishing	11.7	13.9		21.6
Depreciation	3.2	0.2	2.4	}14.7
Various	6.4	10.5	2.0	
Total expenses	113.9	132.5	117.9	142.4

Income

Income from departments	6.1	7.2	8.2	8.0
Income from investments/ real estate	28.8	38.1	42.9	46.2
Vatican Radio	1.2	2.1	{17.4	{20.1
Publishing	17.1	20.7		
Non-recurring income	.5	.4	3.3	
Various	3.5	.3	2.6	
Sales of securities/real estate				13.5
Total income	57.2	68.8	74.4	87.8
Cash deficit	56.7	63.7	43.5	54.6

2 Vatican City State

	1987	1988
	(in millions of US dollars)	
Income	81.2	83.6
Expenditure	74.1	70.4
Surplus	7.1	13.2

(This sum is partly devoted to staff pension and liquidation funds.)

3 Financial Stewardship of Pope John Paul II at the Vatican

Year	Deficit/Surplus *(in millions of US dollars)*	Peter's Pence
1978	−12	3
1979	−20	?
1980	?	?
1981	+3	15
1982	−30	27
1983	?	27
1984	−28	25
1985	−39	28
1986	−56	32
1987	−63	50
1988	−78	52
1989	−54	48
1990	−86	57

APPENDIX B

Foreign Travel – Pope John Paul II

Date	Days	Countries Visited	Distance (kms)
1979			
Jan/Feb	8	Dominican Republic, Mexico, Bahamas	23,710
June	9	Poland*	3,185
Sept/Oct	9	Ireland, USA	18,093
Nov	3	Turkey*	3,785
1980			
May	11	Zaire, Congo, Kenya, Ghana, Burkina Faso, Ivory Coast	18,914
May	6	France	2,509
June	13	Brazil*	27,673
Nov	5	West Germany	2,880
1981			
Feb	12	Pakistan,* Philippines,* Guam,* Japan,* USA (Alaska)*	35,120

(Attempt on Pope's life, May 1981, forced him to postpone the rest of his travel programme for 1981.)

Date	Days	Countries Visited	Distance (kms)
1982			
Feb	8	Nigeria,* Benin,* Gabon,* Equatorial Guinea*	14,734
May	4	Portugal*	4,433
May/June	6	Britain*	4,880
June	3	Argentina	26,904
June	1	Switzerland*	1,412
Aug	1	San Marino	235
Oct/Nov	10	Spain	7,269
1983			
Mar	9	Portugal,* Costa Rica,* Nicaragua,* Panama,* El Salvador,* Guatemala,* Honduras,* Belize,* Haiti*	24,009

June	8	Poland*	3,597
Aug	2	France	2,096
Sept	4	Austria	1,735

1984

May	10	USA (Alaska), South Korea, Papua-New Guinea, Solomon Islands, Thailand	38,441
June	6	Switzerland	2,218
Sept	12	Canada	26,843
Oct	3	Spain,* Dominican Republic,* Puerto Rico*	16,827

1985

Jan	12	Venezuela,* Ecuador,* Peru,* Trinidad*	29,821
May	11	Netherlands,* Luxemburg,* Belgium*	4,721
Aug	12	Togo,* Ivory Coast,* Cameroon,* Central African Republic,* Zaire,* Kenya,* Morocco*	25,431
Sept	1	Switzerland, Liechtenstein	1,580

1986

Jan/Feb	11	India	20,252
July	8	Colombia, Saint Lucia	21,127
Oct	4	France*	2,031
Nov/Dec	14	Bangladesh,* Singapore,* Fiji,* New Zealand,* Australia,* Seychelles*	48,974

1987

Mar/Apr	14	Uruguay, Chile, Argentina	36,613
Apr/May	5	West Germany	3,169
June	7	Poland*	4,559
Sept	12	USA, Canada	30,465

1988

May	12	Uruguay, Bolivia, Peru, Paraguay	34,420
June	4	Austria	2,503
Sept	10	Zimbabwe, Botswana, South Africa, Lesotho, Swaziland, Mozambique	20,599
Oct	3	France*	2,222

1989

Apr/May	9	Madagascar, Réunion, Zambia, Malawi	21,712
June	9	Scandinavia	11,986
Aug	2	Spain	3,908
Oct	12	South Korea, Indonesia, Mauritius	39,047

1990			
Jan	8	Cape Verde, Guinea-Bissau, Mali, Burkina Faso, Chad	14,384
Apr	2	Czechoslovakia*	2,133
May	8	Mexico, Curaçao	29,233
May	2	Malta	1,537
Sept	9	Tanzania, Burundi, Rwanda, Ivory Coast	18,737
1991			
May	4	Portugal	8,957
June	9	Poland	4,581
Aug	8	Poland, Hungary	4,487
Oct	10	Brazil	20,599
1992			
Feb	8	Senegal, Gambia, Guinea	10,010

*Author accompanied Pope on these visits.

APPENDIX C
Foreign Travel – Pope Paul VI

Paul VI was the first Pope since the Napoleonic Wars to travel outside Italy.

Date	Days	Countries Visited
Jan 1964	3	Jordan, Israel
Dec 1964	4	India
Oct 1965	2	USA (United Nations)
May 1967	1	Portugal (Fatima)
July 1967	2	Turkey
Aug 1968	4	Colombia, Bermuda
June 1969	1	Switzerland
July/Aug 1969	3	Uganda
Nov/Dec 1970	10	Iran, Pakistan, Philippines, Samoa, Australia, Indonesia, Hong Kong, Sri Lanka

Select Bibliography

GENERAL

Boff, Leonardo, *Church, Charism and Power*. SCM Press, London, 1985.

—, *Liberation Theology: from Confrontation to Dialogue*, Harper & Row, New York, 1986.

Brown, Lester, R., *Our Demographically Divided World*, Worldwatch Institute, Washington DC, 1986.

Cornwell, John, *A Thief in the Night: The Death of John Paul I*, Viking, London, 1989.

Del Rio, Domenico and Accattoli, Luigi, *Wojtyla, The New Moses*, Mondadori, Milan, 1988.

Family Planning and the Legacy of Islam, Al Azhar University, Cairo.

Häring, Bernhard, *Fede, Storia, Morale*, (Faith, History and Morals), Borla, Rome 1989.

Hebblethwaite, Peter, *The New Inquisition?*, Collins, London, 1980.

—, *In The Vatican*, Oxford University Press, 1987.

Johnson, Paul, *Pope John Paul II*, London 1982.

Kelly, J. N. D., *The Oxford Dictionary of Popes*, Oxford University Press, 1986

Macciocchi, M. A., *Di là dalle Porte di Bronzo* (Beyond the Bronze Doors) Mondadori, Milan, 1987.

Michelini, Alberto, *Spalancate le Porte à Cristo* (Open Wide the Gates to Christ. 14 Apostolic Journeys of John Paul II), published privately, Milan, 1982.

—, *La Chiesa del Mondo Intero* (The Universal Church. 14 Apostolic Journeys of John Paul II) published privately, Milan, 1985.

Milingo, Emmanuel, *The Demarcations*, published privately, Lusaka, 1982.

Pallenberg, Corrado, *Vatican Finances*, Penguin, Harmondsworth, 1973.

Ranke-Heinemann, U., *Eunuchs for the Kingdom of Heaven: The Catholic Church and Sexuality*, originally published by Hoffman und Campe Verlag, Hamburg, 1988.

Sterling, Clare, *The Time of the Assassins*, Holt, Rinehart & Winston, New York, 1984.

VATICAN PUBLICATIONS

ENCYCLICAL LETTERS (John Paul II)

Redemptor Hominis	Church at end of second millennium, 1979.
Dives in Misericordia	God's mercy, 1980.
Laborem Exercens	Workers' rights, 1981.
Slavorum Apostoli	Common Christian roots of Eastern and Western Europe, 1985
Dominum et Vivificantem	Holy Spirit, 1986
Redemptoris Mater	Virgin Mary in the life of the Church, 1987.
Sollicitudo Rei Socialis	Communism and Capitalism, 1988.
Redemptoris Missio	Missionary challenge in Third World, 1991.
Centesimus Annus	New social teaching of the Church, 1991.

APOSTOLIC LETTERS (John Paul II)

Mulieris Dignitatem	Role of Women, 1988.
Euntes in Mundum	1,000th anniversary of Baptism of Kievan Rus, 1988.
Christifedeles Laici	Laity and the Church, 1989.

Paul VI's Apostolic Constitution *Romano Pontifici Eligendo* (on the vacancy of the Apostolic See and the election of the Roman Pontiff), 1975.

Statistical Yearbooks of the Church 1980–8, Vatican Press 1982–90.

Index